TAPPING DIVERSE TALENT IN AVIATION

For my son
Johnny
in loving memory

Tapping Diverse Talent in Aviation

Culture, Gender, and Diversity

Edited by
MARY ANN TURNEY
Arizona State University, USA

Foreword by
NEIL JOHNSTON

Routledge
Taylor & Francis Group

LONDON AND NEW YORK

First published 2004 by Ashgate Publishing

Published 2016 by Routledge
2 Park Square, Milton Park, Abingdon, Oxon OX14 4RN
711 Third Avenue, New York, NY 10017, USA

Routledge is an imprint of the Taylor & Francis Group, an informa business

British Library Cataloguing in Publication Data
Tapping diverse talent in aviation : culture, gender, and
    diversity. - (Studies in aviation psychology and human
    factors)
    1.Aviation psychology 2.Flight training - Psychological
    aspects 3.Flight crews - Training of 4.Women in aeronautics
    5.Communication and culture 6.Diversity in the workplace
    I.Turney, Mary Ann
    629.1'3252'019

Library of Congress Cataloging-in-Publication Data
Tapping diverse talent in aviation : culture, gender, and diversity /
edited by Mary Ann Turney.
        p. cm. -- (Studies in aviation psychology and human factors)
Includes bibliographical references and index.
    1. Airlines--Employees--United States. 2. Airlines--Minority
employment--United States. 3. Diversity in the workplace--United
States. I. Turney, Mary Ann. II. Series.

HD8039.A4272U58 2003
387.7'068'3--dc22   2003058362

Transfered to Digital Printing in 2011

ISBN 9780754635253 (hbk)
ISBN 9781138258594 (pbk)

Printed in the United Kingdom
by Henry Ling Limited

Contents

List of Figures   *vii*
List of Tables   *viii*
List of Contributors   *ix*
Foreword by Neil Johnston   *xv*
Preface   *xix*

PART I: DIVERSITY

1   Tapping Diverse Talent: A Must for the New Century
    Mary Ann Turney and Robert F. Maxant   3

2   Values and Orientation Differ in Mixed Crews
    Mary Ann Turney   11

3   Teaching Non-Native English Speakers: Challenges and Strategies
    Irene Henley and Wayne Daly   21

4   Learning Style Preferences Affect Training Outcomes
    Merrill R. Karp   45

5   Women's Learning and Leadership Styles: Implications for Air Crews
    Mary Ann Turney and James C. Bishop   61

6   Gender Differences in Learning to Fly
    Ruth Lowe Sitler   77

PART II: LANGUAGE

7   ICAO Language Proficiency Requirements
    Elizabeth Mathews   91

8   The Efficacy of Standard Aviation English
    Robert F. Ripley and James L. Fitch   99

9   Reflexive Communication in the Multi-Cultural Crew
    Taras Stratechuk and Ted Beneigh   105

10   Humor, Stories, and Cultural Context
        Mary Ann Turney   119

11   The Music is the Message: Prosody in Aviation Discourse
        Marsha Hunter   129

12   Nonverbal Cues 'Speak' Volumes
        Mary Ann Turney   153

13   Protocols, Rank, and Social Status Influence Communication
        Mary Ann Turney   161

PART III: ENVIRONMENT

14   'Who Are You Calling a Safety Threat?' A Debate on Safety in
        Mono-Cultural Versus Multi-Cultural Cockpits
        Ashleigh Merritt and Surendra Ratwatte   173

15   Inclusive Versus Exclusive Strategies in Aviation Training
        Mary Ann Turney, Irene Henley, Mary Niemczyk,
        William K. McCurry   185

16   Ergonomics and Diversity
        Patricia C. Fitzgerald   197

17   Clash of Subcultures in On-Gate Communication
        Christy Armentrout-Brazee and Marifran Mattson   207

18   Making Everyone Part of the Team: A Model
        Merrill R. Karp and Mary Ann Turney   221

Index   *231*

List of Figures

Figure 2.1	Hofstede's cultural dimensions	12
Figure 2.2	Comparison of cultural differences	13
Figure 2.3	Diversity and organizational choices	18
Figure 4.1	Kolb's learning style theory diagram	48
Figure 4.2	Integrated Aviation Learning Model	52
Figure 5.1	Comparison of affirmative responses of men and women pilots	68
Figure 5.2	Comparison of affirmative responses of military and civilian women pilots	68
Figure 5.3	Comparison of affirmative responses of military and civilian men pilots	69
Figure 11.1	Intonational contour, after Bolinger, 1972	133
Figure 11.2	*The Music of Everyday Speech*	133
Figure 12.1	Factors related to nonverbal communication	153
Figure 16.1	Items rated on a 5-point Likert scale to assess level of comfort performing each function	201
Figure 16.2	Participant reports of comfort level in training aircraft	202
Figure 18.1	Review of literature and methodology across a broad range of educational areas	223
Figure 18.2	Data-driven interventions	226
Figure 18.3	Diverse Workforce Model	228

List of Tables

Table 1.1   Projected employment growth of aviation occupations
                 2000 to 2010   6
Table 1.2   Percentage of commercial pilots by minority group   8
Table 4.1   Dominant learning styles of women respondents   49
Table 4.2   Dominant learning styles of men respondents   50
Table 4.3   Dominant learning styles of both women and men
                 respondents   51
Table 7.1   References to language found in ICAO documents
                 prior to March 5, 2003   94

List of Contributors

Christy Armentrout-Brazee

Christy Armentrout-Brazee received her doctoral degree in organizational communication from the Department of Communication at Purdue University in 2002 and holds a post-doctoral associate position in the School of Technology. She plays an integral part in the Department of Aviation Technology through both her participation in its research program and her teaching in the undergraduate, graduate, and honors programs. Her primary areas of interest focus upon the role of communication in accomplishing productivity, safety, and security process objectives through workplace interactions. She has worked on numerous research projects with members of the aviation industry and regulatory agencies, and has presented her work in a variety of national and international forums.

Ted Beneigh

Ted Beneigh teaches in the Aeronautical Science Department at Embry-Riddle Aeronautical University Daytona Beach Campus. He holds an Airline Transport Pilot and Flight Instructor Certificates with experience in Boeing 727, 757, and 747 jet transport aircraft. Beneigh developed the graduate Crew Resource Management (CRM) Program at the Daytona Beach Campus.

James C. Bishop

James C. Bishop received a Ph.D. in mathematics from Northeastern University in Boston. His major research work has been in statistical hypothesis testing related to sequential trials and he has published significant findings on this topic. Dr. Bishop is currently a professor at Bryant College specializing in actuarial studies and is the examination administrator for the Society of Actuaries in Rhode Island. His background includes eight years of actuarial and statistical consulting experience for a number of firms in New York and Massachusetts. Dr. Bishop is a member of the American Statistical Association. Dr. Bishop's interest in aviation has led him to participate in several studies related to human factors.

Wayne Daly

Wayne Daly has several thousand flying hours of commercial operating experience. He was Chief Flying Instructor at a major Australian college, where his focuses were Flight Instructor, Multi-engine Instrument Rating and international student training. Daly has flown extensively in domestic and international aeromedical operations with the Northern Territory Aerial Medical Service. More recently, he served the Air Ambulance Service of New South Wales and the Royal Flying Doctor Service of Australia as Senior Base Pilot, responsible for flying operations from Sydney.

Currently, Daly is employed by Eastern Australia Airlines, a wholly-owned subsidiary of Qantas Airways. He holds an Air Transport Pilot Licence, Command Instrument Rating (Multi-engine), and a Grade One Flight Instructor Rating with Multi-engine Training Approval. Having previous experience in law, Daly is a part-time lecturer in aviation law at the University of Western Sydney, where he is also the Distance Education Subject Co-ordinator. Daly studied at the University of Western Sydney with a research focus on the education of non-English speaking student pilots.

James L. Fitch

James L. Fitch (Ph.D., Florida State) is a Professor of Communication Disorders in the Department of Communications, College of.Liberal Arts, Auburn University. He has published in a variety of academic and practitioner publication outlets and is active in several professional organizations. He also consults with various domestic and international companies in the area of language training.

Patricia C. Fitzgerald

Patricia C. Fitzgerald is a Master of Science candidate in Aviation Human Factors at Arizona State University. Studies in which she collaborated have been published in the Journal of Air Transportation and the Journal of Applied Social Psychology. Ms. Fitzgerald enjoyed a career in Information Technology, and became interested in an aviation career when she earned her private Pilot Certificate.

Irene Henley

Irene Henley recently retired as an Associate Professor and Head of the Department of Aviation Studies at the University of Western Sydney.

Her academic qualifications include a doctoral degree, a Master of Education degree, and a Master of Arts degree. Her doctoral dissertation examined "The quality and development of flight instructor training in Canada and Australia" and her Master of Education thesis looked at "The association between student pilot stress and flight instructor training."

Dr. Henley's professional qualifications include a Canadian Airline Transport License with a Class I Flight Instructor Rating and an Australian Commercial Pilot License with a Grade 1 Flight Instructor Rating. She has over 20 years of experience in the civil aviation industry as a flight instructor, an examiner, and an inspector. As a Flight Training Standards Categorization Inspector with Transport Canada (8 years) and as an Australian Civil Aviation Safety Authority Approved Testing Officer.

Marsha Hunter

Marsha Hunter is a founding partner at Trapezium Communications, Inc., a public speaking consulting firm in St. Paul, Minnesota. Since its inception in 1979, Trapezium has focused on a unique specialty: teaching speaking skills to trial attorneys. Trapezium's client list includes major law firms throughout the United States; providers of continuing legal education in the U.S. and the United Kingdom; and the U.S. Department of Justice. The company now provides services in aviation communications as well as the legal field. As managing partner, Hunter is in charge of writing and research for Trapezium. She holds a Masters of Aeronautical Sciences degree from Embry-Riddle Aeronautical University, and an undergraduate degree from Arizona State University. She is an instrument-rated pilot with commercial privileges.

Merrill R. Karp

Merrill R. Karp is an Associate Professor in the Department of Aeronautical Management Technology at Arizona State University. He received his Ph.D. in Administration and Management from Walden University in 1996, with a specialization in Aviation Education and Training. He attained an MA in Business Management and Supervision from Central Michigan University in 1975 and a BS in Aeronautical Technology from Arizona State University in 1967. He also attended the United States National War College in Washington D.C. in 1985. Dr. Karp is a retired United States Air Force officer and was the commander of a fighter wing during the Gulf War. His research and publication agenda focuses on aviation human factors, cockpit/crew resource management, cooperative and collaborative learning, and adult learning in aviation education.

Elizabeth Mathews

Elizabeth Mathews is the linguistic Consultant to ICAO. In particular, she facilitates the work of the Proficiency Requirements in Common English Study Group in its work to establish ICAO provisions for the use of English in international radiotelephony communications. Prior to joining ICAO in 2001, Elizabeth was Director of the Aviation and Academic English Programs at Embry-

Riddle Aeronautical University in Florida. She has a Masters degree in Teaching English as a Second Language and has 20 years experience in English language training and education. For the previous six years, Elizabeth focussed on the development, management, and marketing of aviation English training and testing programmes at Embry-Riddle. She developed the curriculum for and managed English language training programmes for air traffic controllers and for both ab-initio and experienced pilots, and she was leader of a team which developed the first commercially available Test of English for Commercial Airline Pilots.

Marifran Mattson

Marifran Mattson is an Associate Professor of organizational and health communication in the Department of Communication at Purdue University. Through her research and teaching program she explores critical interactive features to improve communication among social actors in a diversity of health and safety contexts including the aviation industry. She has been involved in several aviation research projects over the past five years.

Robert F. Maxant

Robert F. Maxant is a retired business executive who has extensive experience working with multicultural issues and multinational companies in Europe and Asia. Educated at Post College, Long Island University, and Arizona State University, he is bilingual in English and German. A pilot of many years, Maxant has a Commercial Pilot Certificate with instrument and multi-engine ratings. He has flown throughout the United States in private aircraft. He is currently working in computer graphics.

William K. McCurry

William K. McCurry has been the Chair of the Aeronautical Management Technology Department at Arizona State University since the fall of 1995. His research interests are in human factors and safety. He completed a doctorate in Educational Psychology and Research from the University of Kansas in 1989.

He has extensive aviation safety, maintenance, and operational flight experience having left military service as a Lieutenant Colonel and a Master Army Aviator where he was involved in the fielding of the AH-64 Apache Attack Helicopter. Dr. McCurry holds a commercial SEL, MEL, rotorcraft, instrument, advanced ground and CFI certificates. He is a member of the Board of Trustees, Council on Aviation Accreditation and has held positions as Secretary and Treasurer of the University Aviation Association.

Ashleigh Merritt

A native of Australia, Dr. Ashleigh Merritt is a researcher for The University of Texas Human Factors Research Project; she also teaches an undergraduate class in Cross-Cultural Psychology. She co-authored with Professor Robert Helmreich the book, *Culture at Work in Aviation and Medicine: National, Organizational, and Professional Influences.* She worked for the Human Factors consulting group, Dédale, in France for two years, focusing on safety initiatives in commercial aviation and she has also worked in the nuclear industry as a consultant on human performance initiatives.

Mary Niemczyk

Mary Niemczyk is an Assistant Professor in the Aeronautical Management Technology Department at Arizona State University. Her background is a blending of two domains – aviation and instructional technology. She has conducted research in both areas and is interested in improving student learning, particularly in the aviation environment. Her current research interests include metacognition, student self-regulation, determination of the knowledge and skills necessary for flight expertise and the cognitive processing differences between novices and experts. Dr. Niemczyk has also designed numerous instructional units using a variety of technologies, including paper, computer, and web-based instruction. She has presented her work at various international conferences and is widely published.

Surendra Ratwatte

Surendra Ratwatte is the Human Factors Manager at Emirates Airlines based in Dubai, United Arab Emirates. He is a Boeing 777 Captain for Emirates Air. Suren was born in Sri Lanka and learned to fly at Embry-Riddle in the United States, gaining an education in the process. He subsequently graduated with a Masters in Aeronautical Science, with particular emphasis on Human Factors and CRM issues.

Robert F. Ripley

Robert F. Ripley (JD, Jones School of Law) is an Associate Professor of Aviation Management in the Department of Aviation Management and Logistics, College of Business, Auburn University. He has published in various academic and practitioner publication outlets and is active in several professional organizations. He also consults for the airline industry and general aviation. His teaching and research focus is in the areas of Aviation Law and Policy and Aviation Human Factors.

Ruth Lowe Sitler

Ruth Sitler recently retired from Kent State University as an Assistant Professor where she was the Flight Program Manager and Chief Flight Instructor. Ruth has flown over 10,400 hours with over 8000 hours of flight instruction. She holds a Ph.D. in Curriculum and Instruction. Her expertise is in differences in gender learning. Previously, Dr. Sitler was employed by the Cleveland FAA Flight Standards District Office as a Safety Inspector and Safety Program Manager. Ruth holds an FAA Airline Transport Pilot Certificate and a Flight Instructor Certificate, including Instrument and Multi-engine endorsements. She is a NAFI Master Flight Instructor, a Gold Seal Instructor and has been an FAA Accident Prevention Counselor for over 20 years.

Taras Stratechuk

Taras Stratechuk is an Associate Professor at Embry-Riddle Aeronautical University and teaches aviation related courses that include Human Factors in Flight Safety. He has over 15,000 flight hours accumulated in over thirty years of flying. In addition to being a designated FAA examiner and Flight Instructor, he holds the Airline Transport Pilot Certificate. His credentials include a Master's degree in Aeronautical Science from ERAU and he was Project Coordinator for the International Civil Aviation Organization (ICAO) at the Indira Gandhi Rashtriya Uran Academy in Fursatganj India where he designed and implemented human factors and flight safety related programs for the Indian government and the Indian civil transport airline industry.

Mary Ann Turney (editor)

Mary Ann Turney is an Associate Professor at Arizona State University; she teaches graduate and undergraduate courses in aviation and human factors. Dr. Turney is currently engaged in research related to human factors, crew resource management diversity, and retention of women in aviation. Dr. Turney was formerly the Director of Flight Programs at Dowling College, where she administered the flight training program, taught aviation courses, and trained the college's Precision Flight Team for intercollegiate competition. Dr. Turney regularly publishes her research on human factors; her professional credentials include a bachelor's degree in English Literature, a master's degree in Secondary Education, and a doctorate in Higher Education. An active pilot and Gold Seal flight instructor, Dr. Turney holds an Airline Transport Pilot Certificate, and an Instrument and Multi-engine Instructor Certificate. A current pilot, Dr. Turney regularly flies across the United States in her single engine aircraft.

Foreword

Neil Johnston

As someone whose aviation career started in the mid-1960s, it is a particular pleasure to have been invited to contribute a foreword to *Tapping Diverse Talent in Aviation*. I say this because at that time the subject matter and most of the ideas advanced in this book would have seemed eccentric, if not downright bizarre. It would have been difficult to envisage developments such as airlines employing personnel from more than thirty different cultural backgrounds in key positions. Equally, the idea of women airline pilots, not to mention women combat pilots was still a distant prospect and, indeed, the very idea of such developments would have caused bemusement and amusement. So unthinkable were they that the very suggestion would probably have generated more hilarity than opposition.

In those days everyone in the aviation business operated on the basis of a rather simple and essentially implicit understanding. This approximated to the notion that there was one correct model for the aviation endeavour and that 'our' country, 'our' airline, 'our' Air Traffic Control unit, 'our' maintenance facility, etc. represented a very good, if not the best available example of that model. Accordingly, one tended to look at the practices of other organizations with polite indifference and occasional distain. In keeping with the origins and pioneering spirit of the early days of aviation, the general orientation was masculine, western and unreflectively self-confident. It took quite a few years for us to realize, not to mention accept, that culturally mediated operational differences in aviation were a reality – rather than an unfortunate departure from the unarticulated normative standard rooted in the masculine western model. With the passage of time we have come to accept that culture and diversity are issues of significance. We better appreciate that minorities not only play a valuable role in aviation, but that they also bring new perspectives, advantages and challenges. While airlines employing personnel from thirty plus cultures and varied linguistic backgrounds are by no means the norm, there are a growing number of such organizations. These organizations meet, daily, the challenges that face those who would wish to integrate, develop and optimize diversity. For these and other reasons we are ever more conscious of the need to achieve an appropriate 'accommodation' or 'fit' between individuals, technology, culture, work groups and organizational practices. We are ever more sensitive to the fact that diversity brings strengths and weaknesses that often vary relative to specific tasks or activities. However, when it comes to optimizing the advantages of diversity and constraining the impact of its weakness we are perhaps less sure as to what to do than we would wish to be. Similarly, while we increasingly recognize the impact of organizational diversity, sub-cultures, climate and so forth, the real difficulties appear when we try to make tangible use of our insights.

It is for these reasons that I heartily welcome the publication of this informative and groundbreaking text. Its very publication is an acknowledgement of just how far we have come in recent decades. A quick glance at the table of contents will quickly establish that it addresses, essentially for the first time in a single work, a number of important topics that seem likely to be of ever increasing importance to aviation. Those unconvinced of the importance of gender and cultural issues will find the various chapters in this book both enlightening and challenging. The various chapter authors have successfully established the relevance of their respective topics and demonstrate the rich opportunities that await both researchers and those whose primary focus relates to practical day-to-day aviation challenges. Given the relative paucity of attention generally given to the role of language in aviation, the fact that seven chapters are dedicated to various aspects of language is also to be greatly welcomed.

To my mind another particularly interesting feature of the book is the attention paid to perspectives that challenge the conventional wisdom. This is especially the case where tradition normally funnels us towards a uni-dimensional understanding of multi-featured topics such as learning, leadership, communications and so forth. By way of example I would particularly cite the examples of how different 'learning styles' contribute to training outcomes (chapter 4), of how gender differences impact upon leadership (chapter 5) and the nature of reflexive communication in multi-cultural settings (chapter 9).

Similarly, the interesting dialogue in chapter 15 – 'Who are you calling a safety threat' - is a useful reminder that the operational strengths and weakness of mixed-culture crews may turn out to be counter-intuitive. This chapter also serves to remind us that prediction in this domain is especially tricky. Empirical research seems likely to challenge 'obvious' assumptions and also to provide useful practical guidelines. On the other hand, the authors of chapter 15 note that the biggest problem of all might simply be the refusal to acknowledge that culture and diversity do indeed play a key role. This latter point is, in a certain sense, endorsed by the chapter's somewhat gloomy finale; the comments there serve to remind us that the nature of the human condition will always remain unpredictable and historically situated – it must, in other words, inevitably reflect contemporary history and events. The challenge, to which the entire book is an excellent testimony, is for us to learn how best to **manage** all such challenges and to learn how we can best adapt our endeavours to environmental and contextual changes.

Chapter 18 synthesizes much of the data and literature relevant to diversity. It should also prove a useful guide for those who would like to combine an interest in diversity with a programme of research. To my mind this chapter suggests a range of interesting research topics that almost seem to leap off the page. Hopefully the future will see both more research into diversity and the increased benefits that will accrue from a progressive growth and deepening of our understanding.

In concluding, I think it is fair to say that we are now much more sensitive to diversity in its many forms that at any period in the past, even if we have a lot more to learn. I warmly welcome the publication of this book and, in particular, the manner in which it helps orient us in new directions and encourages us to anticipate the kind of changes to which the aviation industry must adapt in the future. This unique and interesting text opens up exciting new territory and I congratulate all who have contributed to its creation. I am especially grateful to Mary Ann Turney for giving me the opportunity to write this foreword. I wish both herself and her fellow contributors a well-deserved success.

Captain Neil Johnston
Aerospace Psychology Research Group
Trinity College Dublin
September 2003

Preface

Our workforce continues to become more diverse as the aviation industry moves into the new century. Future aviation employees will tend to be more divergent in their thinking than they were in the past when the talent pool consisted of individuals with very similar backgrounds and when national aircrews were more the norm than international crews. The new diversity invites us to consider the influences of a variety of cultures, belief systems, and values as we design effective and efficient training programs for multi-national, multi-ethnic, and two-gender crews.

The intent of this work is to identify and define cross-cultural issues, gender differences, and ethnic and minority considerations that affect the aviation environment. Although this book is organized in three subject areas -- Diversity, Language, and Environment -- we do not mean to give the impression that these areas are really distinct from one another. In fact, it will become evident to the reader that the three areas often overlap and our selections will call attention to the interconnections among them. In addition, issues associated with these three subject areas are interlocking issues that apply to the aviation industry in a unique way because the aviation industry itself has a distinct and unique culture.

Our first section presents a conceptual view of *diversity* from several perspectives; the second part focuses specifically on issues related to *language*. The final part presents selections related to the aviation *environment*. We have selected articles and research that have challenged our own thinking about cultural differences with a view to enriching professional exposure to these complex topics.

Part I

This section includes six chapters on the theme of diversity. We begin with a discussion of why the aviation industry needs to embrace diversity. In Chapter 2, important variables that affect individual performance are identified and defined. These include how values, standards, and behaviors that differ in mixed teams influence team performance and why aviation professionals can no longer be viewed as 'all alike.' Chapter 3 explains how language itself both reflects and influences beliefs and behavior, and why non-native, English speaking people do not necessarily interpret meaning in the same way as native speakers.

Chapter 4 describes research on how individual learning styles, frequently ignored in the training process, can strongly affect behavior and learning outcomes. In the final two chapters of this section, we examine how aviation training programs traditionally ignore learning differences linked to gender and why there is need for change.

Part II

Since language is such a crucial part of aviation's organizational context, this section includes seven chapters on important considerations related to language and aviation. We begin with a review of ICAO standards and language proficiency (Chapter 7), followed in Chapter 8 by a discussion of the need for a common, standard language. Communication in the multi-cultural crew is examined in Chapter 9, while Chapter 10 reveals how a speaker's choice of anecdotes, reminiscences, and humor may influence the listeners. Chapter 11 examines the intonation and sound of the individual voice as it affects what is heard. The nonverbal aspects of communication are identified in Chapter 12, and finally Chapter 13 relates how assumptions about protocol, rank, and social status affect messages and may pose barriers to effective communication.

Part III

In this section, we consider the aviation environment and the industry culture. Beginning with Chapter 14, we offer an update of a debate on safety in mono-cultural and multi-cultural flight decks. In Chapter 15, the authors examine inclusive and exclusive training strategies. Chapter 16 is a review of the physical environment and some of the ergonomic considerations surrounding comfort and performance on the flight deck. A clash of subcultures is described in Chapter 17. The final chapter in this section focuses on how incorporating diversity can increase individual empowerment and productivity for the future of the aviation industry.

This book is the result of a collaborative effort among a wide variety of individuals with considerable knowledge and experience in the study of human factors in aviation. A brief description of each contributor's background and expertise can be found in the List of Contributors.

I would like to acknowledge and offer special thanks to my friend W. Kathleen T. Reid for taking time from her busy work schedule to offer many helpful suggestions regarding the manuscript, to my husband Bob Maxant for his tireless assistance with graphics and formatting, and to Pat Fitzgerald for significant research support. In addition, I am grateful to Jim and Pam Bishop, Sharon Camlic, my colleague Merrill R. Karp and John Hindley of Ashgate for their continued and persistent encouragement. Without them, this project would not have been possible.

Mary Ann Turney
Phoenix, AZ

PART I
DIVERSITY

Chapter 1

Tapping Diverse Talent: A Must for the New Century

Mary Ann Turney and Robert F. Maxant

Globalization

Friedman (2000) contrasts the current trend toward cultural globalization with the Cold War Era where the world was divided between East and West with a wall in between. Today's global world has one overreaching feature – integration. Friedman describes the world as 'an increasingly interwoven place', where 'whether you are a company or a country, your threats and opportunities increasingly derive from who you are connected to' (Friedman, 2000, p. 8). This globalization is built around the Wide World Web, a symbol of our connectivity in an ongoing and dynamic world (Friedman, 2000).

As the aviation industry becomes more integrated through expanding alliances, it increasingly encompasses a wider range of diverse talent, which highlights the urgency of building cultural awareness and creating harmony amid differences in customs and ideology. Workplace colleagues are likely to come from a range of different cultures. The first stage in developing the competence of working across cultures is awareness. Without awareness, we tend to define others by our own cultural values and what we consider the 'right' way to do things.

Diversity in a Global World

For an industry like aviation with global ambitions, Burman (2003) implies that success is likely to stem from successful joint ventures and alliances. But there is no guarantee that alliances will survive and their relative success will depend on, among other things, flexibility in managing cultural diversity.

The challenge then is the management of a multi-cultural workforce in a global context, encompassing the ability to vary methods and services across cultures, not simply imposing one culture on another. The ability to develop a true trans-national organization requires managerial approaches and systems that allow for variations based on diversity (Burman, 2003). Managing that diversity can mean *national* cultural diversity between nations, races or ethnic groups, or *international* diversity involving a range of cultures in a single nation. Attitudinal differences reflected in language and behavior may reflect deeper differences in mental structures and value systems.

Nisbett (2003) in his book *The Geography of Thought* asks why Western infants learn nouns at a more rapid rate than verbs, while East Asian infants learn verbs at a more rapid rate than nouns. Why do East Asians group objects and events based on how they relate to one another, while Westerners are more likely to identify by categories? Nisbett's research has led him to the conclusion that two completely different approaches to the world (one Asian and one Western) have existed for thousands of years and are only recently beginning to move toward one another.

The nitty-gritty of everyday working together and the problems of creating protocols, 'in-group' humor and 'out-of-office' relationships are another part of creating harmonious workplace life. Local jokes and in-group stories are examples of what can be very difficult to translate into other cultures; what sounds funny to an American can seem foolish to an Italian (Burman, 2003).

Another significant factor, according to Burman (2003) is language. Although English is the common working language that the international aviation community favors, native English speakers can turn language into a disadvantage when one of them is unaware of the confusion that a regional accent or a rapid speech rate may create, or how language confidence can be perceived as a manifestation of 'arrogance on the part of the native speaker' (Burman, 2003, p. 2).

Non-conformity with the International Civil Aviation Organization (ICAO) standards can also generate unexpected miscommunications in the aviation environment. Even when language barriers are overcome, there may be misunderstandings due to different styles of communication, body language, and differing levels of directness. In addition to significant communication style differences, behind the words on the surface lie centuries of cultural and ideological rivalries that have led to previous wars. Stereotypes and prejudices boil up even in superficially similar cultures. The age of terrorism gives additional impetus to the need for better multi-cultural understanding since resistance to a world of brutal anarchy requires an international cooperative effort.

Cultural training and study is essential to mitigate potential conflict and create genuinely international companies (Burman, 2003). No comprehensive solution to the problems of cultural diversity in the context of the aviation industry has been conceived. Yet it is clear that preparation for the success of global alliances means the management of diversity in all its aspects.

Diverse Workforce

In an extensive work on organizational culture, Adler (2002) states, 'cross-cultural dialogue has become the foundation on which global business succeeds or fails' (Adler, 2002, p. 133). Adler's analysis is based on the current situation in the business world where more than 100,000 firms in high technology countries have operations outside their home countries, making a focus on a multicultural workforce a real necessity.

However, the impact of multiculturalism varies significantly with an industry's overall strategy -- and that can largely influence its degree of success in the marketplace. Sophisticated managers, operating in United States-based firms, for example, train their colleagues to appreciate and effectively manage a workforce composed of African-American, Asian-American, Hispanic, and Native American men and women. Adler (2002) states 'Assuming that the workforce is homogeneous or defined by white male norms was never appropriate and is no longer effective' (p. 134).

In addition, cultural diversity management becomes important not only within the organization, but between the organization and its external environment. In order to be effective, states Adler, 'everyone from the CEO to the lowest level worker must use cross-cultural skills' (Adler, 2002, p. 136).

Multiple culturally distinct populations converge in many countries of the world. Singapore, for example, has four cultural and linguistic groups: Chinese, Eurasian, Indian, and Malay. Belgium includes two linguistic groups, Flemish and French. Switzerland has four ethnic communities: French, German, Italian, and Romansh. Canada, a multi-cultural country by policy, uses two official languages. Many countries, including Israel and the United States, have been historic havens for immigrants from around the world. Each population exhibits a culturally unique lifestyle.

The city of Los Angeles highlights the pervasiveness of multiculturalism in the United States and its impact on the workplace. Of Los Angeles' 550,000 school-age children, 117,000 speak one of 104 languages more fluently than English. Los Angeles no longer has a majority population, but according to Anderson 'adjusts to the quirky, polyglot rhythms of 60,000 Samoans and 30,000 Thais, 200,000 Salvadorans and 175,000 Armenians' (Adler, 2002, p. 137). Other cities in the U.S. reflect similar patterns, making multiculturalism 'a dominant fact of [U.S.] domestic life' (Adler, 2002, p. 138).

The Best and the Brightest

Given the need for a highly technically skilled workforce, the aviation industry seeks to attract and retain the best and brightest talent for its future success and growth. And that of necessity means drawing from a diverse talent pool. Census 2000 confirmed that more than 6.8 million Americans, for example, indicated that they were members of more than one race. Latinos will soon outnumber African Americans in the U.S., while Asian Americans are the fastest growing of the demographic groups (www.npr.org/programs/totn/features/2001/jul/010726.cfoa.html).

Future demographic projections reveal that the relative number of native English speakers will decrease compared to the population of the world (or compared to native speakers of other fast growing languages such as Spanish, Hindi, or Arabic) while the number of speakers of English as an additional language will rapidly increase. Whereas a century ago, native speakers of English greatly outnumbered second language speakers of English, the relationship is now reversed (Graddol, 1997).

Changes in worldwide population indicate that new entrants into the workforce represent much greater cultural and ethnic diversity than in the past. Thus the industry can expect a broader talent pool of increasing diversity, and the challenge will become the management of that diversity.

Demographic Trends

The Aviation Workforce in the United States: Previous Trends

Table 1.1 Projected employment growth of aviation occupations 2000 to 2010

	Employed 2000	Projected 2010	Change Number	2000 - 2010 Percentage
Aerospace Engineering/ Operations Technicians	21,062	22,241	1,178	5.6
Aerospace Engineers	50,434	57,437	7,003	13.9
Air Traffic Controllers	26,645	\ 28,566	1,921	7.2
Aircraft Cargo Handling Supervisors	9,949	12,704	2,755	27.7
Aircraft Mechanics	157,884	184,176	26,291	16.6
Aircraft Structure, Surfaces, Rigging, Systems Assemblers	20,057	22,897	2,840	14.2
Airfield Operations Specialists	4,815	6,118	1,303	27.0
Airline Pilots, Co-pilots, and Flight Engineers	98,080	104,391	6,311	6.4
Avionics Technicians	15,534	17,063	1,529	9.8
Commercial Pilots	19,256	24,431	5,175	26.9
Flight Attendants	124,088	146,864	22,776	18.4

Source: U.S. Department of Labor, Bureau of Labor Statistics (n.d.). Industry-Occupation Employment Matrix. Retrieved from http://data.bls.gov/oep/nioem/empiohm.jsp

Data extrapolated from *Taking Flight: Education and Training for Aviation Careers* (1997), indicated that 737,000 people worked in the air transport industry in 1993. Additionally, 542,000 people were involved in manufacturing aircraft, and 53,000 people were employed by the U.S. Federal Aviation Administration (FAA). Major air carriers and large regional carriers employed about three-quarters of those who identify themselves as holding jobs in air transportation. Occupational surveys conducted by the U.S. Department of Commerce recognize three specialized aviation related transportation occupations: pilots, mechanics, and aerospace engineers. In 1993, pilots numbered 101,000, aircraft engine mechanics numbered 139,000 and aerospace engineers numbered 83,000 (Hansen and Oster, 1997). Projections of future growth in aviation occupations through 2010 indicate a continuing trend toward limited growth in the U.S. aviation workforce.

The International Aviation Workforce: Recent Trends

Despite downsizing pressures, in 2002, the annual average commercial pilot workforce was 129,000 (*U.S. Bureau of Labor Statistics Current Population Survey, 2002*) representing an approximate growth rate of 25% since 1993. Global career trends, described *in Aviation Week & Space Technology*, indicate that large industry stakeholders such as Boeing, Bell Helicopter, the Nordam Group, Northrop Grumman, Rockwell Collins, Airbus, Raytheon, Federal Express, and others continue to forecast hiring trends ranging from 300 to more than a thousand new hires (Hedden, 2001).

The Association of European Airlines, which includes many of the large European Airlines such as Aer Lingus, Air France, British Airways, KLM, Alitalia, Lufthansa, Olympic Air, Air Portugal, SAS, Finnair, etc., reported total workforce data at the end of 2001 as 362,000. Data includes flight deck crews, cabin attendants, maintenance, aircraft handlers, catering, and distribution personnel (http://www.aea.be/Yearbook/FramePage_yb.htm).

The European Regions Airline Association reported 45,220 total personnel in the regional airlines in Europe (http://www.eraa.org).

Employment data for Asian Airlines, reported by the Association of Asia Pacific Airlines (http://www.AAPAirlines.org/content/annualreport) states that 183,500 people were employed by the member airlines in fiscal year 2001/2002. That total was a slight increase over the previous fiscal year, but is not broken down by specific occupational group.

The U.S. Bureau of Labor Statistics Current Population Survey for 2002 reported that the total commercial pilot workforce alone was 129,000 with a very low percentage of minorities in that workforce.

The Future Talent Pool: Where Will It Come From?

Looking ahead to the next decade and beyond, we see a significant shift in the population demographics of those entering the workforce. In the United States alone, recent data indicates that the total workforce will increase by 12% in the

2000-2010 decade (*U.S. Department of Labor, 2002*). However, with the exception of 9% of the new workforce, that new talent pool in the United States will consist of women and minorities. Based on current research evidence, the question remains as to whether or not that population will be attracted to careers in aviation (Turney, 2000).

For example, the percentage of women in the workforce is projected to be 48% in 2010. Yet, the number of women employed in technically oriented aviation careers has not significantly increased in the past two decades. Women still constitute less than 6% of airline-qualified pilots (*Women in Aviation International, 2002*) and less than 5% of aviation maintenance/avionics technicians. This is somewhat surprising since a number of barriers have been lifted in the past two decades, notably the exclusion of women pilots from combat aircraft by the military and the paucity of women airline captains (Turney, 2000). Similarly, increases in the numbers of people of color, indigenous peoples, and individuals of Hispanic/Latino background who now seek careers in the aviation ranks remain small.

Table 1.2 Percentage of commercial pilots by minority group

Minority Group	Percent of Total Employed
Women	3.9
African-American	1.8
Asian	4.2
Hispanic/Latino	0.3

Source: U.S. Bureau of Labor Statistics Current Population Survey
      * Based on this data, nearly 90% are white male.

Diversifying Efforts

In light of demographic projections about the availability of new talent, significant efforts toward diversifying the aviation workforce have already begun. In Europe, Fairchild Dornier aims to build an organization where richness of diversity is taken for granted. International companies, such as Airbus Industries, already recruit multi-cultural employees. Airbus conducts business meetings in English and documents are written in English for the purpose of simplifying cultural differences.

The issue of retention of women and minority employees coupled with potential promotion rates in comparison to those of white men continues to hamper greater diversity in companies primarily based in the United States. Although an African American woman headed Raytheon in the late 1990s, such top executive positions are extremely rare for minorities and women. The Boeing Company is attempting to diversify by recruiting engineers and other professionals from Europe. Nordam is offering incentives to attract older employees. Companies such as Northrop Grumman have lost both women and minority executives due to mergers, and others are recruiting talent from one another. American universities that focus on aviation education and training continue to pursue increased enrollments of women and minorities (most are below 15%), but admit that numbers still need to grow.

The United States National Research Council's committee on education and training for civilian aviation careers suggests that integrating diversity can be addressed in three ways: (1) developing interest among underrepresented populations, (2) insuring academic competencies for success, and (3) removing barriers that remain (Hansen and Oster, 1997). Although broad diversity and cultural balance is a future goal, it is only when more diverse populations are participating in the aviation industry that they will begin to influence behavior and organizational culture.

It is difficult for a traditionally exclusive culture to promote change. However, if the best talent is to be tapped, development and change must be inclusive and sustainable; the aviation industry must 'nurture the diversity of belief systems and traditions that enhance people's self-images and give them confidence to act in their own interests while respecting and supporting the traditions of other groups' (UNESCO, 1998).

Summary

The changing demographics of the aviation workplace and the trend toward greater diversity in the potential talent pool that will be available to the aviation industry worldwide suggest the need to increase awareness of multiple realities and to become proactive in dealing with the dynamics of a diverse aviation workforce. Research on changing dynamics and culturally differentiated populations coupled with the development of international alliances and the demand for high levels of skill and cooperation suggests that future success must include a new focus that will seek expertise and provide support for difficult dialogues about cultural differences.

References

Adler, N.J. (2002). *International Dimensions of Organizational Behavior*, Fourth Edition. South-Western.

Burman, E. (2003). 'Managing cultural diversity in a global world', *M World Europe. http://mworld.mce.be/artView.php?article_id=36&article_area=3.*

Friedman, T.L. (2000) *The Lexus and the Olive Tree*, New York: Random House.

Graddol, D. (1997). *The Future of English.* London: The British Council. Retrieved from www.gse.uci.edu/markw/global.html.

Hansen, J.S. and Oster, C.V. (Eds). (1997). *Taking Flight: Education and Training for Aviation Careers,* Washington, D.C: The National Academies Press.

Hedden, C.R. (2001, March 19). 'Careers 2001: Global Trends', *Aviation Week and Space Technology, 154*(12). S1-S34.

Matyas, M. and Malcolm, S. (1991). *Investing in Human Potential: Science and Engineering at the Crossroads,* Washington, DC: American Association for the Advancement of Science.

Turney, M.A. (Fall, 2000). 'Attracting Women to Aviation Careers: What Recent Studies Reveal', *Collegiate Aviation Review, 18* (1).

UNESCO (1998). *World Culture Report.*

United States Department of Labor (2002). Bureau of Labor Statistics. Retrieved from www.bis.gov/news-release/ecopro.t05.htm.

Chapter 2

Values and Orientation Differ in Mixed Crews

Mary Ann Turney

Introduction

Primarily focused on differences in values and cultural orientation, the purpose of this chapter is to raise awareness of differences that are often unnoticed or easily hidden by similar dress, job definition, and the 'group identity' effect of those responsible for the world's air transportation system. This overview of values and cultural orientation is applicable to a broad spectrum of groups in the aviation industry, i.e., flight deck crews, maintenance teams, ground support teams, administrative and flight support groups, and air traffic control teams.

Intellectually, we understand that appearance is not reality, yet we tend to assume that those who look like us also think as we do. If another is a pilot or is wearing the same uniform, he/she must think similarly. Partly this happens because we can emulate the manners of others, while our internal programs differ widely. Societies train individuals to adopt similar values and orientations. Some of these values, such as truthfulness, love, honor, justice, and gratitude are shared by many cultures. However, individuals usually have different perceptions about these same values. Ethics and truth have many different meanings. 'Common sense' is a concept that varies widely among individuals. Silence has a quite different significance for each individual and is interpreted in many different ways; for example, in Asian cultures, silence is frequently a sign of careful listening, while in Anglo cultures it may be a sign that the speaker's ideas are being rejected or ignored. How often have we believed that someone thinks as we do, only to find the person verbalizing beliefs that are abhorrent to our ideas? A person may speak our language, yet hold values that are very different from our own.

Maurino (2000) suggests that there are 'no "culture-free" endeavours: training, safety, design, research or any kind of human endeavour have strong cultural components.' In fact, our performance is always affected by subtle forms of social biases, status perceptions, mental models, and education (Maurino, 2000, pp. 953-954).

Cox and Beale (1997) state that culturally induced mental blocks can hinder our abilities to understand other viewpoints. For example, in many places and for a long time gay people have experienced hostility in the workplace. Homosexuality can be an uncomfortable issue for some individuals.   Moral positions, lack of contact with openly gay people and unconscious concern about one's own sexuality can produce homophobic reactions. For some, new awareness offers opportunity to substitute information for ignorance; for others exclusion and harassment can result (Cox & Beale, 1997, p. 129).

Our use of words can determine how we think. For example, Eskimos have multiple words for 'snow' and some African languages have many words for 'green.'   This multiplicity is due to deeply rooted connections with nature. Similarly, when word order is changed, thought processes are changed. Language determines how we interpret situations. It is for this reason that the aviation world has selected a common language, and has placed strong emphasis on standard phraseology (Nordwell, 1997). Nevertheless, a common language ground does not address the vast potential for miscommunication as will be evident in Section Two of this text.

Cultural Variations

Cultural conditioning throughout our lifetime convinces us that we are normal and others are eccentric. Hofstede (1991) defines culture as 'collective programming of the mind which distinguishes the members of one category of people from another' (pp. 149-150). Core beliefs, for example, can vary depending on the culture in which they exist. Culture influences not only what is normal, but also what is legal. Since national cultural characteristics, racial traits, and gender tendencies can be identified, they can lead to stereotyping.   Stereotyping is assuming that *all* members of a group have a given set of characteristics. Developing intercultural sensitivity then means trying on many views and beliefs to gain insight and understanding about diversity.

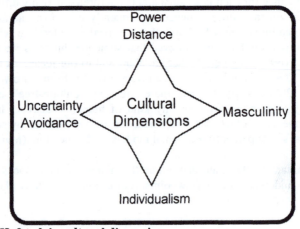

Figure 2.1 Hofstede's cultural dimensions

Hofstede defined the term value as 'a broad preference for one state of affairs over others.' He identified four dimensions or characteristics of cultures, based on research in 50 countries (Cox & Beale, 1997).

1. Power distance - the extent to which people accept inequities in society and consider them normal.
2. Individualism - the extent to which individuals look after their own interests as opposed to collectivism where individuals belong to one or more close 'in-groups.'
3. Masculinity - the use of the biological existence of two sexes to define very different roles of men and women.
4. Uncertainty avoidance - individuals are nervous in situations that are unstructured, unclear and unpredictable.

These characteristics of national cultures strongly affect communication and social interaction among crews (Merritt, 1998).

Power-Distance and Individualism

Individualistic Cultures:	Collectivist Cultures:
independent	interdependent
self-reliant	group oriented
individual responsibility	greater communication
direct talk	group cohesiveness
assertive	avoid questioning
questioning	
fewer emotions	

Figure 2.2 Comparison of cultural differences

Source: Engle, 2000

Individualistic societies, where the power-distance relationship is low, value individual success and achievement; these societies are based on self-interest. Collectivistic societies, where the power-distance relationship is high, value high quality life as defined in family and group terms. Children in collectivistic societies think of themselves as 'we' not 'I'. Preserving face is the collective alternative to preserving self-respect in individualistic cultures. Avoiding shame in collectivistic society takes the place of avoiding guilt in individualistic ones. In Southeast Asia, a powerful motivator is preserving harmony with one's social environment. In Third World countries, preserving national unity is important and people want to serve their country. In collectivistic societies others can be defined as belonging to our 'in-group' or not (Cox & Beale, 1997).

Engle (2000) suggests that aircraft crews from individualistic cultures are more independent and self-reliant and prefer individual responsibility with open and direct talk only as needed (pp. 107-114). These individuals are assertive and comfortable questioning the decisions of those who outrank them. However, they are less likely to share responsibilities and improve interpersonal interactions, often resist any focus on emotions, and the author has heard claims that attitudes *'can be left outside the flight deck.'* Crews from collectivist cultures are the reverse; they prefer interdependence and group oriented activities and a greater volume of communications. They are good at building group cohesiveness, but avoid challenging others, especially those in authority.

Power-Distance and Information Flow

Lie's (1997) study of pilots in a small Italian airline suggests that information flow and feedback is not regarded as significantly important in high power distance cultures. Lie found a clear difference of opinion about communication and information flow between aircraft captains and first officers. This was due to a status gap making those of lower status unwilling to pass information on to those perceived to be 'above' them.

Masculinity

The masculinity dimension identified by Hofstede was examined by Lie. Results suggest that masculine societies believe in the independent decision-maker, and may build walls shutting out critical communication. Accident and incident reports have revealed that there are times on a flight deck when the First Officer consciously lets the Captain make a mistake without saying anything about it. Admitting mistakes and accepting correction with an open mind was found to be difficult, and impeccable performance was frequently sought (Lie, 1997, p. 315).

Cultural Groups

Lewis (2000) groups cultures as linear active, multi-active, reactive, data-oriented, dialogue-oriented, and listening. Linear active cultures use clearly expressed linear thinking. Those individuals in reactive cultures are adept at non-verbal communication and half utterances, assuming that the listener will fill in concepts and nuances. They rely on incomplete, roundabout statements, and they easily deflect blame. Dialogue-oriented cultural groups tend to ignore agendas, and individuals speak out of turn. Data-oriented cultures tend to be driven to provide enormous amounts of information to become convincing while dialogue-oriented cultures already know the information through their networks.

Use of Time

Multi-active cultures believe that completing a human interaction is the best way to invest time. Cyclic time cultures are tuned to nature's cycles and how the past influences the present; they believe that decisions should not be rushed. For Americans, 'time is money.' It flows like a river and individuals have to move quickly to benefit from time. Buddhist cultures believe that time and life itself goes in a cycle. The Japanese have a sense of unfolding time. Time is divided up and there is a marked beginning and end for every event. Doing the right thing at the right time is important (Lewis, 2000).

Culture-Specific Findings

Javidan and House (2001) collected data from 62 countries on nine cultural dimensions. Their study summarizes culture specific findings concerning lessons learned from project GLOBE:

- The United States is among the highest ranked countries on assertiveness and performance orientation.
- Spain is among the highest ranked on assertiveness and power-distance.
- Russia is among the lowest ranked on future orientation and uncertainty-avoidance and high on power-distance.
- Italy is ranked low on future orientation, collectivism and performance orientation.
- Germany is ranked high on uncertainty avoidance and assertiveness.
- Sweden is ranked very high on uncertainty avoidance and institutional collectivism. It is among the lowest ranked on assertiveness and gender differentiation (Javidan & House, 2001, p. 302).

Differences in Values

In describing value system variations, researchers Merritt and Ratwatte (1998) found that Brazilian pilots rated advancement to high level positions as the most important work value, while Taiwanese pilots ranked it next to last. Anglo pilots ranked having sufficient time away from work for family life as number one while Korean pilots feel greatest shame when they make a mistake in front of other crew. Taiwanese pilots show the strongest preference for rules and routines.

Helmreich and Merritt (1997) surveyed pilots from several national groups and found that pilots from every group they surveyed agreed that communication (briefing) and coordination between flight deck and cabin crews was important. However, they found that there were extreme cultural differences about whether junior crew members should question the actions of captains.

Given the broad spectrum of cultural differences, Engle (2000) suggested that Japanese pilots may need to reduce power-distance issues and American pilots may need to work on interpersonal communication and group cohesiveness.

Cultural harmony

Celio Eugenio (Brazilian Pilots Human Factor Group) offers a personal perspective on cultural harmony:

> I believe that we have to be simply human beings -- accepting our limits and, all the time, thinking about our feelings and emotional moments to keep some shared experiences with our colleagues (students, etc.). Unfortunately, we will be (and have to be), sometimes, insecure and defensive. But this situation only occurs with people, not with machines. We must permit ourselves to participate in life's secrets, to stay alive and look for mental. harmony. We do not have to be different. We have to be smart, clever and intelligent to use our faults as a resource to avoid making the same errors in the future. For me, good behavior is connected to mental and physical harmony.

Bridging the Communication Gap

'Silence too is a form of speech'

Although our horizons are limited by education, social rules, and language, we can broaden our horizons by learning about cultural variations and developing individual empathy for others. Successful teambuilding requires the ability to appreciate the views of other team members. Avoiding culturally insensitive behavior supports teambuilding. Working with those of other cultures helps to build understanding of appropriate patterns of behavior.

Language is used in many different ways. Silence, too, is a form of communication. While the British favor understatement, the Spanish and Italians tend to use language in a more eloquent manner. American speech is rapid and opportunistic. Japanese words do not necessarily always offer meaning, but sometimes only mood. Japanese seldom offend with words.

Some languages are direct; others are indirect. Some are more verbose, others are frank and direct, and some lend themselves to humor. Individuals may speak with great emotion; others speak loudly. Some listen for content; others listen for gain or intent. The Japanese do not issue orders; they give hints. In the Middle East, individuals often refer to *Allah* in ordinary conversation. Americans believe that tough talk brings respect.

Meeting of the Minds

Lewis (2000) found that Japanese hate decision-making while Americans love to make decisions. Latin cultures look to leaders to make decisions. Northern Europeans and Americans see decisions as binding. Japanese and southern Europeans see no problems with changing agreements and decisions. Attitudes toward compromise vary widely.

Non-verbal aspects of interactions are very influential (see Chapter 11). Seating hierarchy and 'space bubble' have great impact. Touching and hand-shakes are often regarded differently. Dress and gesture can give multiple impressions. Silence plays an important role in communication. Facial expressions and loudness convey messages. Body posture and foot positions are more significant in some cultures than in others. Many of these ideas are explored further in Section Two.

Status, Leadership and Organization

Organizations have cultural roots. Historical experience, geography, economic experience and leadership combine to create beliefs and values. Individual and collective leadership have differing roots. Leadership can be autocratic or collective. Mistakes are more tolerated in French organizational culture than in German or American. British aviation, for example, has a social status history that permeates its organizational culture. American organizational culture, in contrast, postulates the belief that status is earned through achievement rather than social background. The Puritan work ethic and the right to dissent have characterized U.S. thinking since the 18th century. Latins and Asians base status on age and reputation. In some Asian societies (Malaysia for example) status is inherited. Leaders are paternal. In Asia, managers guide subordinates to support group goals and attach importance to symbols and gesture (Lewis, 2000).

Cultural Impact on Crew Training

Historically, professional crew training was limited to homogeneous social and cultural groups. Participants shared a common cultural framework so that cultural influences were not noticeable. When CRM training was introduced to the international community, it became apparent that the effectiveness of CRM training was dependent on its congruence with cultural values (Woodhouse & Woodhouse, 1999; Helmreich & Merritt, 1997). Problems occur when training is designed and conducted under the assumption that learning processes are similar across national cultures, or even within specific airline cultures.

Diversity and Organizational Costs

In terms of culture, Helmreich and Merritt (1998) remind us that organizations do not operate in a vacuum, but conduct their everyday routines through socially-defined routines. Although these routines may look similar, they are actually unique and distinct. The way in which we do business is biased by the social beliefs prevalent in the context of the operations.

On the organizational level, the industry is challenged by choices regarding differences in values and cultural orientation. Thus, the organization can discourage and minimize differences; it can ignore diversity; it can value and. encourage differences, or it can manage and accommodate differences. Mounting evidence indicates that effectively managing diversity can enhance revenues. The advantage of diversity for problem-solving, better decisions, and improved processes, can lead to higher quality and lower costs. However, a low capacity to manage diversity in work teams can lead to higher costs. The linkages between managing diversity and organizational costs include: (a) employee absenteeism and turnover, (b) barriers to contribution due to poor inter-group dynamics, (c) harassment behavior and discrimination suits, and (d) reduced efficiency of communication (Cox, 1997).

Figure 2.3 Diversity and organizational choices

Summary

This chapter has defined a number of differences in values and cultural orientation. Cultural variations in attitudes, beliefs and acceptable behaviors among a variety of national cultures were outlined, and important differences based on language, social viewpoint, and cultural upbringing or conditioning were suggested. The examples given here reflect only a small sample of differences that can exist among mixed crews.

As political and economic changes continue to accelerate the movement toward global alliances, workplace diversity continues to increase. Gaining insights about differences in values and orientation enables us to interact successfully in the global environment.

References

Cox, T. and Beale, R. (1997). *Developing Competency to Manage Diversity*, California: Berrett-Koehler.

Engle, M. (2000). 'Culture in the Cockpit – CRM in a Multicultural World', *Journal of Air Transportation*, 5 (3), 107-114.

Eugênio, Celio (2003). Personal communication.

Hofstede, G. (1991). *Cultures and Organizations: Software of the Mind, Intercultural Cooperation, and Its Importance for Survival*, Maidenhead: McGraw-Hill.

Helmreich, R.L. and Merritt, A.C. (1998). *Culture at Work in Aviation and Medicine: National, Organizational and Professional Influences*, Aldershot: Avebury.

Helmreich, R.L.and Merritt, A.C. (1997). 'Local Solutions for Global Problems: The Need for Specificity in Addressing Human Factors Issues', in R.S. Jensen (Ed.) *Proceedings of the Ninth International Symposium on Aviation Psychology*, Columbus, OH: Ohio State University.

Helmreich, R. and Merritt, A.C. (1997). 'Cultural Issues in Crew Resource Management Training', ICAO Global Human Factors Seminar, Auckland, New Zealand.

Javidan, M. and House, R. (2001). 'Cultural Acumen for the Global Manager: Lessons from Project GLOBE', *Organizational Dynamics, 29* (4), 289-305.

Lewis, R.D. (2000). *When Cultures Collide: Managing Successfully Across Cultures*, London: Nicholas Brealey.

Lie, A.M. (1997). 'Cultural and Organizational Challenges for Human Factors Training', in Telfer, R. & Moore, P. *Aviation Training: Learners, Instruction, and Organization*. Aldershot: Avebury, pp. 311-322.

Maurino, D. (2000). 'Human Factors and Aviation Safety: What the Industry Has, What the Industry Needs', *Ergonomics, 43* (7), 952-59.

Merritt, A.C. (1993). 'The Influence of National and Organizational Culture on Human Performance', *The CRM Advocate*, Michigan: Western Michigan University Press.

Merritt, A.C. and Ratwatte (1998). 'Who Are You Calling a Safety Threat'? A Debate on Safety in Mono Versus Multi-Cultural Cockpits', in R.S. Jensen (Ed.) *Proceedings of the Ninth International Symposium on Aviation Psychology*, Columbus, OH: Ohio State University.

Chapter 3

Teaching Non-Native English Speakers: Challenges and Strategies

Irene Henley and Wayne Daly

Introduction

The language and cultural differences between students engaged in training using English as a Second Language (ESL) and their native English speaking teachers have been studied in several disciplines and especially within mainstream primary, secondary and tertiary education (Chur-Hansen, Vernon-Roberts and Clark, 1997; Crago, Eriks-Brophy, Pesco and McAlpine, 1997; Hofstede, 1986, 1991; Grant and Secada, 1990; Mezger, 1992; Mpofu, Lanphear, Steward, Das, Ridding and Dunn, 1998; Ortiz and Kushner, 1997; Zoreda, 1997). However, the impact of ESL on the training of *ab initio* pilots has been afforded scarce attention (Daly, 2000; Henley and Berlioz-Nott, 1997; Soros, Henley, Wyndham and Nicoll, 1995). As a result, while strategies based on research conducted mainly in the field of education have been implemented to enhance the effectiveness of teaching and learning in many educational environments where students come from non-native English speaking backgrounds, few programs to assist non-native English speaking student pilots and their native English speaking flight instructors have been developed within the aviation training context. This represents a deficiency in the information required for the effective instruction of student pilots from non-native English speaking backgrounds. Given the highly technical and safety-oriented requirements of flight training and the critical role that clear, unequivocal communication plays in aviation safety, this is an issue that urgently warrants attention (Cushing, 1994). Crew Resource Management (CRM) courses and human factors training within the airline industry seem to be a few of the exceptions to this unsatisfactory state of affairs in aviation education (e.g., Johnston, 1992; Maurino, 1994; Merritt, 1997; Merritt and Helmreich, 1996; Sherman, Helmreich and Merritt, 1997; Soeters and Boer, 2000).

The mediation of any perceived pedagogical difficulties experienced by non-native English speaking students and their instructors in elementary flight training begins with the recognition and identification of challenges or difficulties experienced by both students and instructors. Therefore, the perceptions of student pilots from non-native English speaking backgrounds and of native English speaking flight instructors represents the primary phase in the development of ESL mediation strategies in the flight training curriculum.

Accordingly, small-scale research projects were undertaken in Australia to obtain the perceptions of non-native English speaking student pilots and their English speaking flight instructors in order to determine the occurrence and the nature of communication and learning difficulties encountered during *ab initio* flight training and to identify the types of stressors or challenges experienced by both the students and the instructors when ESL is used in flight training (Daly, 2000; Henley and Berlioz-Notts, 1997; Soros et al., 1995). This chapter highlights the major findings of these research projects and outlines strategies suggested by the participants or gleaned from the authors' personal experience as practitioners in the field of aviation education.

Communication and Culture

Communication difficulties in aviation are the subject of much concern particularly when those difficulties contribute to the occurrence of accidents, such as that experienced at Tenerife, in 1977. This particular accident represents the world's worst aviation accident to date and demonstrates the problems surrounding communication via radiotelephony, combined with the nuances of linguistic diversity (Diedericks-Verschoor, 1997; Job, 1996). Although such major occurrences are infrequent, their potential exists, particularly in operational environments where non-native English speaking pilots must communicate with other non-native English speakers or with native English speakers. For example, between 1993 and 1999, 45 language-related occurrences were reported in Australia, wherein the primary contributing factor was communication difficulties between air traffic controllers and non-native English speaking flight crews (Bureau of Air Safety Investigation [BASI], 1999). Most of these incidents involved elementary training flights, with student pilots in command. Although most were minor, some incidents occurred in close proximity to passenger-carrying flights, which heightens concern for safety.

The growth of the aviation industry, particularly in Asia, has heralded a considerable demand for the training of pilots from different ethnic backgrounds and, as a result, has accentuated the impact of language on communication in elementary flight training (Ostinga, 1994). According to Hofstede (1986) and Samovar, Porter and Jain (1981), Asian and Western cultures rank as the most 'different' of all the international cultures, sub-cultures and sub-groups that were compared, between which communication is frequently difficult. Since Anglo-Western countries are popular training destinations for non-native English speaking student pilots, the potential for language-based miscommunication in flight training exists with the possibility of language problems leading to system failures (BASI, 1999; Lewis, Phelan and Learmount, 1994; Ostinga, 1994).

At the inter-cultural interface, it is also possible to envisage that flight instructors could experience instructional problems and that student pilots will encounter adaptation and learning difficulties since interactions between teachers and students are deeply rooted in the culture of a society (Albert and Nelson, 1993). Studies dealing with stereotyping, interpersonal attitudes, and behaviour in culturally heterogenous groups have also revealed that interaction across cultural barriers often produces substantial problems (Crago et al., 1997; Fiedler, 1966; Fiedler, Mitchell and Triandis, 1971; Hofstede, 1986, 1991; Merritt, 1997; Triandis, 1975, 1976). It is when two cultures come together that behaviors and attitudes are tested. Psychologists, educators, and social psychologists have noted a variety of reactions of individuals in inter-cultural situations or encounters, these being spread on a spectrum from feeling 'excited' to 'ill-at-ease', with a sort of 'wait and see' position in between. The reactions depend on the individuals, their personalities, and cultural backgrounds (Albert and Nelson, 1993; Casse, 1981; Hofstede, 1986, 1991; Merritt, 1997).

The confrontation with the new cultural setting during the initial stages of acculturation can also lead to some emotional reactions and functional or dysfunctional behaviour such as fleeing, withdrawing, being aggressive, being assertive, giving up, or adjusting (Albert and Nelson, 1993; Davidson, Hansford and Moriarty, 1983; Zoreda, 1997). The problem experienced in adjusting to a new cultural setting is often referred to as 'culture shock'. According to Irving (1984), the term culture shock 'expresses the anxiety that results from the loss of commonly perceived and understood signs and symbols of social interaction. The person experiencing culture shock, regardless of his or her customary good will and broadmindedness, often rejects the people and the environment which cause the discomfort' (p. 140). As a result, culture shock can negatively influence effective communication, and thus the learning outcomes for non-native English speaking students (Crago et al., 1997; Zoreda, 1997). Fortunately, the difficulties associated with culture shock usually dissipate over time (Hofstede, 1991; Mezger, 1992; Triandis, 1976).

Among the common difficulties encountered when members of different cultures meet are simple misunderstandings, and according to Hofstede (1986), these cross-cultural misunderstandings can and do occur in teaching/learning situations in which both teachers and pupils come from different cultures. Albert and Nelson (1993) explained that these misunderstandings 'occur in part because individuals from different cultures frequently (a) expect different kinds of behaviour in a given situation, and (b) interpret the same behaviour differently' (pp. 19-20). Landis (1985) also noted that 'two individuals from different cultures can view the same interpersonal situation or event and make diverse attributions regarding the cause of people's behaviour. This perceptual difference may lead to tension and/or conflict, even though the individuals may be well intentioned' (p. 467). These negative effects of inter-cultural interaction and communication can affect both teaching and learning strategies (Crago et al., 1997; Zoreda, 1997).

The status or role of the parties involved in cross-cultural encounters can also influence communication. According to Hofstede (1986) and Mezger (1992), many Asian and Pacific students afford the teacher role high status and respect, which should not be challenged by questioning. This can obviously create a problem in classroom communication between the teacher and the student, where the Western teacher's expectation is that students ask questions, disagree or argue a point, or where students are expected to speak up if they do not understand, whereas the non-native English speaking students would perceive such behaviour as disrespectful or confrontational (Crago et al., 1997; Hofstede, 1986; Merritt, 1996).

Davidson et al. (1983) further underlined that the 'minority culture' is more likely to be disadvantaged as a result of cross-cultural miscommunications and misunderstandings because differences in communication, norms, structures and patterns also predispose the parties toward a misjudgement of academic and communicative competence, which may lead to incorrect assessments of the cause of educational difficulties (Crago et al., 1997; Mezger, 1992; Ortiz and Kushner, 1997; Zoreda, 1997). Therefore, it is important that teachers of second language students be made aware of such misconceptions and that they become sensitive to cultural miscommunications, so they can create a 'stress-free, trusting environment for learning' (Lapp and Flood, 1994, p. 261). This is especially important when the teaching/learning experience takes place in a non-traditional environment, such as the cockpit of a small aircraft, which can be both challenging and threatening for many *ab initio* students. Further, in the aviation context, concerns surrounding student pilots who speak English as a second language relate not only to educational outcomes, but also to possible communication difficulties, which have the potential of leading to a misunderstanding of directions or instructions issued during flight. Aviation safety is the ultimate inheritor of any such misunderstandings or misinterpretations, which may manifest in inadequate aircraft separation or major occurrences such as an aircraft collision.

Challenges Associated with Teaching Non-Native English Speaking Students

Flight instructors who participated in studies conducted by Henley and Berlioz-Nott (1997) and by Soros et al. (1995) identified several stressors or areas of concern associated with teaching non-native English speaking students, supporting the findings of Albert and Nelson (1993) that cross-cultural instruction *is* 'fundamentally problematic' (p. 19). Henley and Berlioz-Nott's (1997) research revealed that language barriers increased the workload of flight instructors teaching students from non-native-English speaking backgrounds and created additional stress to other work and life stressors. Furthermore, it was found that reactions to stress can, at times, adversely affect both the instructor's and the student's performance (Henley, 1987; Soros et al., 1995). Research by Daly (2000) also underlined the potential for ESL to impact upon progress rates, educational outcomes and completion standards in elementary flight training. The issues or problems that flight instructors found particularly challenging are regrouped under five main categories: flight instructor training and education, the level of English proficiency of non-native English speaking students, cultural differences, additional workload, and the training environment and commercial pressures.

Flight Instructor Training and Education

Educators are fully aware that effective communication is essential in any teaching/ learning situation, but miscommunications routinely happen within the classroom, yet, as the literature shows, misunderstandings are likely to be more frequent when teachers and students are from different language backgrounds. Research by Albert and Nelson (1993) revealed that the difficulty, or the inability to communicate effectively with 'foreigners' had some negative effects in the training environment. Davidson et al. (1983) concurred, stating that 'reticence or anxiety about engaging in communication with others may inhibit the oral communication act and deleteriously affect certain types of occupational performance' (p. 98). In addition, a study by Henley (1995) found that many flight instructors lack effective teaching and communication skills which could further aggravate cross-cultural misunderstandings. Consequently, it is possible that the inability to attain a 'shared meaning system', coupled with inadequate teaching and communication skills, could contribute to the stress experienced by flight instructors teaching students of non-native English speaking backgrounds and the anxiety felt by students, and thus, negatively impact on learning outcomes.

The majority of the flight instructors who participated in the Australian research projects confirmed Henley's (1995) findings, stating that their instructor training did not adequately prepare them to cope with the problems that arise when teaching students from non-native English speaking backgrounds. As a result, many instructors, especially inexperienced instructors, said that they found it quite stressful to find ways, mainly through trial and error, of coping with the difficulties of cross-cultural instruction (Daly, 2000; Henley and Berlioz-Nott, 1997; Soros et al., 1995). Instructors noted that although difficulties surrounding the tuition of non-native English speaking student pilots have *'been an issue for at least 15 years, nobody's done anything about it'*, as a result, their *'experience and skills [in teaching non-native English speaking students] were picked-up on the job'* (cited in Daly, 2000, pp. 32-33). Many instructors stressed that if they had had at least some awareness of the kind of problems they would encounter when teaching non-native English speaking students, and if they had been taught strategies to overcome these problems, they would have been able to cope more effectively with the situations in which they found themselves, and they would have been able to adjust more readily to the different teaching approaches needed.

Understandably, novice flight instructors found their work more challenging than did the more experienced instructors. Novice instructors felt that they did not have the depth of knowledge or the experience to efficiently identify learning problems or to find adequate solutions to students' problems. Many reiterated that fault analysis and *'how to handle learning problems caused by poor English'* had not been covered adequately during their flight instructor training (Daly, 2000; Henley and Berlioz-Nott, 1997; Soros et al., 1995).

The Level of English Proficiency of Non-Native English Speaking Students

All the flight instructors who participated in the Australian research projects indicated that they felt that the low level of English proficiency of non-native English speaking student pilots was an important contributor to the learning problems and safety impediments experienced in elementary flight training. Several instructors added that the language barriers they faced with non-native English speaking students was also a main source of stress (Soros et al., 1995).

According to most instructors, some of the major challenges they faced were *'getting the message across'* to students, and *'making sure they've understood it correctly'* (Daly, 2000; Henley and Berlioz-Nott, 1997). The main contributor to these problems, instructors felt, was the non-native English speaking students' inability to understand what the instructor was saying, or simply the lack of confidence and/or command of the English language to be able to explain what they did not understand.

The concern about how to cope when it became obvious that the students did not understand also created stress for the instructors. As one instructor said: *'when they've got the blank looks, but they don't have enough English to be able to ask a question – that's stressful, because you don't know where to start'* (cited in Henley and Berlioz-Nott, 1997, p. 630). Many instructors indicated that their stress level was increased because, at times, they *'simply run out of ways to explain different concepts'*, if the student did not understand. As one experienced instructor explained, when native English speaking students have difficulties, instructors can usually resort to several other methods of explaining something. However, with the non-native English speaking students, introducing different scenarios or different words often has the effect of producing further confusion, and hence creates a more stressful situation for both the instructor and the student.

Another problem faced by instructors is that many second language learners are often 'more familiar with the technical aspects of English, such as the structure, pronunciation, stress and intonation of the language than the more abstract and less accessible, yet very important, rules of how to communicate in a particular cultural context' (Irving, 1984, p. 138). Further, according to Mezger (1992) and Ortiz and Kushner (1997), students take longer to overcome understanding difficulties when the English terminology is complex and technical, because initially students rely heavily on direct translation, which usually proves more problematic.

To further complicate matters, the aviation community has its own technical jargon which could have a negative influence on the learning and performance of non-native English speaking students. Instructors explained that, although *'English speaking students would most likely not have previously heard some of the aviation terms used, they can pick up the meanings quite easily'* (cited in Henley and Berlioz-Nott, 1997, p. 632). However, with the non-native English speaking students, instructors said that they have to take more time to explain new terms, and they have to *'break the explanation down so they [the students] can understand it, which all takes time and can become very frustrating, especially when you're not paid for that time'* (Ibid.). Some of the expressions that were provided as examples included: *'watch your attitude'* or *'bank the aircraft'*. Similarly, many non-native English speaking students initially find the terms 'upwind' and 'downwind' very confusing because here the word 'up' actually indicates a wind coming from the front, a headwind, not a wind from above. Similarly, the term 'down' really means a wind from behind, a tailwind, and not a wind that is below one's position.

Finally, many flight instructors also tend to use colourful language to describe actions or to give instructions to students (e.g., don't let the airspeed 'bleed' off, do a 'teardrop' approach onto final, don't let the wing drop, etc.). Students from non-native English speaking backgrounds could easily become confused when seeking the literal meanings of such dialogue. Understandably, instructors said that having to constantly be aware of the language that they use, and trying to avoid the use of idiomatic expressions or slang, rendered the teaching interaction more challenging and less genuine or spontaneous (Henley and Berlioz-Nott, 1997; Soros et al., 1995).

Ground Instruction   Ground instructors indicated that classes with non-native English speaking students required *'more work and preparation'* (Henley and Berlioz-Nott, 1997). They added that when students from different cultural backgrounds were placed in the same ground school classes, they found it more challenging to cope with the differing learning styles, learning approaches, and learning rates of the mixed group. They also felt that it was more difficult to find a *'happy medium'* to keep everybody interested: *'You've sort of got to balance between not making it too boring, yet you've got to make them all understand – so that's stressful as well'* (cited in Henley and Berlioz-Nott, 1997, p. 630).

Instructors also indicated that it was difficult to provide non-native English speaking students with the same depth of understanding as that provided to native English speaking students because, with non-native English speaking students, they needed to greatly simplify their lessons, use less complex theory and provide more graphic representations of the concepts being presented (Daly, 2000). However, in spite of their best efforts, several instructors said that non-native English speaking students frequently *'missed out on the most important part of their [theoretical] training, the fundamentals, because they haven't understood it'* (cited in Daly, 2000, p. 31). Instructors also emphasised that misunderstanding and misinterpretations arising in class were subsequently manifested in flight *'because the students are not equipped with the right information'* (Ibid., p. 30). Although flight instructors were very concerned about the fact that students often did not possess the fundamentals of aviation theory, they stressed that misunderstandings that manifested themselves in the air were much more problematic because *'when they've got the wrong interpretation in the air it's more dangerous'* (Ibid., p. 31).

Flight Training   All the flight instructors who were interviewed stressed that the current levels of English required for non-native English speaking students by their respective flying schools, and/or the levels displayed by their overseas students, were far from adequate for effective communication, especially within the operational aviation context. In the demanding environment of the cockpit of a small training aircraft, language and communication problems can, at times, create high levels of stress. Instructors reported that, in the air, the major source of instructional problems and stressors was the inability of the students to quickly understand their instruction or the feedback and correctives they provided. One instructor explained: *'When they're doing something incorrectly, you try to explain what to do but they're just confused, and so for the whole flight they wonder why didn't this work because you haven't been able to explain it clearly in a way they would understand. So that's frustrating. They can have the manipulative skills, but it's really the lack of language proficiency that makes it worse'* (cited in Henley and Berlioz-Nott, 1997, p. 630). As mentioned earlier, instructors also identified the restrictions in the usage of their own language as a major challenge and a distraction because they constantly have to watch what they say, and how they say it: *'Having to break words down into simple meanings, and always trying not to use slang can really be a challenging task'* (Ibid.).

Instructors also identified potential operational safety deficiencies arising from language-related difficulties (Daly, 2000; Henley and Berlioz-Nott, 1997; Soros et al., 1995). One instructor explained that because of the poor level of English of the non-native English speaking students, they often will not complete *'a vital action that [they've been] asked to perform'* because they fail to understand the instructor's directions. Obviously, this can compromise safety, particularly in emergency simulations, *'because we're operating the aeroplane in an abnormal situation, with poor communication between the members of the crew'* (cited in Daly, 2000, p. 32).

Many flight instructors indicated that they found sending non-native English speaking students on solo flights, especially at controlled airports, to be particularly stressful because they were never sure how they would deal with non-standard phraseology or possible misunderstandings. Several instructors also reported that they experienced stress caused by time pressures in the air. Flight instructors teach in a dynamic (operational) environment, and as a result, they are often time-limited because of safety considerations (see Henley, Wiggins, Bye and Turney, 2003). Instructors underlined that, in the air, they do not always have the time needed to explain a word or an expression that a student may not have understood. This can create stress and confusion. Nevertheless, one instructor added that even though students were having problems, he tried to refrain from taking over too early because students needed to recognize their mistakes and learn to make their own decisions: *'the student gets upset, but you have to try and hold back from over-riding what they're doing!'* (cited in Henley and Berlioz-Nott, 1997, p. 630). Many instructors underscored that the decision of *'when to take over'* was always a challenging call to make (Soros et al., 1995).

Communication problems in the cockpit are often exacerbated by the fact that student pilots need to interact with Air Traffic Control (ATC) and understand communications from other pilots. One instructor explained that most of the difficulties encountered during flight training surrounded the *'misinterpretation of directions from ATC and a loss of situational awareness by the student, when trying to coordinate their activities with other pilots'* (cited in Daly, 2000, p. 29). Instructors also mentioned that non-native English speaking student pilots frequently did not communicate *'the information that's necessary'* to other pilots and to ATC and that they seldom understood *'communications from other pilots'*. This led to situations where the non-native English speaking students *'are not able to resolve things such as traffic conflicts, on the basis that they can't tell other people where they are'* (cited in Daly, 2000, p. 30). Another instructor added that the students *'just can't visualize where traffic is, either by positions given to them by [the pilots of] other aeroplanes or from traffic [information] given by ATC'* (Ibid.). Hofstede (1986) relates this mode of difficulty to the differing cognitive profiles of non-native English speakers which might predispose one ethnic society to an enhanced or a reduced potential toward the learning of some skills.

Instructors also indicated that communication can deteriorate further if controllers or other pilots used non-standard phraseology: *'It's a very busy environment, there's a lot of traffic, a lot of radio calls to be made, and if the controllers start cutting words off, or using slang, then it makes it even more difficult for the students'* (cited in Henley and Berlioz-Nott, 1997, p. 632). Further, if any non-standard phraseology was used by ATC, the instructors found that they again had to spend more time on the ground during the post-flight briefing going *'through each [new] word in the dictionary because he [the student] didn't understand it and couldn't see what was happening!'* (Ibid.).

In-flight decisions are made based on information received by the pilot from numerous sources, including from radio communication. Instructors noted that non-native English speaking students frequently *'made decisions based on misinterpreting traffic [situations]'* (cited in Daly, 2000, p. 31). Such misinterpretations usually lead to poor decisions, compelling instructors *'to countermand their decisions, otherwise it would've led to a breakdown in safety'* (Ibid.). Another instructor described the following incident as an example of poor decision-making due to misunderstanding and an inadequate comprehension of the traffic situation in-flight. This particular occurrence happened during the conduct of a flight test for the initial issue of a multi-engine instrument rating. The candidate was a non-native English speaking student who had recently completed his commercial pilot training and successfully passed the Commercial Pilot Licence flight test. During departure, the pilot of a transport category aircraft used non-standard phraseology to request traffic information and *'sort out separation'* between his aircraft and that of the student. The use of non-standard phraseology compounded the difficulties experienced by the non-native English speaking student, who *'was quite happy to maintain a level attitude that was on a collision course [with the other aircraft]'* (cited in Daly, 2000, pp. 31-32). Although the other pilot spoke to the student by radio to clarify the traffic situation, *'the student just acknowledged, as they do, but he didn't understand. So the other fellow assumed it was OK and he just kept climbing through our level'* (Ibid., p. 32). Had the examiner not intervened, safety would have been compromised. The instructor stressed that this was not an isolated case and added that in many situations *'it certainly could have been dangerous if they were on their own'* (Ibid.).

Many flight instructors also indicated that in addition to the constant vigilance required for safety reasons, instructors of non-native English speaking students had the added burden of continually having to monitor exactly how their students responded to each radio transmission received from ATC, because *'even when the students do not understand what they hear, they do not question ATC'* (cited in Berlioz-Nott, 1995, p. 24). This sometimes leads to potentially dangerous situations, increasing instructor stress because the students do not realize the gravity of the situation. One instructor explained: *'They just keep going – they're not disturbed at all by what's occurred! It's things like that that make you anxious about letting them go out by themselves, if they're going to make those sorts of mistakes!'* (cited in Henley and Berlioz-Nott, 1997, p. 632). Consequently, instructors indicated that they usually end up doing more flying with overseas students because they are afraid to send them by themselves (Henley and Berlioz-Nott, 1997; Soros et al., 1995).

Cultural Differences

Another impediment to effective communication, identified by the instructors, was that non-native English speaking students generally fail to indicate any apparent misunderstanding that occurs during training (Daly, 2000; Henley and Berlioz-Nott, 1997; Soros et al., 1995). Moreover, despite being aware of their lack of comprehension, non-native English speaking students often indicate that they understand. However, according to Hofstede (1986) and Mezger (1992), the cultural norms of individuals of Asian ethnicity usually dictate that students should understand teachers' instructions upon first explanation. Furthermore, such norms also discourage students from making subsequent requests for explanation and elaboration of instructions, requiring instead that students conduct personal research to improve their level of understanding. This is not the case in Australia, or in most Western countries, where the expectation of instructors is that students query misunderstood lesson elements and ask for clarifications or for further explanations (Hofstede, 1986; Mezger, 1992). Such differences between the cultural expectations of the two groups necessitate the development of an awareness and subsequent adaptation on the part of the instructors, rather than on the part of the students (Hofstede, 1986; Mezger, 1992). Sadly, as mentioned earlier, instructors did not receive specific training to prepare them for their role as flight instructors of students coming from different ethnic backgrounds. As a result, many are initially unaware of these different expectations.

Many instructors labeled some students, who were predominantly from Asian backgrounds, as '*Yes people because they say yes even when they don't understand you*' (cited in Henley and Berlioz-Nott, 1997, p. 630). However, as mentioned above, for many foreign students, this unwillingness to admit that they do not understand stems as much from their cultural background as from a lack of proficiency in English. Indeed, non-native English speaking students interviewed by Daly (2000) confirmed that their native culture normally prevented them '*from asking questions of their instructor*' (p. 28). Merritt (1996) explained that 'each participant brings to the interaction his or her own culturally influenced perception of the difference in power between themselves and the other' (p. 137). Therefore, while the Anglo instructor may construe the student's behaviour as denial or non-participation it may be that the student would consider it rude or disrespectful to indicate that the instructor's explanation was not clear or was not understood.

Finally, an additional source of stress for some female instructors, who teach students from different ethnic groups, arose from the fact that, in general, males of certain cultural backgrounds and societies regard '*females as the one that looks after you, does the housework and that sort of stuff*' (Henley and Berlioz-Nott, 1997; Soros et al., 1995). Most aggravating for some female instructors was the lack of respect for women or the '*arrogance*' of some of the students. One instructor noted: '*It's not in their culture to be in a position where they have to take directions from a female. And I don't think they respect females. They try to undermine you. It's very frustrating and quite rude'* (cited in Henley and Berlioz-Nott, 1997, p. 630). Most female instructors said that, given the choice, they would prefer not to instruct a student who displayed such sexist tendencies.

Additional Workload

Research by Henley, Nicoll and Soros (1994) revealed that flight instructors found teaching non-native-English speaking students particularly stressful because language barriers added to their workload. As most instructors stressed, having to spend additional time in the briefing room with students would not normally be a problem, however, many instructors still are not paid for the time they spend on the ground briefing students. In the words of one instructor this *'is an appalling situation'*. Another instructor explained: *'You have to spend three times as much time briefing before a flight with these students. If we were paid for that briefing time, then it would not affect you as much. I'm not earning a lot of money, so to spend three hours briefing a student for a one hour flight – it's a big drain on your pay – it's half a day gone!'* (cited in Henley and Berlioz-Nott, 1997, p. 631).

Understandably, flight instructors indicated that, because of their financial plight, having to spend additional time in the briefing room with non-native English speaking students was very problematic (see Henley, 1995; Henley and Berlioz-Nott, 1997; Soros et al., 1995). Many instructors noted that they were often torn between endeavouring to provide cost effective training for their students by giving them appropriate ground preparation so that they would get the most out of the flying hour, and the internal pressures of earning enough money to live on.

Training Environment and Commercial Pressures

Many instructors reported that they were under pressure from the management of their flying school to get non-native-English speaking students through their training in the minimum number of hours in order to keep the students or their sponsoring agency (national airline or government) happy, and to establish and maintain a good reputation for the school in the industry and overseas. The main problem, according to some instructors, is that in some cases, management succumbs to commercial pressures and accepts students with a sub-standard command of the English language, thus increasing the workload and stress of instructors. As one instructor put it, *'Operators are trying to get students in for commercial reasons, irrespective of their level of English'* (cited in Daly, 2000, p. 33). Most instructors believed that *'it all comes down to the big dollar'*, and that *'most CFIs [Chief Flying Instructors] are under commercial pressures to accept all the students they can take, so, it's <u>not</u> in their best interest to say: No, you don't speak English well enough – see you later!'* (cited in Henley and Berlioz-Nott, 1997, p. 631). While instructors stressed that accepting students who lack proficiency in English obviously increased their workload, they stressed that more importantly it *'compromised safety [and] certainly compromised the effectiveness of the instruction, because they've allowed people to come in with poor levels of*

English – in some cases zero level of English!' (cited in Daly, 2000, p. 33).

Finally, many instructors also felt that they did not have enough flexibility with scheduling. They explained that the less time allocated between flight bookings, the more money the company made. One instructor noted: *'Some students have problems and would require more time for some lessons or after the lesson, yet you have to end the lesson because you know you have another booking'* (cited in Soros et al., 1995, p. 957). As a result, many misunderstandings or misinterpretations remain unclarified leaving both students and instructors frustrated.

Effect of Stress on Flight Instructor Behaviour

In a study examining flight instructor stress, Henley, Nicoll and Soros (1994) determined that, under periods of stress, instructors 'often develop maladaptive behaviours ... which can affect student learning and performance' (p. 4). This is supported by Blase's (1986) and French's (1991) findings which suggested that under stress teachers may develop behaviors and attitudes which might interfere with their teaching. Blase (1986) listed anger in the form of frustration, rage and resentment as the predominant feeling associated with student-related stressors.

The majority of the flight instructors who participated in studies conducted by Henley et al. (1994) and Soros et al. (1995) recognized that their stress was often reflected in their behaviour and that it affected their own performance as well as their students' performance (see Henley, 2003). Instructors indicated that in times of high stress they tended to be more irritable and became more easily impatient with students. One instructor explained: *'When I'm under pressure and start to get impatient with students, whether you recognise it or not, they can tell, they get feedback from it and usually their performance gets worse, so I just have to take a deep breath and say to myself, okay, cool it, just shut up and calm down. But it affects the student's performance'* (cited in Soros et al., p. 958). Indeed, student pilots in a previous study by Henley (1987) agreed, indicating that their learning and their performance were adversely affected by instructors who displayed impatience by scolding, yelling, or yanking the controls.

Most instructors admitted that they felt bad when they became impatient with students, but sometimes the stress level is very high, due in part to the dynamic environment in which they teach, so it can be difficult to maintain composure. One instructor explained: *'We're emotional beings too. When your emotions are such that you feel this person has just screwed up again and you just want to yell and scream and pull your hair out. It's not that you don't care, but you've got to let out some steam. You feel bad after, but it's too late, the student has gone home'* (cited in Soros et al., 1995, p. 958). At least half of the flight instructors also indicated that they became more easily frustrated or impatient with difficult students, such as those who experienced learning problems or students who were having problems understanding, especially in the air. One instructor explained:

I'm a relatively patient character, yet I'll catch myself being very irritable or impatient sometimes. Again those times I'm not so patient, when I'll snap at the student or whatever, they're not necessarily things about the student. I can really narrow them down to situations where irrelevant of the instructing that I have done, I CAN'T SOLVE that problem. You're at the end of your rope. You've tried all your tricks and it doesn't work. You don't know how to put it across to the student, so you start getting impatient with him. But in reality, it's me. I'm impatient with myself for not knowing how to solve the student's learning problem (cited in Soros et al., 1995, p. 958).

These data are consistent with data from Blase's (1986) research which emphasised that 'while under stress, teachers behave differently with students; they become less tolerant, less patient, less caring, and, overall, less involved. Humor, elaboration of subject matter, and creative involvement are noticeably lacking when the teacher is experiencing significant stress. All in all, the interaction between teacher and student is depreciated' (pp. 32-33).

Challenges Faced by Non-Native English Students

The interviews with non-native English speaking student pilots highlighted some of the problems that they encountered and corroborated, in many respects, the issues raised by the instructors. The students interviewed in the Australian research projects were from Korean, Malaysian, Chinese, and Fijian backgrounds, some of whom displayed a very poor command of the English language. The major difficulties faced by these students involved overcoming communication and language barriers in the initial stages of training, adjusting to a new culture, and for many, adapting to a distinctively different training approach and learning environment (Daly, 2000; Henley and Berlioz-Nott, 1997; Soros et al., 1995).

Language and Communication Problems

Non-native English speaking student pilots indicated that one of the major challenges they faced surrounded differences between the English they studied in their country and that used by their flight instructors, air traffic controllers and other pilots in the country where they were training. In particular, the fast rate of speech and the range of accents in spoken English made comprehension difficult (Berlioz-Nott, 1995; Daly, 2000; Henley and Berlioz-Nott, 1997). Adding to the language problem was the use of slang or local idiomatic expressions by many of the flight instructors (Daly, 2000; Soros et al., 1997). Many students said that they felt that their instructors '*talk really fast*' and that their '*accent [was] very different and difficult to understand*' (Berlioz-Nott, 1995, p. 24). However, the dynamic environment of flight training and safety considerations mean that instructors sometimes have to speak quickly during flight, even though they know that this could be a major challenge for non-native English speaking students.

In Daly's (2000) study, participating non-native English speaking student pilots also indicated that they experienced difficulty learning the skills necessary to achieve the requisite levels of competence in both ground theory and flight instruction because of their lack of proficiency in English. As one student stated: '*I make some mistakes, but I don't know why, and sometimes my flying instructor give information to me, but my English is not sufficient, and so I don't understand fully – just understand half. If my English is good – fully I understand, and come to next flying, I don't mistake again. That's problem*' (cited in Berlioz-Nott, 1995, p. 24). Studies in other disciplines have indeed shown that inadequate English proficiency tended to lead to a decrease in academic performance (Chur-Hanson et al., 1997; Mpofu et al., 1998; Ortiz and Kushner, 1997). Most student pilots underlined that their poor level of verbal and oral comprehension skills were major impediments, especially in the air. One student explained that his '*English training was writing and reading, so my skill listening and speaking did not begin good enough [for flight training]*' (cited in Daly, 2000, p. 20). Another student agreed, indicating that '*most Korean student[s'] reading and writing is good, but listening is very poor! At school we learn [English] through writing, and reading. Have no chance to learn communication [skills]*' (cited in Berlioz-Nott, 1995, p. 25).

Radio communication proved particularly problematic for non-native English speaking students. However, this is understandable because someone learning a different language initially relies heavily on non-verbal cues besides verbal communication in order to understand what is being said (Chur-Hanson et al., 1997; Crago et al., 1997; Hofstede, 1986; Merritt, 1996). Indeed, in addition to verbal cues, some of the non-verbal elements include gesture, expression, and posture (body language), each forming a part of the component element of communication known as a signal. The reception of components of the communication process is synergistic. Accordingly, effective communication usually relies on the reception of signal elements in combination, not individually (Weiten, 1995).

Many admitted that they experienced serious difficulties communicating with ATC and understanding what controllers or other pilots were saying. In addition, many stated that there were many occurrences in flight when ATC did not understand their radio transmissions and during which the students were unable to resolve the ambiguities. One student explained that '*half of time traffic controller say unpredictable things, so I have no idea what he said*' (cited in Daly, 2000, p. 23). The student felt that unless the instructor covered every possible in-flight communication exchange during pre-flight briefings, there was a high probability that he would misunderstand radio transmissions with ATC. Understandably, most students indicated that they felt '*very nervous ATC might not understand*' them, which is a common feeling among non-native English speaking students in most domains, according to Mezger (1992). Many students indicated that they attempted to overcome the communication problems experienced in the air by memorising the radio calls they were supposed to use for a particular flight, the success of which, as mentioned by the instructors, was dependent on the phraseology used by ATC and/or other pilots and the situation being normal or as anticipated.

These difficulties in understanding instructions are compounded by the fact that students have to safely manipulate the aircraft controls at the same time as process verbal information. When instructors or air traffic controllers give instructions or directions, students need to shift their attention from the aircraft to the instructor or controller at a time when attention demands to simply fly the aircraft are already very high. As a result, stress increases and performance usually deteriorates (Henley, 1987).

Not surprisingly, non-native English speaking students found communication easier with instructors from non-native English speaking backgrounds, concurrent with findings by Hofstede (1986) and Ortiz and Kushner (1997). Students felt that these instructors were more understanding because they had experienced similar difficulties themselves. However, while non-native English speaking students feel more comfortable being taught by instructors from non-native English speaking backgrounds, unless the teaching is in the students' native language, Hofstede (1986) stated that having a non-native English speaking instructor provides few learning advantages for the non-native English speaking student.

Cultural Problems

Many non-native English speaking students indicated that, because of their cultural background or their poor command of English, they were reluctant or unable to question their instructors or ask for clarifications if they did not understand the instructor's explanations. One student said: '*Sometimes I don't understand what he say. There are lots of questions during learning to fly, but sometimes I can't question my instructor because I don't have [the] word*s' (cited in Berlioz-Nott, 1995, p. 23). Students also admitted that quite frequently they proclaimed that they understood instructions from their instructor, ATC or other pilots even though they did not understand, mainly because they wanted '*just to keep going*' for the benefit of other students in a class, or to save face (Berlioz-Nott, 1995; Soros et al., 1995).

Some students also explained that even if they had undertaken language training prior to commencing flight training, it had taken them up to four months to be able to understand the language well enough, or to be confident enough in talking to their instructor to indicate that they did not understand, and to ask clarifications or explanations. However, many students also noted that they still indicated that they understood in some situations even though they did not fully understand because, in their culture, it would be a rude lack of respect to point out to their instructor that his or her explanation was unclear or inadequate. One student explained that in his culture, he had '*to respect [the] instructor, not asking too much, and [I] have to understand by myself*' (cited in Daly, 2000, p. 25). Hofstede (1986) and Crago et al. (1997) describe such feelings as common in educational settings involving non-native English speaking students. Samovar et al. (1981) added that the reluctance to acknowledge misunderstanding is more evident when the cultures involved are so diametrically different, as is the case with Asian and Western nationalities.

New Learning Environment and Different Teaching Style

Students who were interviewed indicated that coming to grips with the idea of actually flying a small aircraft and adapting to the new (foreign) situations in which they found themselves were indeed challenging, making learning in the initial stages of training quite overwhelming and difficult. One student said: *'Back home I didn't even get a chance to get close to a light aircraft – the only aircraft you see is at the airport, or flying across. So when I came here, it's like Wow! – fascinating at first. Secondly, everything happened so fast, everything was so new, it really took me some time to adapt to that situation!'* (cited in Berlioz-Nott, 1995, p. 24). Another student explained that at first he was overwhelmed and apprehensive: *'the first time in the air, you can't believe you're up there in a small plane. In the air there's a lot of pressure on you, and if it's turbulent – at first you're scared and you can't think clearly!'* (Ibid., p. 22). These reactions or feelings, however, are not limited to non-native English speakers. Most student pilots feel overwhelmed or apprehensive during the initial stages of flight training (see Henley, 1987).

Finally, some overseas students indicated that they had problems adapting to the teaching style generally used in flight training. The practical (applied), interactive approach used by instructors was seen as challenging because until now they had been used mainly to a teacher-centred, didactic approach. Many Korean students indicated that the one-on-one, participative nature of flight instruction conflicted with their previous learning experiences which consisted mainly of mass lectures where students were not expected to interact and where they were expected to memorise the content as presented (Daly, 2000). Hofstede (1986), Mezger (1992) and Merritt (1996, 1997) agree that non-native English speaking students, particularly those of Asian ethnicity, often experience difficulty adapting to the teaching methods of their Western teachers due to the appreciably different cultural expectations of the two groups. According to Hofstede (1986) and Mezger (1992), these differing expectations can lead to educational problems, the preponderance of which can cause a reduction in the rate of learning.

Strategies to Address the Cross-Cultural Learning/Teaching Issues

Both flight instructors and non-native English speaking student pilots who participated in the Australian research projects suggested several strategies to address the issues highlighted above. Most suggestions centered mainly around the provision of better training for both instructors and students and the requirement for higher levels of English proficiency for non-native English speaking students undertaking flight training. Flight instructors also underlined the leading role that both the accreditation agency and the flight training organisation needed to play in addressing some of the challenges encountered in providing flight instruction to non-native English speaking students.

Higher Entry Level of English Proficiency for Non-Native English Speakers

The participating flight instructors suggested two primary ways of improving the present situation regarding the inadequate level of English proficiency of non-native English speaking students. Firstly, they felt strongly that the flight training industry should be regulated in order to ensure that all overseas students meet minimum English language requirements, and they stressed that the onus should be on the regulatory body to set the standards. They also emphasised that the specified mandatory level of English competency needed to be appropriate to the demands of the aviation operational environment (Daly, 2000; Henley and Berlioz-Nott, 1997; Soros et al., 1995). This concurs with recommendations made by BASI (1999) and ICAO (2001). The primary objective of the instructors' recommendation was to *'take the pressure off the industry, because the commercial pressures are always going to out-weigh turning away a guy because he can't speak English'* (cited in Henley and Berlioz-Nott, 1997, p. 633).

Secondly, all the flight instructors stressed that the present minimum level of English competency required by most flying schools had to be much higher and that students needed to achieve the specified level of English proficiency *before* they undertake flight training. One instructor stated: *'We have a minimum English level for our students, but I think it's not high enough, it needs to be higher – especially in the environment that they're flying in – they need a much higher level of English because safety is at stake here'* (cited in Henley and Berlioz-Nott, 1997, p. 633). The typical International English Language Testing System (IELTS) ranking required by the few flying schools that do require a minimum standard of English for the overseas students they accept is usually an overall ranking of five, which qualifies the student as a 'modest user' of the English language, who 'has partial command of the language, coping with overall meaning in most situations, though is likely to make many mistakes' (International English Language Testing Systems, 1998, p. 26). Most instructors felt that such a ranking was inadequate for the aviation context.

Instructors suggested that the minimum level should be an IELTS ranking of six, which describes the student as a 'competent user', who 'has generally effective command of the language despite some inaccuracies, inappropriateness and misunderstandings' (Ibid.). Some instructors insisted that the ranking should even be higher than six because as one instructor noted, piloting is *'a fairly demanding job as far as English goes. You've got to be competent on the radio – you've got to be competent when you're receiving information, and you've got to be able to translate it into practical use and sometimes very quickly'* (cited in Henley and Berlioz-Nott, 1997, p. 633). Another instructor added: *'the environment for aviation is more demanding than normal tertiary education. Perhaps an IELTS of 7.0 would be a reasonable minimum'* (cited in Daly, 2000, p. 33). Several flight instructors indicated that while a ranking of six might be acceptable for writing and reading skills, a ranking of seven should probably be required for speaking and oral comprehension (Henley and Berlioz-Nott, 1997; Soros et al., 1995).

To achieve the higher standards of English, instructors also proposed that the students should not only undergo English instruction, but should also be given '*a grounding in aviation English*' to facilitate their learning in ground briefings, and during air exercises (Daly, 2000; Henley and Berlioz-Nott, 1997). They added that a course in aviation terminology would help to improve overseas students' ability to communicate more effectively with their instructors and especially with ATC and other pilots when using the radio in the aircraft.

Most overseas students agreed with the instructors indicating that they '*needed [a] higher level [of] English*'. Several students suggested that more contact with the instructors would help to improve their communication skills as well as their instructor/student relationship. Some students also indicated that living with a native English speaking family would be invaluable to accelerate their progress in learning English. One student echoed the views of most saying: '*During the English school, I lived Australian home-stay, and this very good. We always talking with each other, I learnt a lot of English. If all overseas students lived with Australian, that's better. But if the school doesn't give information about that, it's very difficult to find by yourself*' (cited in Berlioz-Nott, p. 25).

The Role of the Flying Organisation

Most instructors indicated that they did not feel that the flying school where they worked was catering adequately for overseas students primarily because '*they're not giving the instructors an understanding of where the students are coming from!*' (cited in Henley and Berlioz-Nott, 1997, p. 633). Some instructors insisted that if flying schools apply to have contracts with overseas airlines to train their cadet pilots, or if the schools have a considerable number of overseas students as their customers, then '*it's the responsibility of the school to give the instructors and the students a greater understanding of each other's cultural backgrounds*' (Ibid.). Most instructors suggested that flying schools could provide their instructors with an orientation course or seminar on the language and culture of the overseas students they marketed, highlighting that '*it would make you understand, and let you know what you're in for*' (Ibid.). Hofstede (1986) and Mezger (1997) stress that an awareness of cultural heterogeneity is the foundation for the development of intervention strategies, which are enhanced by training the teachers of non-native English speaking students.

According to Triandis (1976) and Zoreda (1997), only when instructors are trained to recognise the contribution of cultural heterogeneity to misunderstanding will they be equipped to plan for and avoid cultural misunderstandings. In line with what Hofstede (1991) suggested, complimentary to instructor education in ESL principles could be the development of instructors' awareness of the Western cultural expectations in education. A comparison of those expectations to the educational expectations of other cultures could identify differences, which could be used in the development of pedagogical approaches to be employed in flight training. This may further alleviate training difficulties and aid in the improvement of aviation safety.

Teaching Principles and Techniques and Cross-Cultural Awareness

Instructors also stressed the need to place more emphasis on '*teaching instructors how to teach, rather than teaching them what they've got to say for the first fifteen lessons!*' (cited in Henley, 1995, p. 128). To do this, instructors believed flying schools should require their trainee instructors to complete an in-depth study of the principles and methods of instruction and be exposed to different teaching strategies '*so that people know how to explain things in different ways*' (cited in Henley, 1995, p. 128). They also stressed that flight instructor rating courses should dedicate part of the syllabus to '*giving the trainees the proper way of dealing with the problems they will face, particularly problems that come from the cultural side – because that's something we can't change*' (cited in Henley and Berlioz-Nott, 1997, p. 633). Hofstede (1986) and Mezger (1992) both stressed that expanding instructors' awareness of cultural heterogeneity is the foundation for the development of intervention strategies which are further enhanced by training the teachers of non-native English speaking students.

Senior instructors also suggested that in order to avert the problem of having students proclaiming they understood when in reality they did not fully understand, instructors should be taught to use more effective evaluating strategies. As one instructor advised, '*instead of simply asking students if they understand, instructors should ask them to explain the concept or manoeuvre in their own words*' (cited in Henley, 1995, p. 199). One instructor stated that if the students say 'Yes!', then '*I'll ask them to explain it back to me – it's the only way to really check if the students do understand what has been said*' (cited in Henley and Berlioz-Nott, 1997, p. 632). Instructors also noted that if they took the time to provide students with extra tuition on the ground, in pre-flight briefings, their time in the air could be less stressful. Instructors also emphasised the importance of using standard phraseology with non-native English speaking students in order to minimise confusion and misunderstanding as well as the likelihood of stress-producing occurrences or safety breaches in the air. Finally, instructors stressed that perseverance and patience were key traits needed when dealing with the stress experienced in teaching non-native English speaking students (Henley and Berlioz-Nott, 1997; Soros et al., 1995).

Summary

The review of studies undertaken in Australia has highlighted the fact that cross-cultural aviation instruction can be problematic and can increase the stress experienced by both flight instructors and non-native English speaking students. Stress stemming from cultural and language barriers was experienced because instructors and students find it hard to develop or utilise 'a shared meaning system'. The problem is often exacerbated by external factors experienced by instructors, such as the dynamic or operational teaching environment, pressures from management, working conditions imposed on instructors, and inadequate instructor training. Further, research by Henley (1987, 1995) revealed that stress is at times linked to negative feelings and behaviours that made satisfactory interactions with students much more difficult because the instructor's reaction to stress can affect both the instructor's and the student's actions.

The data also underlined some implications for organisations and regulatory bodies involved in the training of overseas students, and the development and maintenance of training standards. Foremost on the agenda is the need to increase the present level of English language skills required by overseas students. Secondly, there is a need for training organisations to place greater emphasis on instructor training and the preparation of instructors for cross-cultural instruction.

As the overseas aviation training market expands, it is obvious that these issues need to be addressed for the benefit of both the instructors and the non-native English speaking students and to improve the quality of cross-cultural aviation education. A better understanding of the issues raised here could be achieved through future research probing such areas as the effectiveness of various teaching techniques in promoting understanding for overseas students, the development of cultural training programs (for training staff), the effectiveness of a specific syllabus or training schedule for overseas students, and the evaluation of the effectiveness of an 'Aviation English' course for overseas students. It is only through further research to address these issues that the present problems encountered in cross-cultural training can be rectified for the benefit of not only the instructor fraternity, but also the overseas training industry as a whole.

The flight training industry stands to benefit significantly from the continued enrolment of international students, in a manner not dissimilar to that experienced by other educational institutions in which diverse students are enrolled (Mezger, 1992). Mezger (1992) suggested that the revenue increases experienced by educational institutions in which diverse students are enrolled improves profitability, and subsequently, the range and quality of education and facilities available. Similarly, benefits to the flight training industry are manifested in the improved financial ability of the relevant institutions to engage in research, development and capital growth, thus improving the overall product (Ostinga, 1994). Furthermore, as the revenue from this type of flight training originates from overseas markets, export trade earnings expand, thereby providing the added benefit of aiding the national economy. Overall, there is much benefit for all parties derived from the education of overseas pilots. Therefore, an industry focus on appropriate methods for the improvement of the training product can be very advantageous, particularly to student pilots and flight training organisations.

References

Albert, R.D. and Nelson, G.L. (1993). 'Hispanic/Anglo-American Differences in Attributions to Paralinguistic Behaviour', *International Journal of Intercultural Relations, 17*, 19-40.

Berlioz-Nott, L. (1995). *Stress of Flight Instructors Teaching Students of Non-English Speaking Backgrounds*, Unpublished Directed Research Project, Australia: University of Newcastle.

Blase, J.J. (1986, Spring). 'A Qualitative Analysis of Sources of Teacher Stress: Consequences for Performance', *American Educational Research Journal, 23*(1), 13-40.

Bureau of Air Safety Investigation. (1999, September). 'The Language Barrier', *Asia Pacific Air Safety, 23*, 28-29.

Casse, P. (1981). *Training for the Cross-Cultural Mind* (2nd Ed.), Washington, DC: The Society for Intercultural Education, Training and Research.

Chur-Hansen, A., Vernon-Roberts, J. and Clark, S. (1997). 'Language Background, English Language Proficiency and Medical Communication Skills of Medical Students', *Medical Education, 31*, 259-263.

Crago, M.B., Eriks-Brophy, A., Pesco, D. and McAlpine, L. (1997). 'Culturally Based Miscommunication in Classroom Interaction', *Language, Speech and Hearing Services in Schools, 28*, 245-254.

Cushing, S. (1994). *Fatal Words: Communication Clashes and Aircraft Crashes*, Chicago: University Press.

Daly, W. (2000). *Perceptions on the Impact of English as a Second Language in Flight Training in Australia*, Unpublished Master's Directed Research Project, Australia: University of Western Sydney.

Davidson, G., Hansford, B. and Moriarty, B. (1983). 'Interpersonal Apprehension and Cultural Majority-Minority Communication', *Australian Psychologist, 46*(2), 159-184.

Diederiks-Verschoor, I.H.Ph. (1997). *An Introduction to Air Law* (6th ed.), The Hague: The Netherlands: Kluwer Law International.

Fiedler, F.E. (1966). 'The Effect of Leadership and Cultural Heterogeneity on Group Performance: A Test of the Contingency Model', *Journal of Experimental Social Psychology, 2*, 237-264.

Fiedler, F.E., Mitchell, T. and Triandis, H.C. (1971). 'The Culture Assimilator: An Approach to Cross-Cultural Training', *Journal of Applied Psychology, 55*(2), 95-102.

French, N.K. (1991), 'Elementary Teachers' Perceptions of Stressful Events and Stress-Related Teaching Practices, *Perceptual and Motor Skills, 72*, 203-210.

Grant, C.A. and Secada, W. (1990). 'Preparing Teachers for Diversity', in W.R. Houston (ed.), *Handbook of Research in Teacher Education*, NewYork: Macmillan, pp. 403-22.

Henley, I. (1987). *The Association between Student Pilot Stress and Flight Instructor Training: A Study of Perceptions*. Unpublished Master's Thesis. Winnipeg, Canada: The University of Manitoba.

Henley, I. (1995). *The Quality of the Development and Evaluation of Flight Instructors in Canada and Australia*. Unpublished Doctoral Dissertation, Australia: University of Newcastle.

Henley, I. (2003). 'Factors That Affect Learning', in I. Henley (ed.), *Aviation Education and Training: Adult Learning Principles and Teaching Strategies*, Aldershot: Ashgate, pp. 135-172.

Henley, I. and Berlioz-Nott, L.P.H. (1997). 'Stress of Flight Instructors Teaching Students of Non-English Speaking Backgrounds', in R.S. Jensen and L.A. Rakovan (eds.), *Proceedings of the 9th International Symposium on Aviation Psychology*, Columbus, OH: Ohio State University, pp. 629-634.

Henley, I., Nicoll, H. and Soros, S. (1994, October). 'Flight Instructor Stress', *Australian Aviation*, 36-38.

Henley, I., Wiggins, M., Bye, J. and Turney, M.A. (2003). 'Teaching Complex Psychomotor Skills', in I. Henley (ed.), *Aviation Education and Training: Adult Learning Principles and Teaching Strategies*, Aldershot, UK: Ashgate, pp. 239-274.

Hofstede, G. (1986). 'Cultural Differences in Teaching and Learning', *International Journal of Intercultural Relations, 10*, 301-320.

Hofstede, G. (1991). *Cultures and Organizations*, London: McGraw Hill.

International English Language Testing System. (1998, April). *IELTS Handbook*, Cambridge, UK: University of Cambridge Local Examination Syndicate.

Irving, K.J. (1984, Spring). 'Cross-Cultural Awareness and the English-as-a-Second-Language Classroom', *Theory and Practice, 23*(2), 138-143.

Job, M. (1996). *Air Disaster* (Vol. 1), Aerospace Publications, Australia: Fyshwick.

Johnston, A.N. (1992), *CRM – Cross Cultural Perspectives*, Aviation Psychology Research Group, Dublin: Trinity College.

Landis, D. (1985). 'Attributional Training Versus Contact in Acculturative Learning: A Laboratory Study', *Journal of Applied Social Psychology, 15*(5), 466-482.

Lapp, D. and Flood, J. (1994, November). 'Are We Communicating? Effective Instruction for Students Who Are Acquiring English as a Second Language, *The Reading Teacher, 48*(3), 260-264.

Lewis, P., Phelan, P. and Learmount, D. (1994, December 14-20). Gravy Training: How Are Pacific Rim Airlines Coping with a Growing Need for Ab Initio Trainee Pilots? *Flight International*, 37-38.

Maurino, D.E. (1994). 'Crosscultural Perspectives in Human Factors Training: Lessons from the ICAO Human Factors Program', *International Journal of Aviation Psychology, 4*(2), 173-181.

Merritt, A. (1996). 'Facing the Issue: Indirect Communication in Aviation', in B.J. Hayward and A.R. Lowe (eds.), *Applied Aviation Psychology: Achievement, Change and Challenge*, Australian Aviation Psychology Association, Aldershot: Avebury Aviation, pp. 135-142.

Merritt, A. (1997). 'Replicating Hofstede: A Study of Pilots in Eighteen Countries', in R.S. Jensen and L.A. Rakovan (eds.), *Proceedings of the 9th International Symposium on Aviation Psychology*, Columbus, OH: Ohio State University, pp. 667-762.

Merritt, A. and Helmreich, R.L. (1996). 'Human Factors on the Flight Deck: The Influence of National Culture", *Journal of Cross-Cultural Psychology, 27*, 5-24.

Mezger, J. (1992). *Bridging the Intercultural Communication Gap: A Guide for TAFE Teachers of International Students*, National TAFE Overseas Network, Australia: Hobart.

Miles, M.B. and Huberman, A.M. (1994). *Qualitative Data Analysis: An Expanded Sourcebook* (2nd ed.), London: Sage Publications.

Mpofu, D.J.S., Lanphear, J., Stewart, T., Das, M., Ridding, P and Dunn, E. (1998). 'Facility with the English Language and Problem-Based Learning Group Interaction: Findings from an Arabic Setting', *Medical Education, 32*, pp. 479-485.

Oberle, J. (1990, April). 'Teaching English as a Second Language', *Training, 27*, 61-67.

Ortiz, A.A. and Kushner, M.I. (1997). 'Bilingualism and the possible impact on academic performance, *Academic Difficulties, 6*(3), 657-677.

Ostinga, J. (1994 Mar/Apr). 'Blue skies ahead'? *Australian Flying*, 22-27.

Samovar, L.A, Porter, R.E. and Jain, N.C. (1981). *Understanding intercultural communication*, Belmont, USA: Wadsworth Publishing.

Sherman, P.J., Helmreich, R.L. and Merritt, A.C. (1997). 'National Culture and Flight Deck Automation: Results of a Multination Survey', *International Journal of Aviation Psychology, 7*(4), 311-329.

Soeters, J.L. and Boer, P.C. (2000). 'Culture and Flight Safety in Military Aviation', *International Journal of Aviation Psychology, 10* (2), 111-133.

Soros, S., Henley, I., Wyndham, B. and Nicoll, H. (1995). 'Flight Instructor Stress', in R.S. Jensen and L.A. Rakovan (eds.), *Proceedings of the 8th International Symposium on Aviation Psychology*, Columbus, OH: Ohio State University, pp. 955-960.

Triandis, H.C. (1975). 'Cultural Training, Cognitive Complexity, and Interpersonal Attitudes', in R. Brislin, S. Brochner and W. Lonner (eds.), *Cross-Cultural Perspectives on Learning*, New York: Sage/Halsted/Wiley, pp. 39-77.

Triandis, H.C. (1976). *Interpersonal Behavior*, Brooks/Cole Publishing, Monterey, CA.

Weiten, W. (1995). *Psychology: Themes and Variations* (3rd ed.), Pacific Grove, CA: Brooks/Cole Publishing.

Zoreda, M.L. (1997). 'Cross-Cultural Relations and Pedagogy', *American Behavioral Scientist, 40* (7), 923-935.

Chapter 4

Learning Style Preferences Affect Training Outcomes

Merrill R. Karp

Introduction

Projected long-term shortages in the commercial pilot population, coupled with the low representation of women and minorities in career pilot positions, suggests that institutions providing aviation education and training should re-examine the structure and organization of the aviation knowledge transfer process to assure that the aviation industry is able to attract and retain the best pilots candidates. This chapter examines how aviation education can best serve the aviation student's learning style needs, with the goal of providing the best education to meet the desired training outcomes for a diverse student population. The chapter looks at how students learn best and considers knowledge transfer opportunities which colleges and universities can use to enhance aviation education retention and application.

Specifically, learning style theory will be discussed, from the viewpoint of the wide diversity of aviation learners who are dominantly visual, auditory, or hands-on, tactile, or kinesthetic learners, and how individuals' dominant learning styles are pivotal to their success. By exploring how people learn best, and then providing those learners with the tools to take advantage of their dominant learning styles, the next generation of pilots, both women and men, should be better prepared to enter the aviation industry trained to be highly flexible and more adaptable that ever before. Expanding the size of the potential commercial pilot pool by providing for the learning styles of all individuals interested in aviation will also help reduce the long-term projected commercial pilot/technical workforce shortage.

Background

Certainly ongoing research will improve aviation flight training and simulation; however, less has been done to improve the classroom component of aviation education. A pertinent long-term commercial pilot supply factor is the question of the depth and quality of aviation academic education as well as the flight training, of those future commercial pilots. Because of the increasing sophistication of modern aircraft and its high technology equipment, this topic underscores a need to examine, and restructure where necessary, the training options for potential commercial pilots. Any academic program must ensure that the aviation education process involves an in-depth, effective transfer of knowledge across a broad spectrum of aviation subjects. When considering aviation education, the academic component of flight training plays an important role in providing the knowledge base for a new pilot. This academic education has the potential to build an exceptionally solid foundation for ensuring the high standard of technical and flying knowledge needed for future airline pilots.

In developing educational programs, it is important to know how people learn best, and why they succeed. Because of the depth and complexity of the subject matter, aviation academic instructors must present the course material in ways that satisfy the different needs and learning styles of aviation students. Likewise, students must understand their own learning style and try to maintain more focused attention to information being presented in a teaching style that is not easily compatible with their individual learning style.

Learning Style Research

There is some concern in academic circles that traditional higher education is producing students with only a surface approach to learning, rather than the more desired in-depth, or deep learning (Booth & James, 2001). In a highly demanding and technically complex field such as aviation, it is critical for students to have a thorough understanding of the subject, in order to be able to apply acquired knowledge acquired across the broadest spectrum of new situations.

Learning Style Theory and Correlated Strategies

Learning style theory - the way people learn best - is of considerable importance in developing and delivering aviation academic programs. There are many models that have been developed to consider learning styles.

One descriptive concept classifies preferred learning styles into five groups: sensory/intuitive, visual/verbal, inductive/deductive, active/reflective, and sequential/global. This model concludes that the teaching style of most teachers does not generally match the learning style of most students; the students appear to learn better from processes that are sensory, visual, inductive, and active, while lectures tend to be verbal, deductive, and passive (Felder & Silverman, 1988).

Another closely aligned concept is that of visual-spatial aptitude. Visual-spatial aptitude is the ability to form and control mental images by manipulating and orienting an object mentally to create mind-structures (Trindale, Fiolhais, & Almeida, 2002). Visual-spatial aptitude has been further subdivided into two parts: spatial orientation, concerning the awareness or appreciation of spatial relations and image constancy; and spatial visualization, concerning mental manipulations into other visual patterns (Lord, 1985). Research has revealed that visual-spatial learners frequently do not feel comfortable in the traditional classroom because of the emphasis on lecturing, rote memorization, drill, and practice exercises (Trindale, et al, 2002).

Research has also indicated that the following strategies are effective in teaching students with visual-spatial aptitudes: (1) using computers for visual presentations, (2) emphasizing creativity, imagination, new insights, and new approaches, rather than passive learning, (3) using manipulative materials to allow hands-on experience, (4) having students use problem-solving methods, (5) using inductive approaches, in-lieu of rote memorization, (6) engaging students in independent studies or group projects which involve problem-finding and problem-solving, (7) finding out what the students have already learned before attempting to teach them new subjects, (8) allowing students to construct, draw and create visual representations, and (9) emphasizing mastery of higher-level concepts rather than perfection of simpler concepts (Silverman, 1998).

Additionally, there is strong evidence that employing virtual environments and 3-D graphics facilitates the formation of conceptual models to take advantage of visual-spatial aptitude. These environments provide the opportunity to develop applications using acquired higher skills (Trindale, et al, 2002).

A widely used model proposed by Bloom (1964) divides knowledge into three domains: (1) cognitive skills, which start with surface learning knowledge and increase through comprehension, application, analysis and synthesis, until reaching evaluation and deep learning; (2) affective skills, or emotional skills, which start with receiving, responding, valuing and organizing, until reaching characterization; and (3) psychomotor skills, which involves repetitive use of the hands, body, and movement to product learning. All three of these domains should be considered when developing academic curriculum programs.

Noted learning-style theorist David Klob (1984) suggests that there are four types of preferred learning styles (Figure 4.1): (1) Diverger, the imaginative problem-solver; (2) Assimilator, the rational theory-builder; (3) Converger, the practical solutions developer; and (4) Accommodator, the hands-on experience learner. In Kolb's model, each learning style is depicted as a quadrant of a cross defined by how an individual prefers to *perceive* the information on one axis and how they prefer to *process* the information on the other axis. The axes are defined as: (1) Concrete Experience (CE), the 'feelers'; (2) Reflective Observation (RO); the 'watchers'; (3) Abstract Conceptualization (AC), the 'thinkers'; and (4) Active Experimentation (AE), the 'doers.'

Kolb's preferred learning styles can also be characterized by the following questions: *Assimilators* ask 'what?', *Accommodators* ask 'what if?', *Convergers* ask 'how?', and *Divergers* ask 'why?' A typical lecture format, in contrast to these four broad questions, tends to address only the question of 'what?' (Booth & James, 2001).

Kolb's learning theory suggests that the cycle of learning starts with the learner's active involvement in a specific experience. It begins with a *concrete experience*. The learner then *reflects* on the experience by looking at it in a variety of different ways. From this reflection on the experience, the learner draws

conclusions in the cognitive process of *abstract conceptualization.* The learning
cycle is completed when the learner takes action as result of these conclusions in
active experimentation (Heywood, 1997).

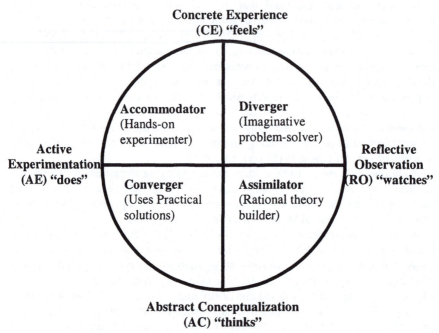

Figure 4.1 Kolb's learning style theory diagram

Using Kolb's model, the learning style is determined by the boundaries of the axes
where the individual prefers to learn, that is: *Convergers'* dominant learning styles
are abstract conceptualization and active experimentation; *Divergers'* dominant
learning styles are best in situations of concrete experience and reflective
observation; *Assimilators'* dominant learning styles are abstract conceptualization
and reflective observation; and *Accommodators'* dominant learning styles are
concrete experience and active experimentation (Heywood, 1997).

Another related learning theory on processing styles considers two types of
learners (Filipczak, 1995): *Global processors,* who need to have an overview of
the material first, then be presented the particular facts, and *analytic processors,*
who need to be given the individual facts first, then be given the composite picture
after all the facts have been received. Filipczak's research deduces that about half
the population are global processors, one-quarter are analytical processors, and the
rest of the population adjusts to either processing style (pp. 43-48).

While the preceding learning style models are all valid and predictive in
various situations, for aviation education a model is needed that can be easily

employed in the classroom for both the learner and the educator to assure that knowledge is transferred on the highest level of effectiveness.

One model that meets these requirements suggests that there are three recognized primary, or dominant, learning styles: First, *visual learners*, who learn best by reading or looking at pictures. Second, *auditory, or aural, learners*, who learn best by listening. And third, *hands-on, tactile, or kinesthetic learners*, who need to use their hands or whole body to learn (Filipczak, 1995). If knowledge transfer is to take place within the entire classroom population, then all of these dominant learning styles should be addressed in the academic environment.

In a study dealing with this specific learning style model, an assessment instrument (Appendix A) was administered to 390 collegiate aviation students (195 women and 195 men) from representative aviation students of university and college members of the University Aviation Association (UAA) from around the country (Karp, Turney, Green, Sitler, Bishop, & Niemczyk, 2002). This instrument was part of a larger research project administered for the overall effort of 'Maximizing retention of women students enrolled in collegiate aviation programs.' The individual university and college aviation faculty representatives who assisted in the data collection distributed the surveys to all of their female aviation students and an equal number of their male aviation students.

Results of Learning Style Research in Aviation Settings

Women Respondents Of the 195 women respondents, 112 (57.4%) were either dominant hands-on learners, or an equal combination of hands-on and visual and/or auditory learners (Table 4.1).

Table 4.1 Dominant learning styles of women respondents (n=195)

Learning Style	Number	Percentage
Visual (dominant)	62	31.8%
Auditory (dominant)	15	7.7%
Hands-On (dominant)	87	44.6%
Visual/Auditory (equal dominance)	6	3.1%
Auditory/Hands-On (equal dominance)	7	3.6%
Visual/Hands-On (equal dominance)	15	7.7%
Visual/Auditory/Hands-on (equal)	3	1.5%
Total	195	100%

Men Respondents Of the 195 men respondents, 118 (60.5%) were either dominant hands-on learners, or an equal combination of hands-on and visual and/or auditory learners (Table 4.2).

Comparison of Women and Men Respondents Comparing the results of the women and men respondents, a picture becomes apparent that women and men in collegiate aviation are very similar in their dominant learning styles. For example, 44.6% of the women indicated that they were dominantly hands-on learners, compared to 45.1% of the men respondents.

Table 4.2 Dominant learning styles of men respondents (n=195)

Learning Style	Number	Percentage
Visual (dominant)	56	28.7%
Auditory (dominant)	15	7.7%
Hands-On (dominant)	88	45.1%
Visual/Auditory (equal dominance)	6	3.1%
Auditory/Hands-On (equal dominance)	10	5.1%
Visual/Hands-On (equal dominance)	14	7.2%
Visual/Auditory/Hands-on (equal)	6	3.1%
Total	195	100%

A quantitative analysis was performed comparing male and female learning styles (without consideration of equal dominance). For this analysis, each respondent was considered to have a percentage of responses in each of the three categories. Percentages were used because males tended to give more responses than females and so accurate analysis required the use of proportions.

A two-sided unpaired t-test was used to compare the male and female responses for each of the three learning styles. The resulting p-values for the visual and hands-on responses showed no significant result at any reasonable significance level. The responses in these two categories were clearly very close. The auditory p-value was .18, which does not show significance at a reasonable level (.05 or .10). However, this does suggest the possibility that males are slightly less auditory-oriented than females.

Composite of Women and Men Respondents Of the total of 390 women and men respondents, 221 (56.7%) were either dominant hands-on learners, or an equal combination of hands-on and visual and/or auditory learners (Table 4.3). Individuals in collegiate aviation, whether they are women or men, are very dominantly hands-on learners and need that 'tactile' connection to process and retain knowledge.

Table 4.3   Dominant learning styles of both women and men respondents (n=390)

Learning Style	Number	Percentage
Visual (dominant)	118	30.3%
Auditory (dominant)	30	7.7%
Hands-On (dominant)	175	44.9%
Visual/Auditory (equal dominance)	12	3.1%
Auditory/Hands-On (equal dominance)	17	4.3%
Visual/Hands-On (equal dominance)	29	7.4%%
Visual/Auditory/Hands-on (equal)	9	2.3%
Total	390	100%

Evaluation of Results

In spite of the research indicating that a majority of pilots are predominantly either hands-on or an equal combination of hands-on and visual and/or auditory learners, previous research indicated that most classroom environments are auditory in nature, with visual supplementation, and very little, if any, hands-on learning applications (Karp, 2000). What is needed is an integrated approach to aviation education that includes all learners' needs.

The Integrated Aviation Learning Model

Considering the theoretical underpinnings and previous research conducted with aviation students, an integrated aviation learning model, the *Aviation Education Reinforcement Option* or *AERO model*© (Figure 4.2) has been developed to increase retention and enhance application of aviation education with a focus on airline flight operations. The major components include adult learning, in-depth theory, immediate application, group learning, and learning style theory (Karp, 2000).

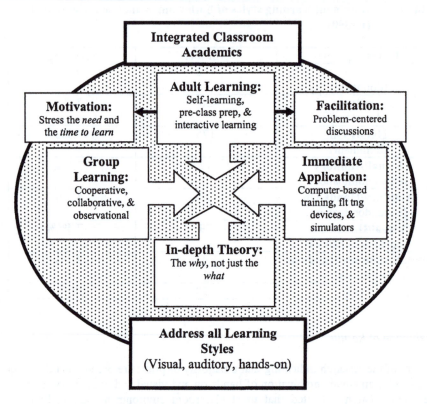

Figure 4.2   Integrated Aviation Learning Model
Aviation Education Reinforcement Option (AERO Model)©

Adult Learning

Since university-age students are in a transition from adolescent learning to adult learning, beginning aviation students must be 'focused' toward self-directed learning to attain their maximum potential. This includes *motivating* the learners by stressing the need to acquire the knowledge and to recognize that this is the time to learn it. While a lecture alone can provide limited information, a learner has little or no knowledge of a subject, *facilitating* the knowledge transfer is more effective to increase knowledge by engaging learners in an exchange of ideas in *problem-centered discussions* and by tapping into their prior experiences.

In-Depth Theory

In order for pilots to apply recently acquired knowledge to new situations, they must have an in-depth understanding of systems and procedures. That is, a detailed comprehension of the *why*, and not just the *what*. Lectures on foundational information should be delivered in the classroom using a video projector to display computer presentation programs and personal computer-based flight simulator programs, to visually reinforce the lessons.

Immediate Application

Then, following each classroom lesson, learners should go to a laboratory for immediate, hands-on application of the lesson components to reinforce the knowledge transfer using PC-Based Aviation Training Devices (PCATD) personal computer-based flight simulator programs, Flight Training Devices (FTD), or flight simulators. Immediate application of acquired knowledge is critical for adult learning and reinforcement to take place.

Computer programs for instruction and tutoring in technical subjects are also particularly useful in aviation education. Computer-Based Instruction (CBI) programs can be used extensively for pre-class preparation, as well as post-class review and reinforcement. CBI programs allow the student to accomplish self-paced learning in a non-threatening environment. In addition to supporting the CBI programs, the same basic computer equipment can be augmented with a control yoke and a throttle/avionics package to be used with flight simulator programs such as a PCATD. The FAA approved PCATDs are relatively low-cost training vehicles that can be easily and effectively integrated into an aviation education curriculum. They are well suited as an educational bridge between the basic, traditional aviation classroom, and the advanced, high technology aviation flight environment (Karp, 1996). Additionally, the CBIs and PCATDs using flight simulator programs help provide educational components to accommodate multiple learning styles, thereby meeting more individuals' learning needs than are met by classroom lecture alone.

Group Learning

Group learning in small 'praxis teams' is particularly applicable to aviation students. Group learning includes cooperative, collaborative, and observational learning. *Cooperative learning* takes place when learner teams give presentations and fly simulator missions as assigned by an educator. In contrast, *collaborative learning* takes place when the educator makes an overall assignment to the group for presentations or flight simulator missions, and the group itself determines who will do what, and how. In the collaborative learning laboratory, the teams 'fly' approaches or Line-Oriented Flight Training (LOFT) profiles, using 'pilot-flying/

pilot-not-flying' procedures early in their training to reinforce multi-crew concepts, as well as airline-oriented challenge-and-response type checklists and procedures. Collaborative learning has proven to be an especially reinforcing process for aviators. The *observational learning* element in group learning includes a non-flying team observing the team that is presenting or flying, either in the classroom or in the collaborative learning personal computer-based flight simulator laboratory. These observational teams then provide a post-presentation or post-simulator flight assessment. This group learning component provides direct peer feedback for the team that is flying or presenting, and objective observational learning for the non-flying or presenting team.

Computer-supported collaborative learning (CSCL) is emerging as the most promising computer-mediated instruction model by improving team performance through enhanced peer group decision-making, communication, and collaborative activities using electronically-based mediation (Wang, Hinn, & Kanfer, 2001).

Learning Style Theory Application

Throughout the various stages of aviation learning (educator lecture, learner cooperative and collaborative presentations and flight simulator missions), the material should be delivered in visual, auditory, and hands-on learning approaches to *address all students' dominant learning styles*. This is a major component of the Aviation Education Reinforcement Option Model (Figure 4.2).

Increasing the Use of Computer Technology to Implement Learning Style: Considerations in Aviation Education Knowledge Transfer

> In this new era, time is the master. Everyone not only needs access to information but also needs to keep up with the ever-changing nature of the knowledge bases. Although many learners will continue to expect their colleges and universities to provide them with the type of education their parents received in the last half of the twentieth century, many more will expect their colleges and universities to be more responsive to their increasing knowledge needs. Many learners who need college educations will want alternatives to the traditional models, alternatives that will provide them with learning opportunities when and where they want them.
>
> Rowley, Lujan, & Dolence, 1998

A working knowledge of available, off-the-shelf aviation computer-based programs is critical to successful pilot training curriculum development. By integrating a comprehensive understanding of learning style theory with the available technology, aviation students can be delivered a course of study that is in-depth in content, as well as highly reinforcing for hands-on, visual, and auditory learners.

Most students arrive at institutions of higher learning already computer-literate and ready to interact with the latest technology. Publishers are producing more high-quality interactive course materials. With this type of learner-centered material available, it could be considered a waste of classroom time to devote it to a 'lecture' that is not interesting, interactive, or engaging. That classroom time could be free for other uses, such as problem-solving and small group discussion, or, as laboratory time for simulators and experimentation with new procedures and techniques.

There are so many new computer-based learning opportunities such as computer-based simulators; CD-ROMs packed with data and interactive programs; on-line access to the latest information; digital libraries, databanks, search-engines, and the Internet to link the classroom to other places where learning can occur. Additionally, the increased use of laboratory setting to examine and solidify learning experiences, along with continual development of group interactions, will help make the learning experience meaningful, realistic, and relevant (Rowley, Lujan, & Dolence, 1998). The challenge facing the educator in the twenty-first century is to maximize teacher-student facilitation opportunities, by planning for, and fully using, all available computer-based assets for non-classroom learning.

Recommendations

1. Educators should administer to all aviation students a 'quick and easy-to-take' learning style assessment instrument (similar to Appendix A), to help them identify, for themselves, their own dominant learning style. The educator should then facilitate a discussion with the learners on how they might maximize their dominant learning style in day-to-day learning situations (by using an aid similar to Appendix B).

2. Educators should present their aviation curriculum using all three learning style environments (visual, auditory, and hands-on) so that *all students* have the best opportunity to reinforce the material using their dominant learning style(s). Employing PC-based training, including PC-based flight simulator programs, immediately following the classroom experience, is an excellent reinforcing vehicle to provide the hands-on learning opportunities which are critically needed by a large number of both women and men aviation students.

3. Students must both understand their particular dominant learning style and pay more attention to information that is being presented in a style in which they are not as effective a learner. Additionally, students must develop 'work-arounds' for comprehending material that is not being presented by an educator in their dominant learning style.

Conclusions

National Science Foundation in the United States reports that research on effective methods of instruction indicate that active, participative, and collaborative techniques, which engage students in real problems and issues, enhance learning. Student-centered active learning and demonstrated performance are the variables that correlate with learning and competency.

Division of Undergraduate Education, 1996

Summary

This chapter has considered aviation educational enhancements through the implementation of learning style theory strategies, as well as exploring gender specific learning style differences and similarities, to create a model to help assure that all aviation students' learning needs are addressed. The emphasis on the use of PC-based flight simulator programs is not aimed at reducing flight training or corresponding simulator training, but is rather focused on providing immediate, hands-on application following each academic class, to reinforce visual and auditory knowledge transfer. Providing immediate, hands-on application is directed toward on improving understanding and long-term retention of the subject matter, as well as increasing knowledge application across a broader spectrum.

By presenting classroom academic components so as to also accommodate hands-on learners, in additional to the historical presentation of the material in visual and auditory formats, more students (both male and female) should be able to maximize their learning potential because their specific learning needs will be addressed. For individuals who are not learning the subject matter fast enough because their learning style needs are not being met, presenting the material in visual, auditory, and hands-on formats should lead to increased student retention in aviation, if all other factors remain constant.

In order to retain the best people in aviation programs, aviation academic providers must design their academic curriculum and delivery vehicles to meet their students' specific learning styles, whether they are women or men. The investment in time to include all learning styles in an integrated aviation education program should pay high dividends in expanding the aviation learners' knowledge base, in enhancing their flexibility to address new situations, and in preparing the next generation of pilots to undertake their critical role in the global aviation industry.

References

Bloom, B. (1964). *The Taxonomy of Education Objectives*, London: Longman.
Booth, K. and James, B. (2001). 'Interactive Learning in Higher Education Level 1 Mechanics Module', *International Journal of Science Education, 23* (9), 955-967.
Division of Undergraduate Education (1996). *Division of Undergraduate News 1996*. Washington D.C.: National Science Foundation.
Felder, R. and Silverman, L. (1988). 'Learning and Teaching Styles in Engineering Education', *Journal of Engineering Education, 78*, 674-681.
Filipczak, B. (1995, March). 'Different Strokes: Learning in the Classroom', *Training, 32*, 43-48.

Heywood, J. (1997). 'An Evaluation of Kolb's Learning Style Theory by Graduate Student Teachers during their Teaching Practice', *Proceedings of the Annual Meeting of the Association of Teacher Educators, Washington D.C., February 1997.*

Karp, M. (1996). *Theoretical Aviation Training for Future Airline Pilots.* Doctoral Dissertation, Walden University, Minneapolis, MN. UMI 9713644.

Karp, M.R. (2000, October). 'University Aviation Education: An Integrated Model', *Collegiate Aviation Review, 18* (1).

Karp, M.R., Turney, M.A., Green, M., Sitler, R., Bishop, J. and Niemczyk, M. (2002). 'Retaining Women in Collegiate Aviation by Implementing Learning Style Considerations', *Collegiate Aviation Review, 20* (2).

Kolb, D. (1984). *Experiential Learning: Experience as the Source of Learning and Development,* New York: Prentice-Hall.

Kozma, R. and Johnston, J. (1991, January). 'The Technological Revolution Comes to the Classroom', *Change,* 16-18.

Lord, T. (1985). 'Enhancing the Visuo-Spatial Aptitude of Students', *Journal of Research in Science Teaching, 22,* 395-405.

Rowley, D., Lujan, H. and Dolence (1998). *Strategic Choices of the Academy,* San Francisco: Jossey-Bass.

Silverman, L. (1998). 'Effective Techniques for Teaching Highly Gifted Visual-Spatial Learners'.

Available at www.gifteddevelopment.com/articles/EffectiveTechniques.html.

Terry, M. (2001). 'Translating Learning Style Theory into University Teaching Practices: An Article Based on Kolb's Experiential Learning Model', *Journal of College Reading and Learning, 32* (1), 68-85.

Trindale, J., Fiolhais, C. and Almeida, L. (2002). 'Science Learning in Virtual Environments: A Descriptive Study', *British Journal of Educational Technology, 33* (4), 471-488.

Wang, X., Hinn, D. and Kanfer, A. (2001). 'Potential of Computer-Supported Collaborative Learning for Learners with Different Learning Styles', *Journal of Research on Technology in Education, 34* (1), 75-85.

Appendix A

Personal Characteristics

Directions: Circle the phrases that you think best reflect your personal characteristics. Circle as many phrases as you feel are applicable.

Observe rather than talk or act

Organized in approach to tasks

Like to read

Usually a good speller

Memorize by seeing pictures or graphics

Not easily distracted

Find verbal instruction difficult

Have good handwriting

Remember faces

Use advanced planning

Doodle

Quiet by nature

Meticulous, neat in appearance

Notices details

Talk to myself aloud

Enjoy talking to others

Easily distracted

Have more difficulty with written directions

Like to be read to

Memorize steps in a sequence

Enjoy music

Whisper to myself while reading

Remember names

Easily distracted by noises

Hum or sing

Outgoing by nature

Enjoy listening activities

Enjoy programs where a speaker tells stories

In motion most of the time

Like to touch people when talking to them

Like to handle objects

Tap pencil or foot while studying

Enjoy doing activities

Reading is not a priority

Usually a poor speller

Like to solve problems by physically working through them

Will try new things

Use hands when talking

Express emotions through physical means

Dress for comfort

Outgoing by nature

Like working with hands

Characteristics and suggested aids adapted by Dr. Merrill R. Karp, Arizona State University, from instrument by Jan R. Amstutz, Director, Intensive English Language Center, California State University, as presented to "Aviation Communication: A Multi-Cultural Forum Symposium," April 11, 1997, Embry-Riddle Aeronautical University, Prescott, AZ.

Appendix B

Suggested Aids for Learning Styles

Directions: Add each individual column of the "Personal Characteristics" assessment instrument. The first column indicates characteristics of "visual learners," the second column indicates characteristics of "auditory learners," and the third column reflects characteristics of "hands-on, tactile, or kinesthetic learners." The column with the highest number of annotated occurrences reflects the most dominant learning style, the column with the second most occurrences reflects the second most dominant learning style, etc. There is a possibility that two or even three of the columns are the same. If so, then those styles are equally dominant. The following aids may be helpful to enhance your particular dominant learning style, or to strengthen a weaker one. Some of the suggestions are the same for more than one learning style, but for different learning and processing reasons.

Visual	Auditory	Hands-On/Kinesthetic
Read	Use video & audio tapes & watch TV	Physically "do" the task
Form pictures in your mind		Practice by repeated motion
Take notes in class	Speak/listen to speakers	
Use notebooks to summarize class notes	Make up rhymes/poems	Pace/walk as you study
	Read aloud & talk to self	Take a lot of notes in class
Draw/use drawings	Repeat things orally	Make lists & write down thoughts during day
Use charts/graphs/maps	Use rhythmic sounds	
Watch lips move in front of mirror while speaking	Have discussions with classmates	Write on surface with finger if paper is not available
Use photographs and pictures	Listen carefully	Role play
	Use oral directions	Think or practice while exercising
Watch TV/Video	Sound out words	
Use acronyms, visual chains, and	Say words in syllables	Stretch/move in chair
Mind maps		Watch lips move in front of mirror while going over lessons
	Use word links, like rhymes, poems, lyrics	

Chapter 5

Women's Learning and Leadership Styles: Implications for Air Crews

Mary Ann Turney and James C. Bishop

Introduction

Aircraft accident analyses suggest that most accidents are attributable to human factors' failures, often related to crew performance. Ambiguity, assumptions, lack of communication, confusion, discrepancies – all have contributed to serious loss of life. Therefore, continual examination of the factors that affect air crew performance is essential.

Increasing numbers of women in professional pilot crews and the elimination of the combat exclusion for military women pilots necessitate greater emphasis on appropriate assimilation for this newly emerging segment of the pilot workforce. Because effective assimilation of women in air crew teams is important to flight safety, training programs need to address learning and leadership styles that do not conform to the traditional paradigms of the current single gender operational culture.

This chapter describes an ongoing study of women pilots that began in 1994 and continues to collect data regarding women's learning and leadership on the flight deck. The purpose of the study is to: (1) examine how women's learning and leadership styles differ from those of men; (2) determine if there are barriers to gender integration and crew teamwork; and (3) make recommendations for more effective crew training programs. The literature review continues to make new data available and herein we have reported the most recent findings from relevant studies, and have summarized data previously collected through a series of studies incorporating methods such as surveys and in-depth interviews with both men and women civilian and military pilots. Results indicate that conceptions of command, leadership, effective communication, decision-making and shared authority differ in meaning between men and women.

The Pilot Image

Traditionally, the ideal pilot image once portrayed a dominant male figure with 'the right stuff.' (Nagel & Wiener, 1988). Today, however, few would disagree that the 'right stuff' has changed, and the piloting job requires higher levels of team-oriented, interpersonal skill. Karp's (1999) studies in crew resource management (CRM) suggest that meaningful contrasts exist among flight crews. He states, 'Often behavioral and motivational contrasts become a barrier to crew coordination, flight integrity, and cooperation. One of the primary objectives of Cockpit/Crew Resource Management training should be to overcome these barriers when working in a multi-cultural environment. Although CRM training has broadened considerably to include all those contributions assure a safe, successful mission, CRM has still to grapple with the deeper aspects of human interaction and motivation which affect the ways in which air crews perform' (Karp, 1999, p. 2). If we are going to promote the functional effectiveness of every member of an air crew, gender-related differences should be understood.

King and Retzlaff (2003) studied gender-related differences at the United States Air Force Academy. They indicated that the much-heralded 'right stuff' for military aviation rests on a male foundation. However, since women are entering military aircraft, the traits that women bring to the flight deck become important. King and Retzlaff measured the cognitive and personality characteristics of 50 female and 64 male pilot candidates. Although they found no significant cognitive differences, 'female pilots were found to have greater extraversion, conscientiousness, and agreeableness. These traits may be ideally suited for modern and future military and space operations which will emphasize increased collaborative functioning' (King and Retzlaff, 2003, p. 1).

Women's Learning Styles

Women do not learn as men do. Jensen (2000), in his discussion of *Brain-Based Learning*, states that 'there are distinct, measurable, structural differences between male and female brains' (Jensen, 2000, p. 86). *The New York Times* reported that Shaywitz was first able to demonstrate the functional differences between the brains of men and women. Her study showed 'actual differences in the parts of the brain used when men and women were thinking and coming up with the same answers'.[1] With magnetic resonance images of a man's brain and a women's brain, Dr. Shaywitz was able to demonstrate clearly that in decoding words, men use a small area on one side of the brain, whereas women use areas on both sides of the brain simultaneously. Donovan (1998) reported that a study using Positron Emission Tomography found definitive evidence that male and female brains function differently. Researchers also suggested that women perform differently from men on spatial tasks; for example, women are more rapid at identifying matching items, a skill called perceptual speed (Kirmura, 1992).

Using various scanners for interactive multi-modality imaging to measure brain hemisphere activity, scientists have learned that women use both right and left brain simultaneously to perform reading functions while men tend to use only one side of the brain.[2]

Earlier gender studies in the United States reflect some of the major differences between women and men. For example, Tannen (1990) found that men prefer debate-like situations in which they pursue knowledge by ritual opposition, while women like to share and learn by interacting in a collaborative manner. According to Gilligan (1982) authoritative systems are more important to men in defining relationships than to women and Belenky et al (1986) contends that women value affiliation and acceptance more than do men. Females tend to be more participatory in their learning styles and males are more independent (Emanuel and Potter, 1992). Gilligan differentiated between men and women's thinking with the metaphors of the web and the ladder. Women operate in a web, suggesting interconnectedness and relationship-building; men operate on a ladder, suggesting achievement orientation and hierarchical thinking (Bannister, 1990).

Heffler, 2001 found that 'a significant gender difference was obtained in the concrete experience learning mode with females scoring higher, i.e., a more experience-based approach to learning, feeling-based judgments, people-oriented, concrete role-play simulation learning, and feeling comfortable with ambiguity' (Heffler, 2001, p. 313).

Through administration of the Armstrong Laboratory Aviator Personality Survey (ALAPS), King and Retzlaff (2003) collected preliminary data from candidates for USAF undergraduate pilot training program (N-1131, 124 of which were female) with an average age of 22.6 (sd=2.9). They reported finding a significant difference only in the area of *dogmatism* where males scored higher (male raw score equal to 6.06, female raw score equal to 4.64; r=4.9 (p<.00001).

After 20 in-depth interviews of female and male pilots (many of whom were collegiate aviation students), Sitler (1998) reported that 18 of the 20 interviewed said that they had observed gender differences in learning. According to Sitler (1998), the time has come to make major changes in curriculum and instruction in order to make flight careers more appealing to women. These changes include restructuring curriculum.

Women's Leadership

The differences between female- and male-oriented leadership are often characterized in a context of heroic and post-heroic leadership constructs. Traditionally, a heroic leader was pictured as possessing stereotypical male characteristics of individualism, assertiveness and dominance (Fletcher, 2002). In contrast, the post-heroic model, described as the transformative leadership model, emphasizes traits such as empathy, relational abilities and the capability to listen. These are sometimes regarded as feminine traits (Fletcher, 2002), thus posing difficulty for an industry that holds onto the more traditional 'heroic' constructs and uses them to define leadership abilities.

One factor challenging women's leadership on the flight deck is the problem of role congruity. Eagly and Karau (2002) studied role congruity prejudice toward female leaders. They found that women were perceived less favorably than men as potential leaders and were evaluated less favorably in leadership positions. This was due to perceptions of incongruity between women's characteristics and what is perceived as leadership ability. They also found that sex is the strongest basis for categorizing individuals; therefore, women are first identified by sex rather than by career role. Finally, the study found that some men dealing with women leaders are uncomfortable when women don't behave in stereotypical roles, such as providing emotional support. Role incongruity may therefore cause confusion and misunderstanding. Another difficulty lies in the perception that women are primarily responsible for family care. These kinds of assumptions generate doubts about women's professional commitments. Also, if women appear to put their work first, they are somehow considered to be inappropriate (Sitler, Turney, and Wulle, 1996). Many women report that their contributions in the workplace are not recognized and some report that they feel almost invisible. Sandelands (2002) attributes this condition to be the result of the separation of the sexes in the human species. Paradoxically, when women violate gender role expectations and display male attributes they are evaluated unfavorably because this behavior is perceived less desirable in women. In a meta-analysis of 162 studies examining gender in leadership styles, women in leadership positions were found to be devalued most strongly when their leadership evidenced a stereotypical masculine style that was perceived as directive (Eagly, Makhijani, and Klonsky, 1992; Eagly and Karau, 2002; Van Vianen and Fisher, 2002). 'Women leaders' choices are thus constrained by threats from two directions - conforming to their gender role would produce a failure to meet the requirements of their leader role, and conforming to their leader role would produce a failure to meet the requirements of their gender role' (Eagly and Karau, 2002, p. 580).

Rutherford (2001) studied gender and management style in a large airline in Britain. Results indicated that status was important, but much less for women than for men. Regarding management styles, 74% of the respondents said that women managed differently from men (84% female respondents; 55% male respondents). Women were also reported by respondents to possess better people skills and were found to be more creative, adaptable, and flexible.

Significant differences in communication styles in men and women have been studied during the past decade or more. Sociolinguistic studies, according to Weiss (1993), reveal actual gender differences in language, including vocabulary, intonation and sentence structure. Male language is direct and female language contains greater imagery. 'Women use intensifiers (e.g., so, such, quite, very, etc.), modifiers, tag question (e.g., isn't it?), and mild expletives. Lakeoff (1990) contended that women are less direct in their speech and have a tendency to end statements in a questioning tone even when they are not asking questions. Male language is more absolute; female language is more abstract and emotional. Men tend to dominate conversation and dispel their knowledge and expertise, viewing life as a hierarchy where they are in competition. Women see themselves as part of a community network, desirous of closeness, intimacy and consensus' (p. 57). Belenky et al. (1986) reported that when women are not heard for long periods of time, they tend to stop communicating. Case (1995) claimed that women speak in a style that is 'facilitative and personal, which appears to be relational, self-disclosing, and integrative' (Case, 1995, p. 4) while men are assertive and appear to be directive and commanding.

Results of Hellman's (2000) study on team dynamics found that women expressed a significantly stronger preference for relationship-building in teams compared to men. The study also revealed that women favor a participatory style of conflict resolution rather than a directive approach. This result agrees with Rogelberg and Rummery's (1996) finding which suggests that female team members are aware of the importance of coordinating, integrating and resolving different viewpoints in a participatory rather than directive manner (Rogelberg and Rummery, 1996 as cited in Hellman, 2000). Further, Hellman's study suggested that if conflict were resolved through shared input from the stakeholders, rather than through a leader-directed approach, there would be greater ownership of the resolution by both parties.

Gender Differentiation

Weiss (1993) stated that 'assumptions about masculinity and femininity, characterizing the male as sexually dominant, unemotional, confident, authoritative and strong and the female as vulnerable, weak, emotional, passive and dependent pervade Western culture' (p. 56). These assumptions tend to create barriers for women in leadership roles in many cultures. However, certain countries like Hungary, Poland, and Denmark are reported to demonstrate the least amount of gender-differentiation in the workplace. 'Such societies tend to accord women a higher status and a stronger role in decision-making' (Javidan and House, 2001, p. 294). In contrast, countries such as Korea, Egypt and China tend to accord women a lower status and thus have fewer women in positions of authority (Javidan and House, 2001). Although many states, such as Israel, have committed themselves to gender equity, studies show 'a wide gap between the egalitarian vision and the daily reality' because women's status is determined largely by family roles (Yishai and Cohen, 1997, p. 460). Similarly, a study of job satisfaction in Taiwan's organizations revealed that 'male employees had higher rank and higher task, team, and status satisfaction than did female employees' (Cheung and Scherling, 1999).

Gorman (2001) looked at women's potential for promotion and job advancement in comparison to men's potential in United States' law firms. The study found that decision-maker's inferences concerning the qualification of potential candidates for promotion are likely to be biased toward men. This was partly due to interpreting what characteristics are required for a job based on the majority population's characteristics. Decision-makers' impressions were also found to be influenced by cultural assumptions about the 'right' characteristics of men and women.

CRM Research

Since today's professional pilots are in cross-functional work teams, they require new operational styles (Rollins, 1995). Skills required for professional pilots include communication, crew coordination and teambuilding, situational awareness, judgment, problem-solving, leadership, and workload management (Antersijn and Verhoef, 1995; Faulkner, 1996; Houle, 1995; Orasanu, 1994; Smith and Hanebuth, 1996; Young, 1995). Some research suggests that the essential skills are specific to particular cultural environments, i.e., skills needed by Anglo pilots may not be the same as those needed by Latin or Oriental pilot groups (Merritt and Helmreich, 1996). In addition, Adams and Driskell (1992) determined that CRM training methodology should address differences in learning styles.

Machado (1994) reported that women are better at communication in the cockpit. He agrees with Tannen that women are more inclined to 'negotiate' in their communication style in contrast to men's tendency to be 'matter-of-fact' (Machado, 1994). Men speak to both exchange information and establish status in a group; women talk to exchange information and establish cohesion.

A sizable cache of literature clearly indicates that women and men exhibit differences in their styles of learning, an important consideration for proponents of crew resource management (CRM) since cognitive processing differs in men and women. Men are more competitive and women are more collaborative. In a study focusing on the relationship between gender identity and workplace team conflict, Randel (2002) found that men, unaccustomed to working with women in highly technical environments, feel the effects of heterogeneity to a greater extent than women. Women report struggling with leadership roles particularly when other crewmembers expect and require behavior that is associated with males alone. The machismo traditions of the aircraft flight deck create challenges for emerging female professional pilots.

Summary of Literature

Researchers have identified a number of differences between men and women in learning and leadership styles. For example, men were found to prefer competition and opposition, while women prefer cooperation and collaboration. Women focused on building relationships; men focused on building achievements. Men seemed to work best with numbers and logic and women were people-oriented and process-oriented. Male language was more direct than female language. Women were participatory in their leadership style while men were more autonomous. Men were more independent of others, while women viewed themselves as part of a community.

With regard to CRM, the literature revealed (1) interpersonal skills have become essential for the flight deck and (2) women face leadership challenges on the flight deck that may affect retention of women in the aviation industry.

Study of Male and Female Pilots

An initial study was conducted in 1994 among professional civilian and military pilots. The study had two objectives: (1) to learn whether or not there were perceived differences between women and men in learning and leadership styles and (2) if there were differences, whether they were perceived to pose barriers on the flight deck. Respondents (total 33) were asked to answer 'yes' or 'no' to the following questions:

1. Are there differences between women and men in learning styles?
2. Are there differences between women and men in leadership styles?
3. Are there differences between women and men in communication styles?
4. If you answered 'yes' to the above, do the differences create barriers?

In order to obtain richer and more in-depth data, open-ended questions were also posed through individual follow-up interviews. Examples were:

1. If yes to #4, what barriers have you encountered?
2. If yes to #4, what recommendations would you make to improve air crew teamwork?

The data was collected in person, by telephone and through email. The original 33 participants were equally composed of women and men and represented all branches of military and civilian aviation.

A quantitative analysis was done on responses to the first four survey items; later, a qualitative analysis was done using thematic coding of the responses from the open-ended questions and the expanded interviews.

Quantitative Data Analysis

A quantitative analysis of the data was performed for the four survey questions pertaining to the four groups in the study: military women pilots, civilian women pilots, military men pilots, and civilian men pilots. The data in these four categories were considered binary and the three unclear responses were omitted. One main result of this analysis regards the question of perceived barriers to air crews. A Chi-squared test was performed on question 4 (Do differences present barriers?) with 1 degree of freedom resulted in a test statistic of 3.4 corresponding to a p-value of .065. This suggested potential differences between the four groups. Further investigation compared the answers of women and men to question 4. Note that 78.6% of women answered yes to question 4 as opposed to 33.3% of men. A t-test using pooled variance results in a p-value of .02. Therefore, there is a significant difference between male and female responses with regard to this item (see Figure 5.1).

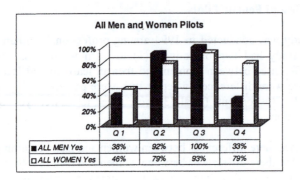

Figure 5.1 Comparison of affirmative responses of men and women pilots (survey questions 1-4)

Other interesting results compare the questions as a whole for the four groups. There is a clear difference between civilian women pilots and military women pilots with regard to the four questions overall. For each of the four questions, more of the civilian women perceived that there were differences between men and women than did the military women. This trend does not appear to exist for the men. The responses from the military men and the civilian men were similar. A test confirms these results (see Figures 5.2 and 5.3).

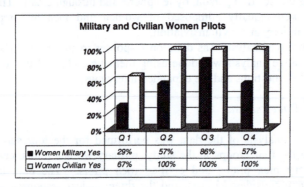

Figure 5.2 Comparison of affirmative responses of military and civilian women pilots (survey questions 1-4)

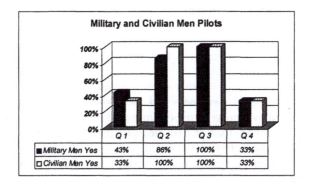

Figure 5.3 Comparison of affirmative responses of military and civilian men pilots (survey questions 1-4)

Qualitative Data Analysis

A number of themes regarding learning and leadership styles emerged from the coded interview data. This data included responses to expanded research questions beyond those in the survey.

- Men and women were reported to have different leadership styles.
- Men were reported to be more task-oriented and to exhibit more confidence as members of a crew.
- Women were reported to be better communicators, to exhibit more sensitivity to people and to be good negotiators.
- Women were reported to work harder at learning technical information.

Both the men and women interviewed reported barriers to women's integration in the crew team:

- Lack of understanding of gender differences.
- 'Macho' pilot image.
- Men are perceived as the leaders.
- Stress on women to continually earn the respect of their male peers. Both men and women surveyed agreed that mistakes made by women become generalized and are perceived as gender weaknesses.
- Small number of women pilots-in-command.
- Men's belief that women have logged fewer flight hours.
- Lack of ability to view women crewmembers as professionals. (Taking care of women or making sexual advances.)
- Language choices by both men and women.

With regard to factors that improve crew teamwork, the following themes emerged:

- Men and women reported that better teamwork emerges from better communication.
- Men and women agreed that all crewmembers should 'do the job.'
- Better situational awareness and the ability to listen and evaluate were considered by men to be important ingredients to cockpit teamwork.
- Women agreed that shared decision-making, conflict resolution and patience were factors, which improve crew teamwork.
- Women believed they should behave in a confident manner, particularly toward men.
- Men reported favorable reactions to self-critiques of behavior in cockpit simulation situations.

Some additional information emerged from the interview data. For example, more than half the pilots interviewed said that they didn't believe there was a difference in learning styles between men and women. There were concerns regarding hiring practices and unequal treatment. The issue of the exclusion of pregnant female pilots from flight duties emerged. A female airline pilot reported that although the job requires assertiveness, men see that trait in females as aggression. One male reported that it is time for women to learn how men see things differently.

Differing Characteristics of Men and Women

A body of research clearly identifies differences between men and women in learning and leadership styles. Results of the initial survey and interview data indicated that the majority of respondents either were unsure or did not perceive differences in learning styles.

Interviews with professional pilots, however, continue to reveal awareness of differences between men and women in leadership styles and communication styles. Generally, women are deemed to function more successfully than men in leadership areas such as communications skill and interpersonal relationships. The following statements from interview data are indicative:

- Women are more sensitive to others feelings and have compassion.
- Women try to empower others to do the job.
- Women are more subtle, less domineering.
- Women are more adept at addressing issues and talking things out.
- Women are better negotiators.
- Communication is easier for women.
- Men are more directive.
- Men are assumed to be the leaders by virtue of gender.
- A pilot needs to be an aggressive type - independent and self-reliant.
- The best women pilots are not feminine; they adopt masculine qualities.

Both women and men stated the desirability of demonstrating confidence; however conflict was reported in situations where women were perceived to act in a manner that was ascribed to men. This included assertive behavior, strong language and a forceful demeanor.

Implications

Based on the data to date, there appears to be a need to provide training for crewmembers regarding differences between men and women in learning and leadership styles. Lack of understanding of these differences inhibits communication and continues to cause gender-related bias.

Some of the issues and attitudes revealed in the data suggested barriers to effective crew teamwork. For example, leaders were perceived as strong and more confident when they were assertive. However, forceful behavior and language was considered masculine. Therefore, women who exhibited this behavior were considered by some men to be inappropriate. Women and men agreed that all individuals should be regarded as professionals first. However, both men and women continue to experience situations in which they were demeaned in their sexual identities.

Practical Application

Based on the collected data acquired to date in this study, a number of recommendations can be made to improve the aviation operational culture.

A. Assess the existing culture in the organization.
  1. Conduct focus groups to identify the level of awareness of gender-based research.
  2. Develop and administer a survey to ascertain perceptions regarding gender-based differences and awareness of barriers.
B. Involve air crews in training and discussion groups to create a common base of knowledge regarding gender differences research.
C. Offer air crews opportunities to practice self-assessment of communication styles, leadership skills, and ability to evaluate attitudes.
D. Develop check pilot and instructor training workshops.
  Instructors are key personnel. These individuals should receive up-to-date information about current research regarding gender differences. Bell (1992) found that training for instructors should involve awareness of small inequities that may have a cumulative effect. Instructors should consciously encourage both sexes to succeed, elicit responses equally, and be aware of attitudes, tone of voice and choice of language. They should dispel stereotypes and select anecdotal material with which both women and men can relate. Expertise in interpersonal relationships has become as crucial as recurrent training on aircraft systems.

E.   Provide both male and female role models. Role models provide a way to learn
      about differences and combat sexism (Parrish and Nordbrock, 1992).

'We cannot afford,' stated Antler (1990),' to let the different ways of seeing remain
isolated from one another' (Antler, 1990, p. 6). We each have much to learn from
the way our diverse peers experience the workplace. The same energy that goes
into aircraft systems training ought to be invested in developing the interpersonal
skills that make successful teamwork. Human systems, in fact, are truly much
more complex than mechanical systems - a reality that we cannot afford to neglect
if we are to prevent even a single aircraft tragedy.

Summary

Air crew populations are changing and the necessity of assimilating women into
the operational environment of aviation needs to be addressed.   Both civilian and
military air crews in many countries now include women. However, women's
learning and leadership styles have been found to differ from those of men.
     Differences in learning, leadership, and communication styles between men
and women have been identified in studies throughout the past two decades. With
regard to learning preferences, women tend toward collaborative learning and men
prefer competition and debate, and frequently learn in a more autonomous style.
Desjardens (1993) contrasted the leadership styles of women and men.   She
indicated that men wish to make important contributions, seek challenges, and
exhibit a pattern of casual interaction with people in the workplace. Women,
however, tend to be less concerned with their rank, are careful about risk-taking,
and attuned to personal relationships.
     In spite of what has been learned, cultural, social and organizational factors
affecting women's employment in the aviation industry remain largely undefined.
If effective air crew diversity is the goal, then it becomes necessary to continue to
study differences and integrate diversity in the workplace.

Notes

1 *New York Times*, February 16, 1995.
2 *New York Times*, March 12, 1997.

References

Adams, R.J. and Driskell, J.E. (1992). *Crew Resource Management: An Introductory
     Handbook,* Washington, DC: US Department of Transportation, Federal Aviation
     Administration.

Antersijn, P.A.M., & Verhoef, M.C. (1995). 'Assessment of Non-Technical Skills: Is It Possible'? in N. McDonald, N. Johnston, and R. Fuller (Eds.). *Applications of Psychology to the Aviation System*, Aldershot: Avebury, pp. 243-250.

Antler, J. and Bikley, S.K. (1990). 'Educating Women Students for the Future', *Changing Education*, 3-7.

Bannister, L. (1990, October). 'Women's Rhetoric as Literature', Salt Lake City, UT: Report presented at the Annual Meeting of the Rocky Mountain Language Association. (ERIC Document Reproductions Service No. ED 325 846).

Belenky, M., Clinchy, B., Goldberger, J., and Tarule, J. (1986). *Women's Ways of Knowing: The Development of Self, Voice, and Mind*, NY: Basic Books.

Bell, S.R. (1992). 'Gender Influences in the College Classroom: Optimizing the Learning Environment for Women', Unpublished MARP. NOVA Southeastern University, Ft. Lauderdale, FL.

Case, S.S. (1995, January). 'Gender Differences Influence Decision-Making: Language Style Is Key to Organizational Success', *Strategy Magazine*, Cleveland, OH: Case Western Reserve University, 4-11.

Cheung, C. and Scherling, S.A. (1999). 'Job Satisfactions, Work Values, and Sex Differences in Taiwan's Organizations,' *Journal of Psychology, 133*(5), 563-575.

Desjarens, C. (1993). 'Leadership Competencies', National Institute for Leadership Development, Phoenix, AZ.

Donovan, P. (1998, October). 'Men's Brains, Women's Brains: Study Overturns Century-Old Assumptions about Cognitive Functions', *University of Buffalo Reporter, 30* (7), 1-3.

Eagly, A.H. and Karau, S.J. (2002). 'Role Congruity Theory of Prejudice Toward Female Leaders', *Psychological Review, 109* (3), 573-598.

Eagly, A.H., Makhijani, M.G., and Klonsky, B.G. (1992). 'Gender and the Evaluation of Leaders: A Meta-Analysis,' *Psychological Bulletin, 111*(1), 3-22.

Emanuel, R.C. and Potter, W.J. (1992). 'Do Students' Style Preferences Differ by Grade Level, Orientation toward College, and Academic Major'? *Research in Higher Education, 33*, 395-414.

Faulkner, J.P.E. (1996). 'Evaluating Crew Resource Management in Ab Initio Pilot Training: The First Seventy Hours', in B.J. Hayward and A.R. Lowe (Eds.), *Applied Aviation Psychology*, Aldershot: Avebury, pp. 143-147.

Fletcher, J. (2002, August). 'The Greatly Exaggerated Demise of Heroic Leadership: Gender, Power, and the Myth of the Female Advantage', *Insights*, Center for Gender in Organizations, Briefing No. 113.

Gilligan, C. (1982). *In a Different Voice*, MA: Harvard University Press.

Gorman, E.H. (2001, September). 'Gender and Organizational Selection Decisions: Evidence from Law Firms', Doctoral Dissertation, Harvard University. Available through UMI Dissertation Abstracts database.

Heffler, B. (2001). 'Individual Learning Style and the Learning Style Inventory', *Educational Studies, 27*(3), 307-316.

Hellman, P.S. (2000). 'Diverse Perspectives on Team Dynamics: The Effects of Cultural Values, Personal Values, Gender and Job Level on Preferences for Team Processes', Doctoral dissertation, The George Washington University, Dissertation Abstracts International, 61(4-B), 2256.

Houle, T.W. (1995). 'An Operational Model for the Evaluation of Crew Resource Management (CRM) Skills in Line Operations Simulations (LOS)', in N. McDonald, N. Johnston, and R. Fuller (Eds.), *Applications of Psychology to the Aviation System*, Aldershot: Avebury, pp. 251-255.

Javidan, M. and House, R.J. (2001). 'Cultural Acumen for the Global Manager: Lessons from Project GLOBE', *Organizational Dynamics, 29* (4), 289-305.

Jensen, E. (2000). 'Sex, the Brain and Learning, in *Brain-based Learning*', Brain Store Inc.

Karp, R. (March, 1999). 'Communication: A Multi-Cultural Perspective,' *The CRM Insight, 3* (3).

Kimura, D. (1992, September). ' Sex Differences in the Brain', *Scientific American*, 119-125.

King, R.E. and Retzlaff, P.D. (2003). 'Psychological Research on Gender Differences and Similarities of USAF Pilots and Pilot Candidates', Retrieved from: http://mirror.apa.org/ppo-OLD/nsf/dodexhibit.html.

Lakeoff, R. (1990). *Talking Power: The Politics of Language in Our Lives*, New York: Harper Collins.

Machado, R. (1994, January). 'A Happy Cockpit: Reducing Cockpit Stress between the Sexes', *Flight Training*, 50-52.

Merritt, A., and Helmreich, R. (1996c). 'Culture in the Cockpit: A Multi-Airline Study of Pilot Attitudes and Values', NASA/University of Texas/FAA Aerospace Crew Research Project, Austin, TX: University of Texas.

Nagal, D.C. and Wiener, E.L. (1988). *Human Factors in Aviation*, San Diego: Academic Press Inc.

Orasanu, J.M. (1994). 'Shared Problem Models and Flight Crew Performance', in N. Johnston, N. McDonald, and R. Fuller (Eds.). *Aviation Psychology in Practice*, Aldershot: Avebury, pp. 255-281.

Randel, A.E. (2002). 'Identity Salience: A Moderator of the Relationship between Group Gender Composition and Work Group Conflict', *Journal of Organizational Behavior, 23*, 749-766.

Rollins, M.L. (1995). 'A Descriptive Study of Crew Resource Management Attitude Change', in N. Johnston, R. Fuller, and N. McDonald (Eds.), *Aviation Psychology: Training and Selection*, Aldershot: Avebury, pp. 45-50.

Rutherford, S. (2001, July). 'Any Difference? An Analysis of Gender and Divisional Management Styles in a Large Airline', *Gender Work and Organization, 8* (3), 326-345.

Sandelands, L.E. (2002). 'Male and Female in Organizational Behavior, *Journal of Organizational Behavior, 23*, 149-165.

Sitler, R. (1998). The Cockpit Classroom: Women's Perceptions of Learning to Fly and Implications for Flight Curriculum and Instruction', *Proceedings of the Tenth Annual International Symposium on Aviation Psychology*, Columbus, OH: Ohio State University.

Sitler, R., Turney, M.A. and Wulle, B. (1996). 'Attitudes Reflective of Gender Based Issues in the Aviation and Transportation Work place', in B.J. Hayward and A.R. Lowe (Eds.), *Applied Aviation Psychology: Achievement, Change and Challenge*, Aldershot: Avebury, pp. 332-342.

Smith, G.M and Hanebuth, C.E. (1996). 'Differences in CRM Evaluation between LOFT Facilitators and Line Check Captains', in B. J. Hayward, and A. R. Lowe (Eds.), *Applied Aviation Psychology: Achievement, Change and Challenge*, Aldershot: Avebury, pp. 148-155.

Tannen, D. (1990). *You Just Don't Understand: Women and Men in Conversation*, NewYork: Ballentine Books.

Van Vianen, A. and Fisher, A., (2002). 'Illuminating the Glass Ceiling: The Role of Organizational Culture Preferences', *Journal of Occupational and Organizational Psychology, 75*.

Young, J.P. (1995). 'Cockpit (Crew) Resource Management: Development of a collegiate course', in N. Johnston, R. Fuller, and N. McDonald (Eds.), *Aviation Psychology: Training and Selection*, Aldershot: Avebury,   pp. 11-16.

Weiss, M.J. (1993).   'Integrating Communication and Gender in the Medical Setting', *Proteus, A Journal of Ideas, 10*, 55-59.

Yishai, Y. and Cohen, A. (1997, February). 'Unrepresentative Bureaucracy', *Administration and Society, 28*(4), pp. 441-465.

Chapter 6

Gender Differences in Learning to Fly

Ruth Lowe Sitler

Introduction

A number of cultural, social and organizational factors define the aviation workplace for women. These factors should be understood if women are going to successfully participate in the aviation industry. Given that the industry intends to tap all the potential talent available, further investigation is needed on how women learn and progress in career development. With the advent of women on flight decks, the study of gender differences becomes essential in order to facilitate communication and conduct commercial air travel in the safest, most efficient manner.

Developing excellence in both men and women pilots necessitates learning about gender differences in learning to fly. When operators, educators, trainers, and regulators become aware of these differences, they become better able to motivate both men and women to maximize their learning strengths and succeed as career pilots.

Field Study

A field study was completed by the author over a period of thirty years as a Certified Flight Instructor in the Akron/Kent area of Ohio. The first five years of the study was done while teaching at a family-owned flight school operating under Federal Air Regulation (FAR) Part 61 and transitioning into a more stringent FAR Part 141 flight school operation. Ten years took place at a FAR 141 flight school combined with an FAR 135 air charter operation. The last 15 years took place while teaching at Kent State University under FAR Part 141 where the author was Chief Flight Instructor administrating phase checks as well as issuing FAA certificates for Private, Instrument and Commercial ratings. The author's accumulated flight hours in this capacity amounted to over 8,500 hours of a total of 10,450 hours of flight time.

The final phase of the study included a research review of gender differences in learning with regard to dramatic changes in educational and career choices, environment and behavioral differences, spatial ability, influences from play, hormonal developmental changes, brain organization and psychosocial sex differences including confidence, anxiety, conformity or dependency, empathy, aggression and self-esteem. This final phase employed a series of taped interviews and observations made by both female and male student pilots. The interview is an important source to provide focused insight (Creswell, 1998; Tellis, 1997). By going to the direct source, the researcher gained fresh information concerning the research questions. Additionally the interviews provided new information for analysis. No other methodology would have provided the kind of fresh, unbiased information that was needed.

The intent of this chapter is to raise awareness by combining a broad review of educational literature with related field study data in order to better define gender differences in learning to fly.

Relevant Studies in Mathematics Achievement

One of the most valuable studies available in the field of education is Klein's *Handbook For Achieving Sex Equity Through Education.* According to Klein (1985), the evidence from the past decade of dramatic changes in educational and career choices of males and females clearly demonstrates the powerful impact of environmental factors on behavioral differences between males and females. The tendency to assume that all differences between males and females are genetically determined and resistant to change is well illustrated by the controversial reporting of Benbow and Stanley's (1980) research on mathematics achievement. Benbow and Stanley's study of mathematically gifted volunteer subjects was erroneously interpreted as suggesting that gender differences in mathematics performance were genetically determined. Media reports overstated the research findings and suggested unproven casual relationships (for example: 'Do males have a math gene?').

Misunderstandings such as those demonstrated in the media treatment of Benbow and Stanley's findings can have serious consequences. Vocational counselors who believe that females have less ability in math and science may discourage females from entering those careers. Parents, believing that their daughters' difficulties in mathematics reflect an innate predisposition, may not encourage their daughters as much as they do their sons.

According to Jaclin (1989), the conclusions of the larger, primary study were that math anxiety, gender-stereotyped beliefs of parents, and the perceived value of math to the student account for the major portion of sex differences in achievement. Using mate-analysis, Rosenthal & Ruben (1982) concluded that they could not pinpoint a cause for this change. They stated, 'We can say that, whatever the reason, in these studies, females appear to be gaining in cognitive skill relative to males faster than the gene can travel.'

According to Pearson & Ferguson (1989), boys are encouraged to excel in math and spatial skills, but not in reading or verbal skills. Although girls are expected to perform well academically across all subjects, they have not been encouraged to excel in math or in experiences thought to enhance spatial abilities (e.g., sports activities). The fact that the women in Pearson and Ferguson's sample obtained comparable ACT math and English scores and that their spatial ability performance was highly related to achievement, suggests that they may have acquired their spatial ability skills through an academic rather than experiential process.

Sadker & Sadker (1994) conducted extensive studies on how females and males fare in America's schools. They identified a need for instructors to provide better support for young women in learning mathematics and technical subjects.

Studies in Spatial Abilities

The construct of spatial ability lacks a uniform definition among researchers. Spatial ability is measured by tests such as mental rotation (Shephard & Melzler, 1971), perception of horizontally hidden figures and paper folding (French, Ekstrom & Price, 1963). Of the three aspects of special ability identified above, (spatial orientation, horizontality/verticality, and visualization), sex differences favoring males are most pronounced and consistent for mental rotations and horizontality/verticality and least consistent for spatial visualization.

One possible method of investigating the role of cognitive factors in gender differences is to examine the effect of training and experience related to these factors. Training can influence performance on the tests for which it is designed, but might not influence school or career performance. The influences of experience stem from play and other leisure activities. For example, play preferences for spatial-type activities such as building with blocks differ for young males and females and appear to be associated with performance on measures of disembedding. Books, television programs and toys for young children reflect sex stereotyping. When successful, training in spatial ability sometimes favors females more than males (Newcomb, 1982), suggesting the ability of experience to alter cognitive sex differences.

Developmental Changes in Hormones

According to Klein (1985), the endocrine system that controls reproduction is established prenatally. There appear to be few sex differences in the development of this system except that the levels, or ratios, of gonadal hormones are different for adult males and females. There appears to be a major need for additional research in this area.

Organization of the Brain

Klein (1985) revealed a popular hypothesis that cognitive functions such as verbal or spatial processing may be more lateralized in one hemisphere for males and the other for females. McGlone (1980), however, in her review of sex differences in laterality, concluded that males are more likely than females to show left hemisphere dominance in processing verbal material, and at the same time seem to exhibit greater right hemisphere dominance for nonverbal material. Females are thought to be less lateralized for either function.

Clear evidence exists regarding brain functional differences between women and men. Jensen (2000) identified the existence of 'distinct, measurable, structural differences between male and female brains' (Jensen, 2000, 86). Specifically, Gron, Wunderlich, Spitzer, et al (2000) summarize that 'regardless of the specific underlying neuropsychological interpretation, left hippocampal activity in men and right frontoparietal activity in women reflect the gender-specific recruitments that differentiate male from female subjects' (Gron, Wunderlich, Spitzer, et al, 2000, 405). In addition, there is some evidence that extent of laterality is dynamic rather than fixed, raising the possibility that laterality can be influenced by experiences, can change developmentally, and, perhaps, can change in response to intervention. Thus, differences in laterality may reflect experiential or biological differences or both.

Psychosocial Sex Differences

Klein (1985) identified five categories of psychosocial behavior revealing gender differences: (1) confidence or anxiety, (2) conformity or dependency, (3) empathy, (4) aggression, and (5) self-esteem. Lack of self-confidence may be one explanation for women's under representation in many careers. In addition, the pressure of social comparisons appears to contribute to lowered confidence in women but not in men (Lenny & Gold, 1982). Peterson, Tobin-Richards & Crockett (1982) summarized recent literature and found that 60% of recent studies revealed consistent differences in expectancies of success, with males more confident than females.

Competition and Anxiety

Women may experience a greater degree of anxiety than men. Block (1981) suggested that females are more fearful, manifest greater anxiety, and have less confidence in themselves and their performance on specific tasks than do males. Aviation culture has historically been characterized as competitive. Gilbert (1999) studied female and male college students, exploring their reactions to positive and negative outcomes in competitive environments. Results indicated that subjects engaged in what were considered gender-role inappropriate tasks, generated greater anxiety or negative affect than those appropriate to the individual's gender role (Gilbert, 1999).

Regarding conformity and dependency, Klein (1985) states, 'Literature on sex differences in conformity was reviewed recently by Eagly (1978), who concluded that females demonstrated more conformity only in group situations characterized by uncertainty.' Dependency, an aspect of conformity defined as the tendency to seek close contact with attachment objects or their surrogates, does not vary consistently by sex (Maccoby & Jacklin, 1974). Block (1976) came to the same conclusion by reviewing Maccoby and Jacklin's studies. A different finding emerged, however, when other studies found in Maccoby and Jacklin's annotated bibliography were considered. All of these 13 studies reported females to be more dependent than males.

Gender Role Influences

Eagly & Karau (2002) define gender roles as 'socially shared expectations' applying to people of a certain social position or who are members of a particular social category. These socially shared expectations are manifest by 'consensual beliefs about the attributes of women and men' (Biddle, 1979; Sarbin & Allen, 1968; as cited in Eagly & Karau, 2002, p.3). Thus, gender role expectations define what members of a group *should* or *ought* to do (Eagly & Karau). For example, women are at a disadvantage in leadership roles because of perceived incongruity between leadership roles and female gender roles. Women are preferred to exhibit communal characteristics, rather than leadership characteristics.

Anderson (2001) looked at factors that influence career choices of professional pilots and found that women experience less positive influencers on career choice due to issues related to bias, such as pressure to select careers involving traditional female work roles, such as social service or humanitarian work (Anderson, 2001).

Sexist Language

Crawford & Unger (2000) suggest that the use of the 'generic' pronoun 'he' in English seems to make men and women think of males, even when the context implies both sexes. Studies have documented the behavioral effects of sexist language. For example, it was found that women's interest in job positions was influenced by the wording of the job advertisements. This resulted in major companies changing their job titles to eliminate gender.

Confidence and Intelligence

Brown (1998) found that gender appeared to be an important factor in perceived intelligence. She noted that self-deprecating women, but not men, were perceived as less intelligent than moderate or self-promoting women. Additional research suggests that modesty in women may have a negative effect upon others' perceptions of women's intellectual abilities (Wiley & Crittendon, 1992). Based on the need for self-efficacy as pilots, it may be necessary for women to better understand that if male colleagues perceive a lack of confidence, this could inhibit a woman's effectiveness on the flight deck.

Summary of Literature

In summary, Klein (1985) concludes that psychosocial differences between males and females have been documented. Differences in aggression are most pronounced; differences in confidence/anxiety, conformity, empathy, and self-esteem are less strong. All observed psychosocial differences reflect a strong contextual component. Thus, females exhibit more anxiety and less self-confidence in situations requiring mathematics than in those requiring verbal skill. Taken together, these findings suggest that females are more sensitive to social cues than are males. Females are more able to put themselves in the place of others and are also more likely to respond to the opinions of others—including opinions about their lack of ability in subjects such as mathematics or science. There has been a general tendency to assume that cognitive differences are more often attributed to socialization (Peterson, 1980). In both cases, there has been only minimal attention to the processes by which biological or socialization factors might operate.

Whatever processes operate at the individuals level, however, they cannot explain the large sex differences observed in educational and occupational attainment in many areas. Situational factors (for example, other roles selected by women) as well as discrimination are clearly important as well.

Findings and Possible Corresponding Reasons

The following section describes findings discovered and observed during this field study with possible rationales:

1. Women may tend to be slower to gain confidence.

    Rationale:
    Lack of confidence appears to be one of the five categories of psychosocial behavior that reveal gender differences according to Klein (1985). According to Block (1981), this may be because females are more fearful of flying and manifest greater anxiety.

    If women students were at ease and encouraged in their efforts and successes, their confidence and self-efficacy would increase significantly.

2. Women may tend to be more apprehensive about first solo and, therefore, they may be slower to solo.

    Rationale:
    There are two major reasons for women being slower to solo airplanes:

    a. Women (and older men) seem to need more time to gain the confidence required for first solo. They are fully aware that this is the part of flying that could hurt them if performed incorrectly; therefore, they are extremely cautious. They would rather take a little more time before first solo than take any chances. In comparison, young men seem to think that nothing can possibly happen to them and this attitude helps considerably to produce an early solo.

b. It appears that women's learned dependency is related. Learned helplessness may hinder women's progress. In addition, sometimes men are socialized with a tendency to over-protect women for what they believe to be for their own good.

Both confidence and dependency are included in the five categories of psychosocial behavior revealed by Klein (1985).

3. Women are quicker to grasp instrument flight.

Rationale:
The reason many women are quicker to grasp instrument flight may be because instrument approaches are methodical and contain much detail, requiring precision and concentration. Most women seem to naturally enjoy procedure and its rewarding results. The details are similar to that of following intricate software instructions. Follow the procedures and finish with an airport. Flight instructors can capitalize on this advantage.

4. Women pilots have far fewer fatal aircraft accidents.

Rationale:
Women pilots have far few fatal accidents according to statistics from the National Transportation Safety Board (NTSB). Statistics show the three main causes of general aviation accident fatalities are: Flying into bad weather, Barnstorming, and Flying while intoxicated. These are the three previously listed items on my list that women usually don't do. This is what makes women's fatal accident record so low in this area.

5. Once women learn a procedure well, they appear to be more consistent and they rarely vary from the procedure.

Rationale:
Most women work so hard at learning the details of each task that, once achieved, they will consistently repeat the task in exactly the same manner in order to be 100% correct. This tendency is effective in normal flight. In emergencies, there is a need fo for initiative and possibly innovation. Women should also be trained to be ready to make the necessary deviations.

6. Women may be more fearful of stalls, spins, and other unusual attitudes.

Rationale:

All of these maneuvers are aggressive. Most probably, women are more fearful of stalls, spins, and unusual maneuvers because of lack of practiced aggressive behavior. Boys grow up shooting play guns and playing pretend battles. Aggression was on their minds much of their growing-up years. They faced the possibility of having to go to war to protect their country. Is it any wonder that most of them enjoy the aggressive maneuvers in flying? Flying aggressive maneuvers may be a woman's first chance at deliberate aggression; therefore, they are understandably timid. After they complete 30 or 40 of these maneuvers, they do not hesitate to complete the maneuver successfully. Most even learn to enjoy them as well. Introducing these maneuvers after thorough explanations may be an effective teaching strategy.

7.　Women tend to operate the controls of the airplane with smoothness and skill.

Rationale:

Since many women have been conditioned to be gentle as children, they naturally treat the airplane in a gentle manner. They don't 'man-handle' the plane. Women's gentle touch on the controls provides smooth handling of the aircraft.

8.　Women may have less technical background from past experience.

Rationale:

As children women have seldom built model airplanes, sailed paper airplanes, or even looked closely at airplanes while growing up. Once they begin paying attention to the details of aerodynamics, their knowledge base is easily developed to appropriate standards.

9.　Women rarely fly into dangerous weather.

Rationale:

Since society doesn't expect women to be 'macho', they have little trouble canceling a planned flight when the weather is bad. They have no image to uphold and naturally opt for safety.

10.　Women pilots rarely show off in airplanes.

Rationale:

Very few women pilots appear to have a need or desire to 'show-off' in airplanes. Therefore, they do little barnstorming or other low-level maneuvers. It's not that they couldn't. Most of them simply prefer not to show-off.

11. Women pilots rarely fly while intoxicated.

   Rationale:
   Women pilots do not generally fly while intoxicated. In fact, the vast majority report that they would not even be seen at an airport in that condition. Their pride and sense of negative community reaction would not allow it.

12. Women's flying accidents usually involve touchdown or taxiing.

   Rationale:
   The fact that women pilots' accidents are usually related to landing or taxiing seems to relate closely to their automobile accident statistics where women are involved in 'fender benders'. (Notice how closely this compares to landings, 'wing dings', and taxi accidents.)

Further Findings

An additional item seems to be emerging. There is the tendency of some women to take a hand off the throttle and flare with both hands on the yoke for landings. This is especially true in transitioning to twin-engine aircraft. It is not clear whether it is because of lesser arm strength or an attempt to have more control of the aircraft. Since taking one's hands off the throttle during landing means the loss of an invaluable landing tool, helping women learn to use the trim tab for all landings is essential. With proper trimming procedures, even smaller women are able to keep one hand on the throttle and the other on the yoke during all landing flares.

   Although empathy and self-esteem have not yet been mentioned, they are the two remaining categories in Klein's (1985) five categories of psychosocial behavior. They play a major part in the possible reasons for all twelve differences.

   Empathy and self-esteem form the overall attitude of all pilots, especially women pilots. If their self-esteem is already low and they can 'feel' low expectations from the people around them, they will most certainly perform in accord with those expectations. If flight instructors can learn what women pilots are feeling, they can better meet their needs. According to Byrne (1978), the prejudice of male workers must share the responsibility with the bias of employers if the fact that the training of women is deficient. Technical dexterity is certainly attained by women to a degree equal to men. Indeed, it should not be accentuated by the tendency for certain subject areas to be taught by men or women only and thus become sex-linked. Second only to this is the need to educate both sexes for the best job or career of which he or she is capable—which 86 percent of the boys and 88 percent of the girls and 89 percent of their parents rated as a major school objective in the Schools Council's survey of nearly 5,000 pupils in 1968.

   In addition, according to Byrne (1978), instructors need to treat girls and boys alike. A shrewd observer will see differences in our attitudes towards girls that are translated into the way we plan what we do, the way girls are handled, the way they are stretched or discouraged in their work. Any school that makes great play of 'interest-based' activities and lacks a program of educational objectives based on needs and not pre-conditioned interests will also be planning a 'hidden curriculum' which is subtly and pervasively different for girls. This is because of the different interests that parents, nursery school teachers, and relatives have encouraged them to regard as 'feminine', acceptable, and praiseworthy. Social behavior spills over into classroom activity (Byrne, 1978; Sadker & Sadker, 1994).

Summary

The following is a list of factors that were found in the accumulated data to be important information in training women to fly. They include:

- Women may tend to be slower to gain confidence; therefore, slower to solo.
- Women may be quicker to grasp instrument flight.
- Women pilots have far fewer fatal aircraft accidents.
- Women may tend to learn a procedure correctly, and be more consistent, rarely varying from that procedure.
- Women may be more fearful of stalls, spins and other unusual attitudes.
- Women tend to operate the controls of the airplane with more smoothness and skill.
- Women may have less technical background from past experience.
- Women rarely fly into dangerous weather.
- Women pilots rarely show-off for spectators.
- Women pilots rarely fly while intoxicated.
- Women's accidents usually involve touchdown or taxiing.

Further studies are needed to focus specifically on insight into the differences in gender with regard to learning to fly, including the aviation environment and the experiences and perceptions of women students involved in aviation. Although gender balance is unlikely in the foreseeable future, the more women participate as aviation students, the more they teach faculty and peers how to behave toward women. If we are going to tap all the potential talent available to the aviation industry, it would appear useful to establish a strong climate for women. Investigation is needed on how women learn, lead, and experience career satisfaction (Turney, 2000). We can then proceed to develop excellence in women pilots, thereby, providing the finest possible women pilots for the aviation industry.

References

Anderson, S.L. (2001). 'An Investigation into Factors Influencing Career Choice among Professional Pilots', Unpublished Doctoral Dissertation, University of Minnesota. UMI Dissertation Services (UMI No. 3010534).

Benbow, C.P. and Stanley, J.C. (1980). 'Sex Differences in Mathematical Ability: Fact or Artifact'? *Science,* 210, 1262-1264.

Block, J.H. (1976). 'Issues, Problems, and Pitfalls in Assessing Sex Differences', *Merrill Palmer Quarterly, 22,* 283-308.

Block, J.H. (1981). 'Personality Development in Males and Females: The Influences of Differential Socialization', Paper presented at the annual meeting of the American Psychological Association.

Bryne, E.M. (1978). *Women and Education,* Great Britain: Tavistock Publications Limited.

Crawford, M. and Unger, R. (2000). *Women and gender: A feminist psychology.* New York: McGraw-Hill.

Creswell, J.W. (1998). *Qualitative Inquiry and Research Design,* Thousand Oaks: Sage Publications.

Eagley, A.H. (1978). 'Sex Differences in Influenceability', *Psychological Bulletin, 85,* 86-116.

French, J.W., Ekstrom, R.B., and Price, L.A. (1963). 'Manual for Kit of Reference Tests For Cognitive Factors' (Rev. Ed.), Princeton, NJ: Educational Testing Service and Related Behaviors.

Gilbert, S. (December, 1999). 'Winning or Losing against an Opposite-Sex Peer on a Gender Based Competitive Task', *Sex Roles: A Journal of Research.*

Gron, G., Wunderlich, M., Spitzer, et al. (2000, April). 'Brain Activation During Human Navigation: Gender-Different Neural Networks as Substrate of Performance', *Nature Neuroscience, 3* (4), 404-408.

Hoffman, M.L. (1977). 'Sex Differences in Empathy and Related Behaviors', *Psychological Bulletin, 84,* 712-722.

Jacklin, C.N. (1989, February). 'Female and Male: Issues of Gender', *American Psychologist,* 127-132.

Jensen, E. (2000). 'Sex, the Brain and Learning, in *Brain-based Learning*', Brain Store Inc.

Klein, S.S. (1985). *Handbook for Achieving Sex Equity Through Education,* Baltimore, MD: The Johns Hopkins University Press, 248.

Lenny, E. and Gold, J. (1982). 'Sex Differences in Self Confidence: The Effects of Task Completion and of Comparison to Competent Others', *Personality and Social Psychology Bulletin, 8,* 74-80.

Maccoby, E.E. and Jacklin, C.N. (1974). *The Psychology of Sex Differences,* Palo Alto, CA: Stanford University Press.

McGlone, J. (1980). 'Sex Differences in Human Brain Asymmetry: A Critical Survey', *Behavioral and Brain Science, 3,* 215-227.

Newcombe, J. (1980). 'Sex Related Differences in Spatial Ability Problems and Gaps in Current Approaches', in M. Potegal (Ed.) *Spatial Orientation: Developmental and Physiological Bases,* New York: Academic Press, pp. 223-250.

Pearson, J.L. and Ferguson, L.R. (1989). 'Gender Differences in Patterns of Spatial Ability, Environmental Cognition, and Math and English Achievement in Late Adolescence', *Adolescence, 24* (4), 421-431.

Peterson, A.C. (1980). 'Biophysical Processes in the Development of Sex-Related Differences', in J. Parsons (Ed.), *The Psychobiology of Sex Differences and Sex Roles*, New York: Hemisphere, pp. 31-55.

Peterson, A.C., Tobin-Richards, M.H. and Crockett, L. (1982). 'Sex Differences', in H. E. Metzel (Ed.), *Encyclopedia of Educational Research (5th ed)* New York: Free Press, pp. 1696-1712.

Rosenthal, R. and Ruben, D.B. (1982). 'Further Meta-Analytic Procedures for Assessing Cognitive Gender Differences', *Journal of Educational Psychology, 74*, 708-712.

Sadker, M. and Sadker, D. (1994). *Failing at fairness: How America's schools cheat girls.* New York: Scribner.

Shephard, R.M. and Melzler, J. (1971). 'Mental Rotation of Three-dimensional Objects', Science, 171, 701-703.

Sitler, R.L. (1998). 'The Cockpit Classroom: Women's Perceptions of Learning to Fly and Implications for Curriculum and Instruction', Unpublished Doctoral Dissertation, Kent State University, Kent, Ohio.

Symons, D. (1981, February). 'Interview by Sam Keen, Eron and Alley Opp', *PsychologyToday*, 52-61.

Tellis, W. (1997). 'Application of a Case Study Methodology', *The Qualitative Report, 3* (2), 1-18.

Turney, M.A. (2000). 'Attracting Women to Aviation Careers: What Recent Studies Reveal', *Collegiate Aviation Review, 18* (1).

Wiley, M.G. and Crittenden, K.S. (1992). 'By Attributions You Shall Be Known: Consequences of Attributional Accounts for Professional and Gender Identities', *Sex Roles, 27*, 259-289.

PART II
LANGUAGE

Chapter 7

ICAO Language Proficiency Requirements

Elizabeth Mathews

Introduction

On March 27, 1977, the worst disaster in aviation history—resulting in the loss of 583 souls—occurred when a Spanish controller and a Dutch pilot, both speaking English, failed to communicate critical information. In, apparently, a circumstance of imperfect understanding, KLM Flight 4805 attempted a take off, crashing into the Pan Am aircraft already on the runway.

On December 20, 1995, American Airlines Flight 965 arriving to Cali, Columbia from Miami, Florida, turned off course, crashing into a mountainside, killing all 160 on board. The air traffic controller last in contact with the aircraft's flight crew later told investigators that the flight's last reported position was incongruent with what he understood the aircraft's position to be, but that he did not know how to either convey that information to the crew in English or to seek clarification of their position.

On January 20, 1990, Avianca Airlines Flight 052, inbound to New York's John F. Kennedy airport, crashed when it ran out of fuel. The National Transportation Safety Board determined that the probable cause of the accident was 'the failure of the flight crew to adequately manage the airplane's fuel load, and their failure to communicate an emergency fuel situation to air traffic control before fuel exhaustion occurred.'

What these accidents have in common is that in each one accident investigators found that insufficient English language proficiency on the part of the flight crew or a controller had played a contributing role in the chain of events leading to the accident. In some instances, the use (or misuse) of language has contributed directly or indirectly to an accident. At other times, language is a link which exacerbates the problem.

As sobering as is any discussion of airline accidents, the focus of this chapter is NOT on the accidents themselves; instead a practical solution is presented: a recently adopted set of Standards and Recommended Practices from the International Civil Aviation Organization which stand to have a far-reaching and significant safety impact. In this chapter we review the role of ICAO to establish requirements, the need for strengthened language requirements, and the scope of the requirements themselves.

International Civil Aviation Organization

The International Civil Aviation Organization (ICAO) is the United Nations organization established to administer the Convention on International Civil Aviation. The 189 ICAO Member States signatory to the Convention agree to abide by the Standards and Recommended Practices (SARPS) contained in the 18 Annexes, which constitute the international civil law for aviation and cover all aspects of aviation. While the Convention, its Annexes and SARPS have immediate application to *international* civil aviation operations only, it is customary for States to apply the provisions to domestic operations as well. Without the Convention, and ICAO to administer it, flight operations would be random, a matter of constant dispute with respect to airspace rights, disorderly and dangerous.

The Preamble to the ICAO Convention

Whereas the future development of international civil aviation can greatly help to create and preserve friendship and understanding among the nations and peoples of the world, yet its abuse can become a threat to the general security; and

Whereas it is desirable to avoid friction and to promote that cooperation between nations and peoples upon which the peace of the world depends;

Therefore, the undersigned governments having agreed on certain principles and arrangements in order that international civil aviation may be developed in a safe and orderly manner and that international air transport services may be established on the basis of equality of opportunity and operated soundly and economically have accordingly concluded this Convention to that end.

While ICAO has no punitive enforcement body, there are a number of ways in which compliance with the Convention and SARPS is assured. The first is by force of the Convention. ICAO was established and is supported and maintained by Member States. Articles 37 through 40 are particularly relevant, and are paraphrased here:

Article 37:   Each ICAO Member State agrees to conform to ICAO SARPS to the highest degree possible.

Article 38:   If a Member State cannot fully comply with an ICAO SARP, they must notify ICAO, which in turn will notify other Member States of the 'difference.'

Article 39:   Any person who is not able to comply with ICAO licensing SARPS must indicate that on his or her license.

Article 40:   Such a person cannot participate in international aviation, except with the explicit permission of the State whose territory is entered.

However, there are other measures by which ICAO SARPS are enforced, as well. The next pertinent measure is through 'peer pressure.' The ICAO Member States monitor compliance. When deficiencies are noticed, it is brought to the attention of the civil aviation authority and to ICAO, who corresponds with the Member State. The industry, both by the influence of insurers and the requirements of individual States, regulators, airlines and air traffic service providers, determinedly self administers the compliance of these provisions Finally, the States themselves recently mandated ICAO to conduct a new safety oversight and audit program which is universal and increasingly comprehensive. Any shortcomings and deficiencies are notified to all Contracting States. States are keen to be found compliant.

What makes this relatively tight system work is the extensive review process through which all proposed amendments to ICAO Annexes travel:

1.   Development of a proposal by the Secretariat or working group;
2.   A preliminary review of a proposal by the Air Navigation Commission, which comprises 18 representatives who debate the proposal;
3.   Review by each of the 189 Member States, all of which have the opportunity to comment to ICAO;
4.   Final review, debate and revision by the Commission;
5.   Review (with adoption or rejection) by the ICAO 36 member Council; and
6.   Final review by Member States (current status of LPRs).

ICAO Language Requirements Prior to March 5, 2003

A review of ICAO documents prior to the adoption of the language proficiency requirements on March 5, 2003 highlighted the need for amendments. While there were a number of references to the use of language for radiotelephony communications, references to the use of English specifically were found only in Annex 10, Volume II, which governs Communications (in bold, Table 7.1).

Two Recommended Practices in Annex 10 and a Standard in Annex 1 (Personnel Licensing) comprised the provisions relating to the use of language. Annex 10, Chapter 5 recommended (5.2.1.2.2) that English be made available whenever an aircraft station is unable to comply with the preceding Recommended Practice (5.2.1.2.1) that radiotelephony communications be conducted in the language used by the station on the ground. The Annex 1 Standard stipulated that controllers demonstrate knowledge of 'the language or languages nationally designated for use in air-ground communications and ability to speak such language or languages without accent or impediment which would adversely affect radio communication.'

Table 7.1   References to language found in ICAO documents prior to March 5, 2003

Document	Chapter and paragraphs	
Annex 10	5.1.1.1	5.2.1.5.2 - 5.2.1.5.5
	5.2.1.2. --	5.2.1.6.2.1.1
	1 5.2.1.2.5	
	5.2.1.4.3.2	
	Attachment B	
Annex 1	4.3.1.2.e	
(Doc 4444) PANS-ATM	Part X, Chpt. 2.1	
Manual of Radiotelephony (Doc 9432)	Forward 1.2	Glossary
	2.1	

In addition to the absence of a similar Standard requiring language proficiency for flight crews, these Standards and Recommended Practices (SARPS) relating to language did not provide a clearly defined required proficiency level. Essentially, recommending the use of a language without defining a proficiency level rendered implementation difficult and assessment uneven. Furthermore, the embodiment of the previously existing provisions concerning the use of English in Annex 10 as Recommended Practices belied the safety critical role of English in aviation communications.

The remaining references to language relate to the use of standard radiotelephony phraseologies, correct radiotelephony transmission technique, with allusions to the use of 'plain language' whenever phraseologies do not apply. However, explicit guidance on the use of plain language when circumstances necessitate a deviation from standard ICAO phraseologies was scant, appearing in two documents:

a)   'Speak slowly and clearly and use standard words and phrases as much as possible.' (Forward to Document 9432)

b)   'Subsidiary phraseologies...should be as clear and concise as possible and designed to avoid possible confusion by those persons using a language other than one of their national languages.' (Document 4444, Part XII, Chapter 2)

The Applications of Language in Aviation Communications

To understand the importance of the revised ICAO Language Proficiency Requirements, it is useful to review the three fundamental applications of language use in radiotelephony communications. First, there is the correct use of ICAO phraseologies. ICAO publishes phraseologies as a means to promote clarity and brevity. Mis-communication can result from an incorrect use of ICAO phraseologies, or from the use of phraseologies other than ICAO phraseologies. An example of such possible mis-communications can be found in the potential confusion between the ICAO phraseology 'Taxi into holding position,' (meaning for the aircraft to stop short of the runway) and the non-standard phraseology used by some States to 'Taxi into position and hold' (meaning to enter a runway and await take-off clearance.) Secondly, proficiency in common, or plain language, is important for safe radiotelephony communications. Early aviation communication specialists had hopes that the requirements of pilot and controller communications would be achieved once there was developed a 'radiotelephony speech' based on a simplified English. Experience shows and safety experts and linguists agree that phraseologies alone, no matter how extensive, are not sufficient to adequately cover all of the potential situations that can arise from human communication, particularly, in aviation, for urgent or emergency situations. There will always exist a need for plain language in addition to phraseologies. So, the first role of language in communication is standardization on ICAO phraseologies and the correct use of those phraseologies. The second is proficiency in plain language. While incorrect application of phraseologies has been determined to be a contributing factor is some accidents, a lack of general proficiency in the language used for radiotelephony communications is more often cited as having played a contributing role in accidents. The controller last in contact with the English-only speaking crew of a flight which strayed off course and crashed into a mountainside acknowledged to accident investigators that the flight's position reports were incongruent with where he understood their position to be, but that he lacked plain English proficiency to clarify his doubts or to notify the crew that they may be off-course. The need for this 'plain' language, which can be described as 'aviation-specific English—not phraseologies,' arises not only during emergency and urgent situations, but also in any instance in which clarification is sought, or negotiation, either of meaning or situation, needs to occur. While there is little, if any, room for 'conversational' English in radiotelephony communications, there is certainly a need for plain English language in many instances.

The third language-related issue as it relates to flight safety concerns the use of more than one language in a single radiotelephony environment. Many pilots, controllers, and safety experts believe that a single language for radiotelephony communications ensures optimal situational awareness, and a runway collision at one major airport in 2000 was attributed by accident investigators to the use of two languages in a single environment. However, it must also be recognized that there are significant and legitimate national, cultural, economic, and organizational barriers to any move to establish a single-language radiotelephony environment, making such a move currently impractical. Because language use is so closely tied to our sense of national and cultural identity, language policies always require sensitive management. In fact, language *exclusion* policies are most often, from a linguistic and political point of view, decidedly wrong. However, in the limited domain of aeronautical radiotelephony communications, the interconnectedness of safety with clear communications makes a single-language policy one that legitimately merits consideration. Indeed, a number of non-native English speaking ICAO Member States, free to set policies more stringent than ICAO Standards, have implemented measures which either require or encourage the use of only English, at least in busy international sectors. The ICAO Language Proficiency Requirements adopted by the ICAO Council in 2003, while requiring that English be made available for use in international radiotelephony communications, do not prohibit or limit the use of local or national languages. Thus, the requirements directly address the first two uses of language as explained here, and indirectly impacts on the third, regarding the use of more than one language for radiotelephony communications.

The Scope of ICAO Language Proficiency Requirements

The Language Proficiency Requirements adopted by the ICAO Council in amendments to Annexes 1, 6, 10, and 11 on March 5, 2003 address these issues in a number of ways. The amendments

- **strengthen** the provisions for the use of the English language to be used in radiotelephony communications, both the language of the station on the ground and, in airspace where it is required, English (Annex 10);
- **establish** minimum skill level requirements for language proficiency for flight crews and air traffic controllers (Annex 1);
- **introduce** an ICAO language proficiency rating scale applicable to both native and non-native speakers (Annex 1);
- **clarify** the use of plain language and phraseologies (Annex 1 and 10);
- **standardize** on the use of ICAO phraseologies (Annex 10);
- **recommend** a testing schedule to demonstrate language proficiency (Annex 1); and
- **provide** for service provider oversight of personnel compliance (Annexes 6 and 11).

The ICAO Language Proficiency Requirements in Annex 10, Volume II— Communications, continue to allow for the use of the language of the station on the ground, but require that English be made available by way of an ICAO Standard, rather than the previously existing 'Recommended Practice' primarily for the reasons elaborated upon in an earlier sections. An ICAO Standard, of course, naturally has more binding value than does a 'Recommended Practice.' Even more important, perhaps, are the Annex 1—Personnel Licensing requirements which specify the level of proficiency which pilots and controllers must attain, and establish testing requirements for the demonstration of proficiency. The proficiency requirements apply equally to native and non-native speakers. That is, all speakers must move to the use of a dialect or accent which is reasonably and readily understood among the international aviation community. Native speakers, too, must take care that any strong regional or local dialect does not interfere with their international communications. The Language Proficiency Requirements also specify, by way of an ICAO Standard, the use of ICAO phraseologies. Previous SARPS directive related to the use of phraseologies had required the use of *standardized* phraseologies, but without specifying ICAO standardized phraseologies. The new SARPS now do so will bring more pressure to bear on those individuals and States whose use of phraseologies deviates significantly from ICAO phraseologies. As important as is the correct use of phraseologies, at least equally important is that controllers and pilots have proficiency in 'plain' (but aviation-related) language, and so the proficiency requirements in Annex 10 apply to the use of both phraseologies and plain language.

Taken together, the ICAO Language Proficiency Requirements stand to have an unprecedented positive safety impact on global aviation communications.

Language Cooperation

Along with the move to establish strengthened ICAO English language proficiency requirements comes, however, a call for close international cooperation and a sharing of the burden. The requirements place a heavy training burden on non-English speaking ICAO Member States. How can native (and highly proficiency) English speaking individuals and organizations assist? There are a number of ways. English speaking individuals can take greater care in their use of phraseologies, and Member States can work to ensure their phraseologies are in accord with ICAO's. Airlines can assist code-sharing partners in the establishment of high quality aviation-specific English programs, either by providing qualified language training personnel in country or by making English language training available at cost for international partners at existing training centres. Between 1995 and 1997, several North American and European airlines provided intensive aviation English language training to controllers from the civil aviation authority of one ICAO Member State. Additionally, much useful language training material can be developed by modifying existing aviation training products, such as videos, CRM training packages, and simulator programs. Organizations can invest in the development of high quality aviation-specific English learning products and materials by contracting with educators. Products so developed may be made available to learners at cost or for marginal profit. In short, those native and highly-proficient English speaking States and organizations naturally favoured by the provisions for the strengthened use of English can facilitate the movement towards a safer communication environment by giving assistance to those non-native English speaking States not so favoured, and by generally factoring this world-wide need for heightened language proficiency into commercial considerations. An aviation community cooperatively committed to communicating better will fly more safely.

Summary

This chapter reviewed the role of ICAO to establish requirements regarding language proficiency standards, and the need for strengthening language requirements for pilots and air traffic controllers.

Accident investigators have found that insufficient English language proficiency on the part of a flight crew or a controller frequently was a contributing factors leading to an accident. Inadequate communications can either be a direct cause, or misuse of language can be a link in a chain of events that eventually produces an accident.

A practical solution to miscommunication problems lies in the adaptation of Standards and Recommended Practices from the International Civil Aviation Organization (ICAO). Such practices offer the opportunity to improve safety through more effective communication among both national and international flight crews and air traffic controllers.

References

ICAO, (2003). 'Language Proficiency Requirements', Amendments to Annexes 1,6,10,11, Montreal, CA.
ICAO, Document 4444, Part XII, Chapter 2, Montreal, CA.
ICAO, Document 9432, Chapter 1, 1.2, Montreal, CA.
ICAO, 'Personnel Licensing', Annex 1, Montreal, CA.
ICAO, Recommended Practices 5.1.1.1, 5.2.1.2.1, 5.2.1.2.2, 5.2.1.2.5, 5,2,1,4,3,2, 5,2,1,5.2-5.2.1.5..5, 5.2.1.6.2.1.1, Chapter 5, Annex 10, Montreal, CA
ICAO, 'Standards and Recommended Practices (SARPS)', Articles 37-40, Annex 1-18, Montreal, CA.

Chapter 8

The Efficacy of Standard Aviation English

Robert F. Ripley and James L. Fitch

Introduction

Aviation is just one of the many areas of society that is coming to the realization that global communication needs to be standardized. Even though English is the primary aviation language, as it is for business, there is not an agreed upon standard for being able to read, speak and understand English. Variations in English (accents and dialects) can interfere with the process of communication by creating misunderstandings, ambiguity and slowing the process of comprehension. Although the Federal Aviation Regulations require that pilots be able to read, speak and understand English when flying in the U.S. airspace, the regulations do not address the very important issue of a performance standard that needs to be met.

Training in the use of Standard English, adapted for the aviation environment, would likely have a far-reaching impact in reducing the number of communication-related accidents and thus the overall accident rates. Standard English can be defined as pronunciation according to the dictionary and using language that conforms to the rules of formal grammar. Using Standard English would remove distractions to, and possible misunderstandings of, the content of a communication.

In aviation, the speed and accuracy of communication is critical to flight safety. It would seem that standard English training, amended to fit the aviation environment, should be included as an integral required skill for all airline personnel worldwide whose communication is vital to safe air transportation.

In this chapter, the authors describe air carrier accidents that have as a primary or secondary cause faulty language or other communications breakdowns and present and discuss the features of speech and language that need to be addressed in the aviation environment. We will also present proposed English language performance criteria that would apply to domestic and international aviation personnel.

Accidents

On April 30,1991, the NTSB found that the crew of Avianca Flight 052, which crashed in 1990 at Cove Neck, N.Y. while enroute from Bogotá, Columbia to Kennedy International Airport, allowed their aircraft to run out of fuel without adequately alerting air traffic control to their pending emergency situation. Of 158 persons on board Flight 052, 73 died in the accident, which occurred 16 miles from the airport.

On March 27, 1977, the worst aviation disaster in history occurred when a Pan American World Airways 747 was struck by a departing KLM 747 on the ground at Santa Cruz de Tenerife, Canary Islands, killing 583 people.

Near Charkhi Dadri, India on November 12, 1996 a Kazakhstan Airline's Ilyushin I-76 collided with a Saudi Arabian B-747 that had just departed from New Delhi, India killing 351 people. This was the worst midair collision in history and the third worst aviation disaster of all time.

What does each of these accidents have in common? These accidents were caused, in part, because the crews did not know or use standard aviation English and they were unable to communicate effectively with air traffic controllers. In the Avianca accident, the crew was Columbian and though they spoke English they did not clearly communicate their low fuel status to air traffic control. The language breakdown was intensified by the highly congested airspace in the New York area. In the Tenerife accident the air traffic controllers were Spanish, the Pan Am crew was American and the KLM crew was Dutch. Even though all parties to this accident also spoke English, there were language and communications breakdowns that clearly contributed to the accident. It is interesting to note that in the Charkhi Dadri accident, the air traffic controller was native Indian and the flight crews were Saudi and Russian. Even though all parties to this accident also spoke English, language or communication differences contributed to this disaster. In just these three accidents 1,006 people died, partly because there were language problems that resulted in communications failures.

It is worthwhile to remember that two of the three worst aviation disasters in history (Tenerife and Charkhi Dadri) had language or communications breakdowns cited as primary or secondary factors.

Need for Standardization

Aviation is just one of many areas of society that is coming to the realization that global communication needs to be standardized. English is the primary language of business and social agencies around the world. However, variations in English (accent and dialects) can interfere with the process of communication by creating misunderstandings and slowing the process of comprehension. In business, speed and accuracy are critical to maximizing productivity, and productivity is vital for increasing profit potential. Training employees to use Standard English is, therefore, an integral part of job preparation. Standard English can be defined as pronouncing words according to the dictionary and using language that conforms to the rules of formal grammar (the type of language used in writing business letters). Using Standard English removes distraction to, and possible misunderstanding of, the content of a communication.

Standard Aviation English

In aviation, the speed and accuracy of communication is critical to safety. It would seem that standardized language training should be included as an integral required skill for those whose communication is vital to safe air transportation. But crew training does not include testing, or training, in standard language skills. Rather, crew-training focuses on communication style, particularly that of the pilot in command. While communication style is important, quality of the content of communication is critical to safety.

Accent and dialect differences are generally due to geography. Accent may be the result of the effect of a speaker's first language or a later learned language. The globalization of aviation introduces the challenge of communication among both native English speakers and those whose native language is not English.

Additionally, there are a great number of regional differences in the speech of native English speakers. An example of a common misunderstanding among American English speakers is found in a phrase such as "ten/tin airplanes." In many parts of the United States, notably the South and Midwest, "ten/tin" are produced the same and the speaker must rely on context for correct interpretation. The dictionary pronunciation of "ten" indicates the vowel should be the same as the vowel in the word "bet" and "tin" should have the same vowel as the word "bit." There are other vowels that can create confusion, such as the pronunciation of "Don/Dawn." "Don" should have the same vowel as in "hot" and "Dawn" should have the same vowel as in "awe." Vowels are normally the sounds of the language most affected by accent.

A second example is in the use of inflection. In some parts of America (notably the South), speakers tend to use upward inflection in declarative sentences, while in most parts of the country an upward inflection indicates a question. An example of a potential for misunderstanding can be found in a sentence such as "you are the pilot of this plane." This sentence can be interpreted as a statement or a question, depending on the inflection.

Another consideration in terms of different domestic dialects is the distraction factor. When individuals who have different regional speech and language patterns talk, the attention of the listener is often drawn to the accent rather than the message. This distraction can result in the listener's either losing part of the content or delay the processing of the content. Obviously in situations in which quick response is critical, a delay could be costly.

Non-Native English Speakers

Another challenge can exist in the evaluation and training of non-native English speakers. Each language requires an individual study to determine sound and language commonalities and differences.

For purposes of consideration in this paper, we will take a brief look at the challenges of native Spanish speakers learning to speak English. Spanish has several sounds that differ significantly from English. For examples, there are no Spanish counterparts for the 'z' and 'sh' sounds. They simply aren't used in the language. The Spanish speaker substitutes the nearest sounds in his own native language which is 's' for 'z' and 'ch' for 'sh.' Because of the 'sh/ch' confusion, he may have problems speaking, and understanding, word pairs such as 'chip' and 'ship,' 'wash' and 'watch,' and 'dishes' and 'ditches.' The confusion of 's' and 'z' results in the same type of confusion in word pairs such as 'seal' and 'zeal,' 'ceased' and 'seized,' and 'loose' and 'lose.'

Vowels are also different, with the tendency of the Spanish speaker to use long vowels for short vowels. For example, a phrase such as 'hit the mitt' spoken with a Spanish accent becomes 'heat the meat.' The difference in vowel sounds is even more significant than consonant sounds, as vowels carry the basic intelligibility of the language.

There are also sounds in Standard English that do not occur in any other language. The English 'r' sound is a different and difficult sound for speakers of any other language. There is just not any sound like it. Also, the 'l' sound, which has similarities in production to the 'r' sound, is one that does not transfer well from one language to another. These sounds are particularly difficult for persons whose native language is of Asian origin.

For non-native English speakers, evaluation/training should include idioms, as idioms comprise a significant portion of the English language and their meaning is not readily apparent to an individual who is not exposed to the language. Examples of phrases just involving the word "one" that could confuse a non-native English speaker include "back to square one," "watch out for number one," "one for the road," and "one of these days." In addition to training non-native English speaker on idioms, native speakers need to be trained to avoid idioms in the aviation environment.

Evaluation of Language Skill

While a description of a comprehensive evaluation/training program is beyond the scope of this chapter, the following are characteristics that should be considered in developing such a program.

- First, the training should be specific to the aviation industry, as a program comprehensive to the language as a whole would not be cost/time efficient.

- Second, the evaluation should be performance-based to determine real-world competence in the aviation environment.
- Third, the program should be available on the Internet so it is accessible at any geographic location at any time.

The increase in air traffic and the number of individuals involved in support positions increases the importance of clear and accurate communication, so these personnel should be included the testing/training of standard aviation English. This is particularly true in light of the recent increase in airport security personnel, where the word 'safety' takes on a new dimension.

Summary

The domestic and international aviation industries should consider the inclusion of standard aviation English testing/training in all areas of activities. A number of post-accident investigations have found that a probable cause factor in several air carrier accidents has been the communication difficulties and misunderstandings related to the use of the English language in both national and international aviation operations. As a result, it is proposed that individuals working in crucial areas of aviation, whether they be native speakers or non-native speakers, should be required to demonstrate proficiency before being placed in situations where safety could be compromised by miscommunication.

References

Aircraft Accident Report (1991). *Avianca, The Airline of Columbia, Boeing 707-321B, HK2016, Fue Exhaustion, Cove Neck, New York, January 25, 1990*. NTSB/AAR-91-04, Washington, D.C: National Transportation Safety Board.

Aircraft Accident Analysis (1998). Saudi and Kazakhstan accident available at http://users.senet.com/au/~wingman/collision.html.

Aviation Safety Reporting System (2001). Pilot Communication Reports, Moffett Field, CA: NASA/Ames Research Center.

Cushing, S. (1994). *Fatal Words: Communication Clashes and Aircraft Crashes*, Chicago: University of Chicago Press.

Orlady, H.W., and Orlady, L.M. (1999). *Human Factors in Multi-Crew Flight Operations*, Aldershot: Ashgate.

'Subsecretaria de Aviacion Civil' Accident Report, 1978 (ICAO circular 153-AN/56), ICAO: Montreal.

Chapter 9

Reflexive Communication in the Multi-Cultural Crew

Taras Stratechuk and Ted Beneigh

Introduction

Imagine an airline crew where the captain turns to the first officer and says, 'We're not in Kansas anymore. Just follow the yellow brick road.' Imagine that after a particularly annoying and lengthy Air Traffic Control rerouting clearance, the First Officer turns to the captain and utters, 'Curiouser and curiouser, said Alice!' Picture a senior flight attendant, frustrated with passengers complaining that the flight will arrive late, turning to her assistant and ordering 'Go see if the captain's nose has grown; he promised us an on-time arrival!' Such unorthodox use of language from *The Wizard of Oz*, *Alice in Wonderland* and *Pinocchio*, would have little meaning to someone from a culture that lacked these childhood stories.

Even more interesting would be the fact that the deliverer of the message, looking at the blank expression on his foreign-born companion's face, would, himself, have little clue of the miscommunication that had just transpired. Unfortunately an additional problem with such culture-induced communication is that it leaves both the message sender *and* the receiver in a state of confusion, possibly leading to frustration, loss of patience, and even hostility.

The above scenarios may have little business on the flight deck of an airliner, but they illustrate the point that an array of culturally provocative challenges face today's air carrier crews. The safety implication of growing diversity as it relates to crew communication is a crucial matter. Crews need the skills to manage cultural differences in communication. Unmanaged differences in communication can lead to unsafe incidents, even accidents. (This management may be as simple as the way a captain greets his/her crew during their first meeting, or how questions are solicited from crewmembers during routine and emergency situations. It may be in the way eye contact is maintained during routine dialogue, or how formalities are observed during the drive from the crew room to the hotel room.)

Culturally shared communications, along with culture-induced values, help to form our overall view of the workplace. In turn, this perspective of the work environment has been shown to affect motivation. And motivation ultimately affects crew behavior as well.

Concerns with Culture

Culture plays a large part in shaping the human being who may eventually end up responsible for the flight of a modern airliner. In the past, pilots speaking of culture and cultural differences may have centered their discussion on the clashing of corporate cultures (culture at the professional or organizational level). Such a clash has, at times, negatively impacted the motivation of an airline crew and resulted in serious safety implications. A number of early safety reports (1989 Air Ontario - Fokker F28; 1992 Mount St-Odile - Airbus; 1993 New South Wales - Piper Navajo) attributed 'corporate/organizational culture' as the cause of serious accidents. These events offered a venue for other cultural issues in aviation, thus further paving the way for attention to be placed on 'national' culture and eventually for our emphasis on communication in all multi-cultural settings.

What we are presently seeing is a transformation that may be going unnoticed by many aviation crew resource management (CRM) educators; that is, the rapid appearance of cross-cultural subgroups in the crews among American domestic carriers, including the regional airlines. These subgroups not only include crewmembers who were born and raised in countries other than the USA, but also include women, African-Americans, and other minorities within American national culture.

This phenomenon has created a need for CRM designers to embrace the process of understanding cross-cultural dialogue through unique, reflexive communication principles. These communication principles will be discussed later in this chapter, but first let us review some of the relevant literature.

A Review of Culture

The word 'culture' has its origins in the Latin language. Beginning in the era of the Roman Empire and continuing throughout the centuries, the term has undergone significant changes. Today it is anthropologically fragmented into often difficult and debatable meanings. One could say: 'Latino culture is very rooted in music,' or 'The Germans have a unique beer-drinking culture,' or 'I have a difficult time handling the culture of bikers.' These examples use 'culture' as a term descriptive of a geographical region, a country, or even a group of people within another culture.

In the late eighteenth century the German philosopher and historian Herder claimed that the human individual is a creature of 'weak instincts' and that *culture* arises as a 'second genesis' that 'occupies the creature's whole life after birth and consists in the acquisition and application of everything that is communicated to it by past generations.' This notion of culture described the features that separate humans from all that is purely instinctive.

The term was further redefined by the mid-nineteenth century pioneer Sir Edward B. Taylor, who called it 'the complex whole of ideas and things produced by humans in their historical experience.' In turn, this definition led to the more modern and generic notion that all peoples and nations have their own specific culture that can be understood as a unified system. In other words, culture was no longer seen as a worldly human helper for all of mankind, as in Herder's view, but rather as a phenomenon ascribed to a specific group of people.

This brought on the unforeseen complication that there could now exist many groups of people within geographical regions, nations, parts of nations, cities, even neighborhoods, each subscribing to its own 'culture'. This notion of a culture within a culture is what anthropology as a discipline has wrestled with since its inception. Often it is the origin of much debate and disagreement among scholars. It is no wonder that Raymond Williams, who helped explain the meaning of the term culture for the International Edition of the Encyclopedia Americana, says that it is 'one of the two or three most complicated words in the English language.'

In 1991, Hofstede defined four dimensions of what was to be coined 'national' culture by the aviation community. Afterwards, the research group at the University of Texas at Austin under Helmreich adopted these dimensions in their work and they soon became the standard in multi-cultural CRM discussions within the aviation industry. The dimensions are PDI (Power Distance), UAI (Uncertainty Avoidance), IDV (Individualism-Collectivism), and MAS (Masculinity-Femininity).

For the purposes of this chapter, the use of the term culture refers to shared behaviors that are generalized to a group of people but not necessarily 'national' in nature. For the purpose of our goal as it relates to crew communication issues, we probably come closer to Hofstede's earlier definition of culture: 'The collective programming of the mind that distinguishes the members of one human group from another' (Hofstede, 1980).

This is a more generalized and all-encompassing use of the term, one that transcends national, corporate, organizational, or any other form of specialized culture. It simply suggests the development of a new order of dialogue for pilots, one that is informed of gender, racial, and ethnic representations within the modern airline workplace. The term culture, for this purpose, could thus best be defined as:

> ...the values, beliefs and behaviors we share with other people and which help define us as a group, especially in relation to other groups. Culture gives us cues and clues on how to behave in normal and novel situations (Merritt and Helmreich, 1995).

Values, Motivation, Attitude and Performance

Safety only partly rests in formal structures and protocols. Fundamentally, it rests in attitudes (Maurino, 1998). What motivates pilots to perform safely and efficiently in the traditional or mono-cultural flight deck of an airliner is not a new topic and has been the discussion of aviation human factors experts for well over 30 years. From the standpoint of CRM and motivational theory in the *multi-cultural* setting, there is still a lot of research to be done.

Our main point here is to show that much improvement can be made to enhance airline crew motivation and performance through the use of communication principles that construct convergent realities for crews of mixed cultural backgrounds. Although we feel that established workplace-related motivational theory is fairly generic to all working environments, it would be helpful to briefly review some of the concepts before continuing our discussion of the multi-cultural aviation application as it relates to crewmember communication.

An individual's decision to participate in any system is determined by the relative magnitude of inducements and contributions when both are measured in terms of the participant's values and motives (Vroom, 1970). Humans have two sets of needs that relate to the work they do: the first is to avoid pain, and the second to grow psychologically. Fredrick Herzberg in his classic work on the motivation-hygiene concept *The Motivation to Work*, explains his theory by comparing job satisfiers and dissatisfiers.

The dissatisfiers (or hygiene factors) are essentially elements in the environment and serve primarily to prevent job dissatisfaction (company policy, supervision, salary, interpersonal relations and working conditions). The satisfiers (motivators) are factors that stand out as strong determinants of job satisfaction from a psychological standpoint (achievement, recognition, work itself, responsibilities and advancement opportunities).

One might therefore conclude that what motivates a person to work in the flight deck of an airliner is related to that person's overall perception of what exists under this duality of needs. In other words, *how an individual's culturally induced values allow him/her to view interpersonal relations with crew members might be considered influential in determining job satisfaction from a pain-avoidance standpoint. How a member of a culturally diverse crew is given responsibilities and recognition by the company or superior might also be considered influential in job satisfaction from a uniquely psychological standpoint.*

It may be safe to expect, then, that our perception of these factors, based on the values we hold due to our cultural background, gender, race, and ethnic representation, ultimately will design our motivation and desire to work in the multi-cultural crew. Values, attitudes and motivation equal behavior, and, as mentioned before, crew behavior is what causes or avoids accidents in aviation.

In a study by researchers A.C. Merritt and R.L. Helmreich at the University of Texas at Austin, Anglo pilots were questioned and compared with non-Anglo pilots. Their extensive database showed that the strongest differences in attitudes were in the areas of command structure and communication flow. They observed that: 'One has to consider the values that underline these attitudes to fully understand their origins' (Merritt and Helmreich, 1995).

Communication

The 'Cultural' Meta-Message

Communication is one of the seven parameters influencing CRM that must be identified and understood by all flight crews (Beneigh, 2001). As early as 1984, researchers S.G. Redding and J.G Ogilvie, of the University of Hong Kong, presented their findings on 'Cultural Effects on Cockpit Communications in Civilian Aircraft'. They argued that cultural levels of difference, although assumed not to affect the behavior of professional flight crews, might, in fact, operate unconsciously and in ways that were difficult to perceive.

A woman invites her mother over for dinner. While watching her daughter make the turkey, the mother says, 'I see you still add onions to your stuffing.' 'Why do you have to criticize everything I do?' exclaims the daughter in frustration. 'I didn't criticize,' her mother replies, 'I just asked a question. What's got into you? I can't even open my mouth!'

The above example comes from Deborah Tannen's book *I Only Say This Because I Love You: How the Way We Talk Can Make or Break Family Relationships Throughout Our Lives*. The author talks about the two messages in the meaning of the words and sentences spoken. The *message* and the *meta message*. The *message* would be what a dictionary and grammar book could tell you about what is being said. Two people in a conversation would easily agree on what the message is with no difficulty.

But what about the *meta message*? ('Meta' meaning, going beyond and higher.) It is the meaning that is not stated, but implied and expected to be understood, a 'heart meaning' Tannen calls it; rather than a 'word meaning.' In the above example, what was really being said was something like the following: 'Daughter, I've taught you how to make a good stuffing and I've told you that adding onions does not make the dressing better. How many times do I have to tell you that? I am very disappointed in you!'

Although Tannen uses this to describe family members talking to one another, an aviation analogy can be made to describe meta messaging in cross-cultural airline crew communication. Tannen says family members have a shared history, everything they say echoes with meanings from the past, and they develop a sixth sense for sniffing out criticism in almost anything a loved one says. Just as each family in every part of the world has developed its own meta messaging, we could say that each person's unique cultural background has also developed a similar shared history and system of sixth-sense communication.

As an example: in the United States a First Officer who uses the word *may* in this context, 'You *may* kindly start the checklist at your convenience,' could easily communicate a meta message to the receiver of usurped leadership and ineptitude. The implied message might be along the lines of: 'Look captain, I'm really the boss here and even though you wear the stripes, I am telling you that you have my permission to do this now!' This is not a very friendly scenario and could easily upset an authoritative captain with a sensitive ego.

But in Indian culture, the word '*may*' in the aforementioned context conveys a totally different meaning. The meta message, in India, would be one of respect, professionalism and even admiration; in contrast to the U.S. use, the meta message *now* would be: 'Captain, I am finished with my part of the procedures and I am now very humbly and politely reminding you that you are the boss; I respect that you are the boss and that it is your turn with the checklist.'

Importance of Communication

Cultural differences in a mixed crew can originate from almost infinite sources within that culture: religion, politics, economics, sense of humor, history, paternalism, shame of failure, proceduralization, and family values, to name just a few. It is the ultimate goal of any airline crew to have unambiguous and effective cockpit/crew communication and interaction in spite of these cultural differences. Safe cockpits in civilian aircraft are characterized by open communication, good fellowship and helpfulness (Redding and Ogilvie, 1984). In 1997 The Aerospace Crew Research Project at the University of Texas at Austin undertook an extensive study to establish the relationship between culture and a pilot's [or pilots'] work values and attitudes (Helmreich and Merritt, 1997).

In their study of 10,000 pilots from 25 airlines in 18 countries, they found an almost universal endorsement by pilots of the importance of communication; however, the actual expression or actualization of this concept varied significantly cross-culturally. They found that subtle differences in communication began emerging as more specific behaviors were rated. In other words, pilots everywhere value the safety implications of proper communication and professional codes (checklists, SOPs, CRM principles), but how those codes are enacted is indeed a function of culture language with their multi-cultural co-workers.

We believe success can be obtained and monochromatic vision avoided through reflexive communication principles that are adopted to fit multi-cultural CRM training. With this approach, the issue becomes a problem to be solved rather than a paradox to lament.

Constructing Converging Realities

The fundamental view of our world is firmly implanted during our formative years (through family, religion, education, politics, language, etc.). A Hindu pilot from Uttar Pradesh might look at a given situation very differently than a Southern Baptist pilot from the Texas Panhandle. Cultural differences imply that we see the world through different realities. CRM needs to be expandable enough to embrace this understanding.

After all, CRM is a *process*, the output of which is improved safety and efficiency of aviation operations. Culture is among the many input factors, and cultural preferences influence CRM factors (Maurino, 1999). As an example, Anglo North American cultures tend to be individualistic whereas South American cultures tend to be collectivist and hierarchical. Communication in individualist cultures is direct, succinct, personal, and instrumental; communication in collectivist cultures is indirect, elaborate, contextual, and affective (Merritt, 1993, 1994).

As mentioned earlier, multi-cultural flight crews in the U.S. are here to stay, and across the globe a number of major air carriers are staffed by crews from many nations. A Draconian strategy for the management of such organizations is simply to impose the values and practices of the parent culture on all members of the organization (Helmreich, Merritt, and Sherman, 1996).

Consider the fact that the English language has no polite or respectful variant for the word *you*, as other languages do (such as Spanish or German). In Anglo cultures there is only one way to address someone, whether it is your best friend or the president, as in 'Do you know what time it is?' On the other hand in Spanish, we have the more respectful *'usted'* as opposed to the familiar *'vos'* or *'tu'*, and in German we find the *'Sie'* instead of the *'Du'*. Loosely translated, these polite versions of 'Do you know what time it is?' would be: 'Do you *sir/madam* know what time it is?'

This difference in communication styles often results in South Americans being perceived as unassertive and submissive while North Americans are perceived as direct and arrogant. Do these differences, which were established through the repeated use of language throughout one's developmental and childhood years, contribute to create a more assertive or submissive pilot? No one may know the answer to this, but [suffice it to say that] empirical evidence from many foreign-born pilots currently flying with major carriers in the Unites States seems to confirm that, at least from a perceptual standpoint, these problems exist -- and can lead to miscommunication, stressful working environments, and perhaps, ultimately, unsafe practices.

The following are comments made by a First Officer who currently flies for a major airline and was born and raised in Buenos Aires, Argentina, under the influence of a highly educated and traditional South American culture:

> ... another example is how my communication style is perceived. Specifically, during the various phases of flight I try to keep the captain in the loop ... I might tell the captain that I am going to warn the flight attendants to prepare for landing and many times they think I am *asking* them if I should do it ... these types of issues happen often on the flight deck. It is only out of respect for his authority and respect for him as a crewmember that I constantly strive to keep him in the loop.
>
> I wish American captains would understand my value system as it relates to my work. I will go out of my way to sacrifice comfort, without compromising safety, to do a job above and beyond the call of duty. This sometimes is misinterpreted as a sign of weakness and can create barriers in the interpersonal relationships I establish on the flight deck.
>
> ... the fact that I speak English with no accent ... many times crewmembers automatically assume that I was born and raised in the

United States with a Hispanic background. Well this is not the case, and many times I do not share the same knowledge of expressions ... therefore when they use a term or expression that I am not familiar with and I ask for clarification, many times I am given a look of surprise as if I am of lesser intelligence or a bit ignorant ...

Culturally unique human beings have different views of the same reality and therefore derive different meanings from the same situation. Mutual understanding of any single situation can thus only result from a construction of convergent views of that situation.

Mutual understanding of cultural differences between airline crewmembers can likewise be 'constructed' and reinforced during CRM and Line Oriented Flight Training (LOFT) so as to improve overall communication among crewmembers. It is our suggestion that these training sessions be uniquely staged with voluntary, multi-cultural, and diverse crews whenever possible, and that the subsequent post-flight briefings focus on reinforcing sound reflexive communication principles as outlined in the following pages.

The Captain Mike and Co-Pilot Miguel Dialogue

(The following is our unique aviation adaptation of the Mike and Miguel dialogue presented by John and Catherine Kikoski in their classic work on reflexive communication.)

Mike and Miguel both work for a major airline here in the United States. Both are experts at what they do and both are highly qualified and experienced in their respective positions on the flight deck. Miguel is an immigrant Chilean-American male who is a naturalized citizen of the U.S. and has been living here for over 30 years. He grew up in Santiago, Chile. Mike is a middle-class, white American male. The airline has paired them for this rather lengthy flight and this is their first time together. Both have been sitting in the crew room for some time making small talk. The captain has already asked Miguel to check the weather and MELs. Both are growing more and more impatient.

Captain Mike (to himself): Why aren't we getting on with it?

Co-pilot Miguel (to himself): Why aren't we getting on with it?

Captain Mike (to himself): It's a quarter to twelve and we are supposed to pull out of the gate in 45 minutes. I haven't heard him talk about the weather briefing I've asked him to do or the MEL check I told him about or anything yet. How can I rely on this guy when all he does is ask me questions about myself, my background, my interests, my family, my 'philosophy?!' He is polite and means well, but why does he have to be so nosey? I don't know him well enough yet to get into that personal stuff. I know he's just invited me to have a cup of coffee by gate eleven, but it's a ten minute walk down there and we are scheduled to depart on time. Look, all I want is for this guy to perform his duties and carry on as is expected of any co-pilot.

Co-pilot Miguel (to himself): It's quarter to twelve and I've been here with this captain for 45 minutes already, and he won't talk about anything important. How can I expect to be comfortable with him on this long flight unless I know something about him? I feel like a dentist pulling teeth, and he doesn't want to know anything about me! Where I come from, you don't sit next to someone for over four hours sharing responsibility for the lives of more than two hundred people without knowing something about that person! If this were Santiago and not San Francisco, I probably would take a little longer. But given how rushed things are here in the U.S., one has to try and make friends in just a few minutes. It's too bad that he's turned me down for the coffee break. With a little more time I think we could have gotten to know each other better. Sometimes I think all these Anglos want is a robot next to them in the cockpit.

Captain Mike (to himself): Oh well, I've never had any luck with Hispanic co-pilots before. Why should it be any different this time?

Co-pilot Miguel (to himself): Oh well, I've never had any luck with these Gringo captains before, why should it be any different this time?

Captain Mike: Thanks for the invitation to have coffee with you but I've got to get going. You go ahead and I'll meet you later in the airplane.

Co-pilot Miguel: Oh that's all right, maybe another time. I'll check on that weather for us and have a look at those MELs.

Reflexive Communication

The above dialogue lends itself to a clearer understanding of reflexive communication. Reflexive communication may be envisioned as a figure eight that reflects and folds upon itself, bringing more information to each conversant (Hoffman, 1991). Reflexive communication involves accessing an individual in the cultural context as reflected in the Ivey Model. It is not about two people but rather about four 'participants' (Mike, Miguel, and their corresponding historical backgrounds), each accessing each other's cultural history through openness of mind, tolerance and constructive dialogue.

There are three components of reflexive communication: 1) Premises, 2) General Stances, and 3) Micro skills. We present them below as they appear in Kikoski's text on the subject.

Premises

There are four premises for constructing mutual realities. They provide the basis for reflexive communication:

Premise 1: Reality always is viewed from a position or background; as one's position changes, so does one's view of reality.

Corollary: Reality always is viewed from a position that is the nexus into which flow the general cultural paradigm and the individual-specific experiences that comprise that person at that point in time.

Premise 2: Mutual understanding of reality becomes progressively clearer with the exchange of different perspectives.

Corollary: We come to know human and organizational realities through conversation with each other.

Premise 3: Separate, un-communicated realities divide us.

Corollary: Co-created realities that are shared provide a common reality so that common vision, purpose, and action can evolve.

Premise 4: Reflexive communication is a process-focused approach.

Corollary: This process of communication brings about the folding back of different views, meanings, and positions so that they eventually overlap and begin to converge.

This premise emphasizes the use of reflexive questions, which emphasis evokes different meanings about a situation and is likely to generate new ways of thinking and acting (Tomm, 1991). Such an approach involves the difference between asking 'This is how I see the situation. Do you agree?' and 'From your position, how would you see this situation developing?'

Reflexive communication focuses more on the process of communication than on the result of communication and generates expressions of multiple views and understanding of a problem more than a solution-focused approach.

General Stances

Three general stances facilitate reflexive communication:

1) The not-knowing stance: This stance involves taking the non-expert position of not knowing (Anderson, 1995). Taking this stance encourages communication by leveling the hierarchies of position and knowledge. While hierarchies exist in all organizations, emphasizing them discourages communication; de-emphasizing them encourages communication. Content and relationship aspects characterize most communication. We all are aware of the content aspect of communication – the information that a message is intended to convey.

We may be less conscious of the relationship aspect of communication – the relationship between sender and receiver that imposes behavior and delineates the hierarchy among communicants. For example, the question 'Do you think the report might be ready by tomorrow?' conveys a different connotation if made by a superior than by a subordinate. It may be perceived as a command by the former or a request by the latter. In either case, the relationship aspect determines an expectation of behavior (Watzlawick et al, 1967). A not-knowing stance conveys the message that everyone is equally qualified to generate ideas, opinions, and perspectives about a situation or a problem.

2) The curious stance: The curious stance simply means that one expresses one's ideas in a tentative manner (Anderson and Swim, 1993). A dogmatic or assertive expression of ideas often hinders the creative process, but a tentative or non-judgmental mode of expression encourages others to take, leave, or develop ideas at will without vesting or territoriality. This climate encourages the free exchange of ideas on their own merit and without threat of penalty.

Taking this stance helps to multiply varying perspectives on a problem and naturally leads to an evolved solution. We express our curious stance by asking questions rather than making statements as well as by beginning our questions with expressions that convey tentativeness – perhaps, possibly, or could it be.

3) The collaborative stance: This is the result of the two preceding stances. The shared perspectives, ideas, and meanings contributed by the conversers evolve into common knowledge (Gergen, 1985). This process filters many levels of perceptions, and triggers deep involvement among participants, making possible the co-construction of a jointly owned outcome.

Micro Skills

Micro skills are specific tools that enhance the communication process. They are relatively easy to learn. The skills are best learned one at a time. Following the discussion of each skill, practice provides a hands-on approach to the mastery of the skill. As one gains proficiency in one skill, another is added and practiced simultaneously. Thus, each remaining skill is added until the complete set of micro skills has been acquired (Kikoski, 1999).

The term 'microskill' was first used, and the actual skills were first developed, more than two decades ago by University of Massachusetts communication theorist Allen Ivey. It is an attempt to make explicit what is presently largely implicit. According to John and Catherine Kikoski, 'It is becoming more difficult to communicate with one another in the increasingly diverse workplace. We need to learn to talk, converse, and transcend the limits of culture. The micro skills give us the tools to accomplish this more effectively.' Although it is beyond the scope of this chapter to outline all the specific communication micro skills that could be used for airline crew training, their development for use by the airline industry would be both beneficial and appropriate.

Summary

Airline crews are becoming more culturally diverse than ever before. Without proper attention and training, this trend toward diversity in aviation can develop into crew communication problems that can lead to low motivation and lessened crew performance on the airline flight deck. Poor performance in an airliner setting establishes a window of opportunity for the chain of events that has been shown to lead to aviation accidents. Communication is one of the most important parameters influencing CRM and it must be identified and understood by all flight crewmembers.

We conclude that the understanding of sound reflexive communication theory, as it applies to multiculturalism and diversity in the airline crew environments of today's globalized world, should be an essential part of any airline CRM and/or LOFT training program. The development of aviation-specific reflexive communication micro skills for airline crews should be a human factors priority. For those of us who believe that intelligent consideration and management of cultural factors will significantly improve the aviation system's performance, we propose to foster a communication environment within which 'cultural differences become natural and compatible to the largest extent possible, so that they can coexist without feelings of shame or blame' (Maurino, 1998).

References

Anderson, H. (1995). 'Collaborative Language Systems: Toward a Postmodern Therapy', in Mikesell, R. , Lusterman, D., and McDaniel, S. *Integrating Family Therapy: Handbook of Family Psychology and Systems Theory.* Hyattsville, Maryland: American Psychological Association.

Anderson, H. and Swim, S. (1993). 'Learning as Collaborative Conversation: Combining The Student's and Teacher's Expertise', *Human Systems: The Journal of Systemic Consultation & Management 4*, 145-160.

Beneigh, T. and Rodriguez, C. (2001). 'A Computer-Aided Educational Method for Enhancing Crew Dynamics', *Proceedings of Computer Aided Ergonomic and Safety Conference*, Maui, Hawaii.

Garland, D., Wise, J., and Hopkin, D. (1999). *Handbook Of Aviation Human Factors*, Mahwah, N J: Erlbaum.

Gergen, K. (1985). 'The Social Constructionist Movement in Modern Psychology', *American Psychologist, 40* (3), 266-275.

Hawkins, F. (1993). *Human Factors In Flight*, Aldershot, UK: Ashgate.

Helmreich, R. and Merritt, A. (1998). *Culture at Work in Aviation and Medicine.* Aldershot, UK: Ashgate.

Herzberg, F. (1966). *Work And The Nature of Man,* World Publishing Company.

Hoffman, L. (1991). 'A Reflexive Stance for Family Therapy', *Journal of Strategic and Systemic Therapies, 10* (3,4), 4-17.

Hofstede G. (1980). *Culture's Consequences: International Differences in Work-Related Values,* Newbury Park: Sage.

Hutchinson, D. (1981). *New Horizons for Human Factors in Design,* New York: McGraw-Hill.

Ivey, A., Ivey, M and Siemek-Downing, L. (1987). *Counseling and Psychotherapy: Integrating Skills, Theory and Practice,* Matawah, N J: Prentice Hall.

Kantowitz, B. and Sorkin, R. (1983). *Human Factors: Understanding People-System Relationships,* John Wiley and Sons.

Kikoski, C., Kikoski, K. (1996,1999) *Reflexive Communication in the Culturally Diverse Workplace,* Westport, CT: Praeger.

Maurino, D. (1999). *Crew Resource Management: A Time For Reflection,* Montreal, Canada: International Civil Aviation Organization (ICAO).

Merritt, A. and Helmreich, L. (1995). 'Culture in the Cockpit: A Multi-Airline Study of Pilot Attitudes and Values', *Proceedings of the Eighth International Symposium on Aviation Psychology,* Columbus, OH: Ohio State University.

Rice, M. and Williams, R. (2001). *The Encyclopedia Americana International Edition, Volume 8,* Danbury, CT: Grolier.

Tannen, D. (2001). *I Only Say This Because I Love You: How We Talk Can Make or Break Family Relationships Throughout Our Lives,* New York: Random House.

Vroom, H. and Deci, E. (1973). *Management and Motivation.* Middlesex, UK: Penguin Books.

Vroom, V. (1970). *The Handbook of Social Psychology,* New York: Addison-Wesley.

Watzlawick, P., Bavelas, J., Johnson, D. (1967). *Pragmatics of Human Communication: A Study of Interactional Patterns, Pathologies, and Paradoxes.* New York: W.W. Norton.

Chapter 10

Humor, Stories, and Cultural Context

Mary Ann Turney

Introduction

Aviators have traditionally enjoyed humor and anecdotes related to aviation experiences. Witness the multitude of tales, cartoons, and jokes associated with aviation, and often understood only by those familiar with the 'lingo' of the industry.

But what is enjoyed as aviation humor is not universal. The following is an example of a joke told with great enthusiasm by one of the author's Asian students:

> 'The controller told the pilot to "say altitude" and the pilot replied "altitude." The student didn't know the rest of the joke, but thought it was really funny even before hearing the punch line from another student. [The controller replied "Say cancel IFR."]'

What's significant is that even without the punch line, the Asian student found the joke much funnier than his Anglo peers. Conversely, the Anglo students laughed heartily at this joke that seemed much less funny to non-American students:

> 'Question: What makes an airplane fly? Answer: Money.'

These examples from an aviation classroom in the United States illustrate why research suggests that the use of humor is likely to be related to such individual differences as sex, age, sense of humor, and culture (Decker and Rotondo, 1999).

The role and constructive uses of humor need to be better understood as 'humor has the potential to improve quality of life, job satisfactions, and performance in organizations' (Consalvo, 1989, p. 285). However, because humor is context-specific, it may give rise to great hilarity in one group and fall flat, or worse, become offensive, in another (Holmes, 2000).

Although it is clear that each individual has a unique sense of humor, research suggests that what is funny among the members of one national, ethnic, or racial group may offend another. What men consider humorous is not the same as what women view with humor (Butcher, 2001). According to a study at Salisbury State

University, men were shown to use a greater variety of types of humor than women (Decker and Rotondo, 1999).

Evidence suggests that shared humor is an important part of the workplace culture and serves a number of important functions. Jokes and shared stories can create solidarity or connection and may mitigate the threat of actions such as directives and criticisms, thus maintaining a sense of cohesion. In contrast, humor can be used in an unequal power relationship for the purpose of either control or subversion. As a socially acceptable strategy, humor may camouflage coercion, or it can signal protest and disagreement and undermine authority (Holmes, 2000).

Cultural Context

Robinson (1991) found that the purpose of humor and laughter depends on the communicator's and the receiver's different perspectives on humor and on their cultural heritage. There are particular types of humor that are preferred in specific workplaces as well as preferred styles in some organizational cultures. Holmes' (2000) study of workplace environments in New Zealand indicated that humor may become a means of integrating differences among a variety of sub-groups into a unified workplace culture. In a culture such as aviation, however, where diversity is only beginning to alter the environment, humor may be more divisive than inclusive, and therefore become a mechanism for subverting those who do not belong to the dominant group.

A Swedish study suggests that humor can serve to bridge the mental and intellectual distance between people of different backgrounds. This study was based on 20 interviews, nine with women and 11 with men; ages ranged from 17-75 years and all were from Sweden. They were asked, what does humor mean to you? The majority of those interviewed suggested that joking is a 'balancing act between what is tolerated and what is not tolerated depending on ethics, culture and the situation where it is used' (Olsson, Backe, Sorensen, and Kock, 2002, p. 25).

White's (2001) study of humor compared 200 students from 65 different institutions with 127 faculty members. Results indicated that as the classroom continues to grow more global in its makeup, humor as perceived by different cultures should be studied, because 'one cannot assume that all cultures respond to humor in the same way' (White, 2001, p. 11). The same humor can be perceived as positive in one culture and negative in another culture. For example, when students in the author's aviation classes were asked what was funny, responses reflected age and gender differences.

Measuring What's Funny

Researchers can measure 'what's funny?' by asking for individual responses. This method has the drawback of asking for a retrospective response. Another method of measuring what's funny is discourse analysis of taped recordings.   How can researchers critically observe 'what's funny' to a particular individual? A review of definitions of humor suggests that the concept of humor can be viewed from a number of perspectives, based on the humor-related literature appearing in business administration and communication journals (Holmes, 2000).

Humor can be defined as what makes people laugh, as what physiological 'signs' indicate that an individual is experiencing a humorous response, or as what social or psychological effect humor may have. Hay suggests that a wide range of clues, in addition to overt laughter, may identify instances of humor. These include the speaker's tone of voice and the audience's response. Responses to humor include such subtleties as a raised eyebrow or a twitch of the lips (Hay, 1996).

Functions of Humor: How it Works

Ervin-Tripp and Lampert (1992) identified four functions of humor: *Equalizing* or creating solidarity, *defending* or protecting the self, *sharing* similarities, and *coping* with weaknesses.

In a study of four professional workplace environments, Holmes (2000) used discourse analysis to examine verbal humor in routine interactions. The data consisted of recordings from informal work-related discussions ranging from 20 seconds to two hours. Analysis consisted of more than 120 hours of recordings consisting of 330 workplace interactions. Participants included a racially/ethnically diverse group of men and women including Anglos, Samoans, Chinese, and Thai. Results confirmed that humor was context-bound and served in this environment to maintain solidarity within a group. It was also used to reduce inequities between those of differing status (Holmes, 2000, p. 160).

Humor and Power

Holmes' (2000) study also found that humor can be used effectively as a means of exerting power and control. Results of the study suggest that it is more acceptable to exert power through humor in an age when informality and equality is valued. In situations where relative power is a significant part of personal identity, humor functions with more complexity. It is a way of 'embedding a risky or unacceptable proposition in a superficially innocuous utterance' (Priest and Swain, 2002, p. 179).

When the underlining intent is controlling or coercive, this use of humor is identified as 'repressive discourse' (Pateman, 1980). Repressive discourse disguises the coercive intent or fudges the power relationships. While it is based on power imbalances, it distracts attention from issues of power (Holmes, 2000). When it is used by the powerful to repress, it may conceal the power structure to gain compliance and control (Priest and Swain, 2002).

While humor can be used by the powerful to maintain control while appearing to be collegial, it may be used by the less powerful to subvert that control. Holmes and Marra (2002) analyzed humor as a socially acceptable means of challenging or subverting authority. Their research focused on the 'dark side' of humor, using critical discourse analysis (CDA) to understand how humor functions as a subversive strategy. Data consisted of recordings of 12 meetings between female and male colleagues in workplace project teams. This study identified 217 instances of humor throughout 875 minutes of business meeting data sets.

Researchers found that group size and personality were relevant variables related to humor in groups. Certain individuals were identified as making the most humorous statements in every group in which they participated. Women were more likely to use humor in small groups than in larger ones. One focus of the study was on humor that subverts the status quo. About 40% of the humor in the organizational meetings was subversive humor (Homes and Marra, 2002).

Subversive humor functions on three levels. On the first level, the focus is on the individual and humor is used to undermine the power or status of an influential individual in a group. This can destabilize a team in relation to the larger organization. On the second level, humor is focused on the group or organization. The humor challenges or criticizes values or goals, thus subverting the larger organization. The third level is the societal level, where humor is used to question the ideology of the industry community as well as broader societal values. This level of humor subverts larger values, often those of conflicting national cultures in the organization (Holmes and Marra, 2002).

Holmes, (2002) study identified several types of subversive joking, including quips, jocular abuse, and role play. Quips are short, witty, often ironic comments about the topic under discussion. They are a subtle way of criticizing. Quips are short and can easily be used in situations where time constraints make longer samples of humor impractical.

Jocular abuse is usually a negative remark aimed at a person. It is concise and, like quips, can easily be inserted in a conversation. It is typically directed at leaders and managers or at those with the most status. Role play is subversive humor in which a speaker quotes and imitates another person by using paralinguistic signals to imitate a speech style. Those quoted in this way in the study were usually members of out-groups and occurred relatively infrequently in the data (Holmes, 2002).

Subversive and Divisive Humor

Bing's (1999) study of humor distinguished between subversive humor and divisive humor. Subversive humor targets ideology and reveals how social practices that exclude people from power can be absurd. Humor can reveal absurdities such as the difficulty women can have in getting their suggestions heard. Subversive humor ridicules unjust social situations rather than the people who benefit from or maintain those situations. Divisive humor is different. It divides groups into 'us' and 'them,' and is based on stereotypes. 'Divisive humor has long been used against women and other out-of-power groups' (Bing, 1999,

p. 51). Yet Bing's study showed that women don't mind divisive humor as long as the 'in-group' is female.

Humor and Gender

As indicated earlier, men and women perceive humor differently. Robinson and Smith-Lovin (2001) completed a study of 29 six-person discussion groups at the University of South Carolina in which humor was considered in the context of remarks that were intended to elicit amusement or make people laugh. Participants consisted of undergraduate Anglo-Americans between ages 17 and 25. There were four groups in each of seven gender combinations, including one all-female and one all-male group. Only the remarks that provoked laughter were deemed successful. Results indicated that men engaged in humor at higher rates than women. However, the all-female group joked more frequently than the all-male group. Researchers concluded that women engage in more humor when no men are present. Results also supported humor as a hierarchy-building mechanism for men, while women use more cohesion-building humor (Robinson and Smith-Lovin, 2001).

Thomas (1997) examined three joke cycles involving humor about gender, sexuality, and stupidity. Based on an analysis of audience reaction, the author concludes that significant themes appear. Thomas stated, 'One significant theme was the emphasis on sexuality (and even stupidity to a lesser extent) in the jokes about a "smart" woman' (Thomas, 1997, p. 307). Some response patterns revealed that such jokes are just as likely to be seen as *not* funny.

Thomas provided an extensive analysis of jokes about 'dumb blondes' in order to illustrate the varying reactions to these kinds of jokes. According to Thomas, the blonde woman's high profile in the United States has become the modern substitute for ethnic jokes that became socially unacceptable. 'Dumb blondes' as the focus of jokes is also partially attributable to a mass media phenomenon stemming from the fame of such women as Mae West, Jean Harlow, Marilyn Monroe, and Madonna. Here are a few blonde jokes collected by the researcher:

Why did the blonde get fired from her computer job?
She kept putting white-out on the screen.

Why can't blondes make Kool-Aid?
They can't fit two quarts of water into the packet.

What's a blonde's mating call?
'I think I'm drunk.'

What do you call 5000 blondes falling out of an airplane?
Air pollution.

These jokes and others like them emerged from those circulating among college students of varying ages, their friends, and families. Detailed commentary from five men and eight women collected in Thomas' study revealed that 'depending upon the context and persons involved, they see the jokes as containing incongruous images, as funny, as not funny, as 'putdowns,' as about women in general as well as blondes, as reflective of competition among women, and as true' (Thomas, 1997, p. 291). By collecting responses to these jokes and others related to dumb blondes, Thomas found that some joke listeners smile or chuckle, not because they like the jokes, but because they are giving the joke teller what they believe to be an appropriate response so as not to challenge the expectation of humor that accompanies the joke, nor to create conflict with the joke teller.

A significant factor determining when a joke is considered funny or offensive is having enough emotional distance from the topic. Thomas indicates that Oring's 1992 research revealed that the context of the interaction in which a joke is told, as well as the individual who tells the joke, affects the type of response from the listener. One young male in Thomas' study reflects awareness of this personal and contextual factor in his observation: 'I do not believe in racism or sexism. However, I am humorous and understand that if a joke can be made about anything in life, it will be. Still, I am very careful about how my audience will react if I am telling these [blonde] jokes' (Thomas, 1997 p. 289).

Humor and Social Norms

Humor and Racism Denial: A Study in South Africa

In studying humor and racial issues, Barnes, Palmary, and Durrheim (2001) found that ethnic prejudices are communicated in standard ways in different countries, and similar strategies are employed to justify racist opinions.

For two months, conversations about race were recorded without the knowledge of the speakers. These conversations took place in South Africa following the decriminalization of interracial sexual relations (1997). The researchers, an interracial couple, found that race and racial issues were frequently discussed in their presence. Informed consent was sought and given when the researchers knew the speakers personally and their identities were protected with pseudonyms. Much of the data was collected at gatherings of family and friends.

The study considered the talk in the context of powerful norms of non-racism associated with the new South Africa. Within this context, blatant talk about race and racist opinions were taboo, thus the study focused on the rhetorical maneuvers used to talk about race in the presence of an interracial couple. Focus was placed on (1) how the topic of race was introduced into a conversation and (2) how race talk was used while distancing the speaker from inferences of racism. Results indicated that humor was used most commonly to introduce the topic of race into the conversation, allowing a speaker to utter potentially racist comments without attributions of racism being made to him or her. Humor also served to ease tension associated with sensitive subjects.

Two functions of humor emerged from the recordings. First, humor creates a light context and invites laughter. It discourages inferences of racism due to the inappropriateness of anger as a response to humor. Second, humor allows the speaker to mock racist beliefs and thus distances the speaker from inferences of racism, while making racist statements. Apte (1985) suggests that humor allows individuals to rationalize prejudice felt toward other ethnic groups, to reinforce one's superior position, and to enhance social cohesion. This analysis looked at humor as a strategy to mitigate potential inferences of racism, while the speaker reproduced racial stereotypes (Apte as cited in Barnes, Palmary, and Durrheim, 2001, p. 331).

Stories of Personal Experience

In Barnes, Palmary, and Durrheim's (2001) study, telling personal experience stories was a common way of saying things that went against the social norm of non-racist attitudes. These stories could not be dismissed as false because personal experiences are not open to verification. The speaker could also deflect accusations of racism by posing as an observer of facts and events. It's not what *they* are saying; it is what was 'heard' or 'seen.' Talk distances the speakers from racism by grounding their opinions in the external world. Their anecdotes imply that reality makes prejudiced opinion inevitable.

The South African study offers some insight into how humor serves as a mechanism that may be in use by individuals wishing to express beliefs and ideas that are politically unacceptable in the current workplace climate, but where the culture has not yet caught up with the 'acceptability' standard. Further study may reveal how such humor-based stories may have implications in the aviation industry as its workforce diversifies.

Humor and Leadership

Priest and Swain (2002) examined the relationship between leader effectiveness and humor in two cadet samples at the US Military Academy. Subordinates were asked to recall good and bad leaders and rate them on leadership and humor. Sixty cadets responded; nine were women. Results indicated that those leaders who were believed to be good had higher humor ratings than those deemed as bad. Analyses also found that the military culture had a strong preference for extraverted styles of conduct and 'boorish' humor was preferred.

The author undertook a study of 19 Certified Flight Instructors in 2003. The instructors were attending a two-day Flight Instructor Refresher Course in the Northeastern United States. The group ranged in age from 22 to 69 years and consisted of 3 women and 16 men. Three members of the group were corporate pilots as well as flight instructors and one was an airline pilot. They were asked verbally to assist the researcher who was collecting data regarding the use of humor in aviation, particularly the use of humor by individuals who were in instructional or leadership roles.

A written response was requested, and the question to be addressed was what type of humor would be appropriate for use by a flight instructor or aviation leader such as an airline captain. Respondents were asked to distinguish between inclusive humor that would be appropriate to use with all types of people and humor that would be offensive or exclude some individuals or groups. Sixteen people responded anonymously. Responses were coded thematically and the following is a summary of results.[1]

Inclusive humor
- Establishes a common ground and makes a person feel part of the 'aviation club'
- Eases fearful situations or anxiety levels
- Recounts instructor's personal mistakes in the learning process
- Adjusts to particular situations, as well as gender and educational background of the listener
- Is relevant to the setting
- Clarifies complicated subject matter

Exclusive humor – Types of humor that exclude some individuals:
- Humor that belittles the student or trainee
- Humor that refers to ethnicity, gender, race, or sexual preference
- Humor that involves 'in-jokes' that are not explained

Summary

The role of humor needs to be better understood in a multi-national and multi-cultural industry such as aviation. Research reflects significant cultural differences regarding what is funny and appropriate among various groups. These differences emerge not only due to nationality, values and cultural background, but age, race, and gender factors also affect what makes an individual laugh or frown at a joke, remark, or anecdote.

Humor may be used to exert power and control and to subvert and divide groups in workplace settings. It can thwart team effectiveness and undermine acceptability standards. Use of humor is a means of both enhancing and subverting effective leadership. Finally, humor is an effective and constructive means of developing cohesion in the workplace. Humor can engender a sense of belonging, mitigate criticism, reduce stress, and support team efforts when it is accompanied by self-censorship and awareness of cross-gender and cross-cultural factors.

Note

1 The author gratefully acknowledges the support and assistance of Aviation Seminars, and Michael Sloan, the seminar presenter. Michael Sloan is an Assistant Professor in the Department of Aviation Science at Bridgewater State College, Bridgewater, MA.

References

Barnes, B., Palmary, I. and Durrheim, K. (September, 2001). 'The Denial of Racism: The Role of Humor, Personal Experience, and Self-Censorship', *Journal of Language and Social Psychology, 20* (3), 321-338.

Bing, J. (Fall, 1999). 'Tendered Jokes: Humor as a Subversive Activity', *Women and Language, 22* (2), 51-52.

Butcher, J. (December, 2001). 'Have You Heard the One about the Prefrontal Cortex?', *The Lancet, 358.* 2136.

Decker, W.H. and Rotondo, D.M. (1999). 'Use of Humor at Work: Predictors and Implications', *Psychological Reports, 84,* 961-968.

Ervin-Tripp, S. and Lampert, M.D. (1992). 'Gender Differences in Construction of Humorous Talk: Locating Power', *Proceedings of the Second Berkeley Women and Language Conference,* CA: Berkeley, pp. 108-117.

Hay, J. (1996). 'No laughing matter: Gender and Humour Support Strategies', *Wellington Working Papers in Linguistics, 8,* 1-24.

Holmes, J. (2000). 'Politeness, Power, and Provocation: How Humor Functions in the Workplace', *Discourse Studies, 2* (2), 159-185.

Holmes, J. and Marra, M. (2002). 'Subversive Humor between Colleagues and Friends', *Humor, 15* (1), 65-88.

Olsson, H., Backe, H., Sorensen, S. and Kock, M. (2002). 'The Essence of Humour and Its Effects and Functions: A Qualitative Study', *Journal of Nursing Management, 10,* 21-26.

Priest, R.F. and Swain J.E. (2002). 'Humor and Its Implications for Leadership Effectiveness', *Humor* 15-2, 169-189.

Robinson, D.T. and Smith-Lovin, L. (September, 2001). 'Getting a Laugh: Gender, Status, and Humor in Task Discussions', *Social Forces, 80* (1), 123-158.

Robinson, V.M. (1991*). Humour and the Health Professions*: Thorofare, NJ: SLACK.

Thomas, J.B. (1997). 'Dumb Blondes, Dan Quayle, and Hillary Clinton: Gender, Sexuality, and Stupidity in Jokes', *Journal of American Folklore, 110* (437), 277-313.

White, G.W. (Winter, 2001). 'Teachers Report of How They Used Humor with Students and the Perceived Use of Such Humor', *Education, 122* (2), 1-11.

Chapter 11

The Music is the Message:
Prosody in Aviation Discourse

Marsha Hunter

Introduction

Prosody is the music of speech. It encompasses the full range of the aural signal in human speech, including frequency, pitch, intonation, loudness, rhythm, duration, pauses, and phrasing. It includes any individual spectral irregularities present in speech, such as the dysfluencies 'um' or 'er', misspeaks, stumbles, or dropped sounds. Prosody provides language-enhancing information, supporting words, grammar, syntax, and semantic meaning with varying degrees of clarification. Prosody provides paralinguistic cues -- those outside of language -- to a listener's ears. Paralinguistic cues include emotional and expressive information that serves to complete the context of an utterance. The meaning of a message may be obscured when speakers use unfamiliar prosodic speech patterns. On the other hand, prosody may contain sufficient intentional force to convey a message even when language is garbled.

Prosody issues abound in aviation communications. Fluency in second languages is dependent on acquisition of language-appropriate prosody. Rate of speech and monotone delivery are prosody issues in radio communications. The relative pitches of male and female voices, on the radio, on the flight deck, or in the passenger cabin, are areas that may be understood at least partly in terms of prosody. Prosody's subtle cues may be processed beneath conscious access, offering opportunities for gender-based preconceptions and cross-cultural misunderstandings of the music of human language.

The body of aviation communications research does not descend from one model of discourse or linguistics, but is derived from an array of sciences that shed light on the unique requirements of spoken language in aviation. The challenges of aviation communications have engendered dynamic, wide-ranging research rooted in many different models. While isolated elements of prosody have been present in many studies, prosody as a basis for study has been largely absent. After a brief history of prosody's theoretical underpinnings, a review of its elements and salient features of cognitive processing, this chapter argues for inclusion of prosody in aviation communications research.

History of Prosodic Studies

The sound of a human voice contains frequency, pitch, intonation, rhythm, loudness, and duration. These elements combine to form prosody, what Wennerstrom (2001) refers to as the music of every-day speech. In pure music, pitches change as a melody unfolds, but the melody is supported and enhanced by underlying harmonies, crescendos and decrescendos, by tempo changes, or by the addition of new instruments. As a person speaks, the pitch of the voice changes from word to word, and across phrases and sentences, forming intonational phrases. If intonation is the melody of speech, then prosody is the rest of the orchestra. Prosody accounts for the rhythm, loudness, and structure that support the melody. This music of speech contains a significant portion of the meaning of a spoken message.

Describing the "particular way in which pitch is utilized in language" (Gandour, 1978, p. 41) has been a challenge for thousands of years. Ancient Indian phoneticians describing Sanskrit and Vedic classified speech sounds as 'high' or 'low'. The Greeks used musical terminology related to the tuning of stringed instruments to designate spoken sounds as 'sharp' and 'heavy,' 'acute' and 'grave' (House, 1999, p. 12). Other aspects of prosody have been given musical descriptors as well. 'Bitonal' described sounds in ancient Greek that combined high and low tones in the same syllable. 'Falling glide' designated intonational movement within syllables containing long vowels or diphthongs that started high and proceeded to a low tone (House, 1999). The study of prosody has relied heavily on musical and metaphorical description well into the 20th century. Bolinger (1972, p. 20) described changes in fundamental frequency in a sea analogy:

> The ripples are the accidental changes in pitch, the irrelevant quavers. The waves are the peaks and valleys that we call accent. The swells are the separations of our discourse into its larger segments. The tides are the tides of emotion.

Intonation and pitch in speech remained largely a metaphorical discussion until 1862, when Helmholz's analyses of resonance, frequency, and place theory spawned physiological theories of tone perception (Sekuler and Blake, 1994). By the 1920s the science of phonology began to distinguish between 'language' and 'speech,' leading to more careful examination of the sounds of human utterances. Still, there was slow progress in obtaining actual measures of intonation and other prosodic elements. Grutzmacher and Lottermoser developed a pitch meter in the 1930s that permitted measurement of fundamental frequency (Hart, Collier and Cohen, 1990). By the 1940s the sonograph was invented, providing a 'convenient way of plotting frequency, energy, and time' (Gregory, 1997, p. 617). Musical analogy was still often the point of departure for intonational studies in the 1950s, when Chang (1958) made recordings of conversations in the Chengdu dialect of Chinese, then used a swanee whistle (a fipple flute similar to a penny whistle) to transcribe them onto musical staff paper using his own system of notation. Chinese is a tone language, in which 'pitch is used to contrast individual lexical items or words' (Gandour, 1978). Coexisting with the Chinese tones for individual words are pitches that denote semantic, emotional, and expressive meaning. Chang referred to this second layer of Chinese intonational meaning as 'the fluctuation of the voice pitch as applied to the whole sentence. It is the sentence melody...' (p. 401).

By the 1960s Lieberman and Michaels (1962) used a Vocoder, an early version of the modern digital 'voice coder'[1] to examine 'the contributions of fundamental frequency and of amplitude to the transmission of the emotional content of normal human speech...to see whether the perturbations of vocal pitch, that is, the irregularities in the fundamental excitation rate, were pertinent...' (p. 235).

Over the last thirty years the study of tone perception has proliferated (House, 1999), maturing in concert with methods applied to other areas of perception and cognition. Prosody is pertinent to an array of communication disciplines, including phonetics, sociophonetics, psychology, sociolinguistics, linguistics and neurolinguistics, rhetoric, pragmatics, and anthropology (Georgakopoulou and Goutsos, 1997).[2] Prosodic studies have developed transcription and coding systems, defined and recorded the spectrum of human speech, and decoded the phonetic sounds of speech for meaning (Fox, 2000). Prosody studies in many of the world's languages document specific intonational patterns for each, enabling comparison among all (Chang, 1958; Warren, 1996; House, 1999). Prosody and intonation challenges for second language speakers are well documented (Wennerstrom, 2001). Studies of the perception of prosody as related to the neural bases of language explain the cognitive complexities of comprehending spoken messages (Stirling and Wales, 1996; Lieberman, 2000; Warren 1996). Prosodic science stands ready to enhance our understanding of aviation communications, and will be especially helpful in decoding and interpreting speech in an increasingly diverse industry.

Elements of Prosody

Prosody encompasses 'intonation, rhythm, tempo, loudness, and pauses, as these interact with syntax, lexical meaning, and segmental phonology in spoken texts' (Wennerstrom, 2000, p. 4). Prosody is akin to the third dimension in speech analysis. Speech can be analyzed as text on a page, or as language heard on an audiotape, but prosody describes the sound of speech in more telling detail. Prosody analysis gives meaning to the rise and fall of the extra-lexical information in every human utterance. While it is true that researchers do not yet agree on all elements to be included in definitions of prosody, there is general agreement on certain basics.

Pitch and Fundamental Frequency

Pitch is the perception of the fundamental frequency (F_0) of a human voice. The F_0 is the lowest of the simultaneous frequencies, or harmonics, present in the spoken sound (House, 1999; Wennerstrom, 2000). Pitch changes continuously during the course of speech (Hart et al., 1990). As F_0 changes and moves, it helps listeners perceive linguistic categories, discern information contained in phrases, and comprehend the emotions, attitude, and involvement of a speaker (House, 1999).

Ohala (1983) argues that there is a 'universal frequency code' that equates meaning with pitch, and which exists not only across human cultures, but also across animal species. Such a code thus has correlates in the animal kingdom, for example among birds, as when a wren chirps in high tones when greeting a mate, but rasps harshly at predators (Bolinger, 1989). Species from the chickadee to the rhinoceros to a wide variety of frogs use frequency extremes on a 'harshness scale' (Ohala, 1983, p. 6). In such a scheme high pitches denote smallness, nearness, nonaggression, supplication, uncertainty, and defenselessness. Lower pitches convey largeness, dominance, power, confidence and finality. The frequency code theory holds that pitch contains nuggets of semantic knowledge, referring to specific non-arbitrary states. Though lacking lexical meaning,[3] pitch may contribute to social, cultural, or emotional meaning. Thus, pitch may convey meaning even when language is indistinct.

Intonation

Intonation is the movement of pitch across spoken language. House (1999) defines linguistic intonation as 'perceptually relevant variations in F_0 used by the speaker to convey information about units larger than a single word (e.g. phrase and sentence)' (p. 15). Intonation contains a significant portion of the meaning of a spoken message, conveying emotion and expressivity. Fox (2000) contends that while pitch, accent, and distinctive boundaries of language help convey a message, intonation is the element of prosody that possesses inherent meaning. As a person speaks, the pitch of the voice changes from word to word, and across phrases and sentences, forming intonational contours.

Intonational Contours

As intonation changes across a phrase or sentence, it forms contours with identifiable elements linked to meaning. The direction of an utterance's intonational contour varies from low to high, or high to low, fluctuating constantly. A falling intonational contour may indicate a completed statement. Rising contours often contain questions or imply uncertainty. Intonational contours 'constitute a *gradient*. A falling intonation, for example, may fall from different heights and to different extents' (Fox, 2000, p. 270). Contours offer a constant stream of cues for the brain to interpret as it decodes a message (Warren, 1996).

In addition to the historic difficulties in describing prosody, linguists have continuously reinvented representations of contours in search of clear intentional depictions. Bolinger's simple but intuitive contour notation (Figure 11.1) accounts for rises and falls, questions and conclusions. This notation gives the sense of meaning without specific acoustic or temporal parameters. Bolinger describes it as having 'the shape of a bumpy suspension bridge' (p. 23):

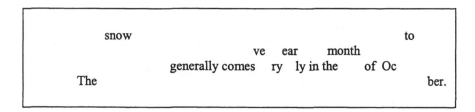

Figure 11.1 Intonational contour, after Bolinger, 1972

Such depictions leave much to interpretation, as did Chang's (1958) musical notation of the Chengdu dialect (not to mention its exclusion of those who do not read music), but the attempt at visual representation of speech sounds begins to lend specificity to individual utterances. Wennerstrom's modern example (Figure 11.2) shows time, frequency, amplitude, spectral data, prosodic symbols, and a kind of word pictograph, packing maximum information into each graphic representation:

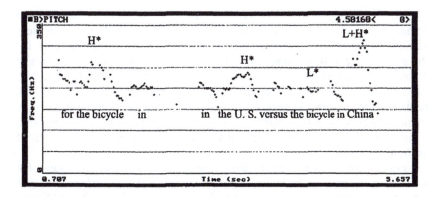

Figure 11.2 *The Music of Everyday Speech*
From *The Music of Everyday Speech* by Ann Wennerstrom, copyright 2001 by Ann Wennerstrom. Used by permission of Oxford University Press, Inc.

Comparing these prosodic depictions with cockpit voice recorder transcriptions from the United States' National Transportation Safety Board (NTSB) accident reports demonstrates how much more information is potentially available, and how open to interpretation NTSB transcripts truly are. Consider this excerpt from the accident on July 2, 1994 at Charlotte, North Carolina, when USAir flight 1096 crashed on a missed approach during a thunderstorm at the airport:

1839:02 Captain:	if we have to bail out
1839:03 First Officer:	(unintelligible)
1839:06 Captain:	it looks like we bail out to the right.
1839:09 First Officer:	amen.
1839:09 Captain:	ten miles to the VOR which is off the end of the runway
	'bout a mile off the end of the runway.
1839:14 First Officer:	yeah.
1839:16 Captain:	so I think we'll be alright.
1839:20 First Officer:	chance of shear.

(NTSB, 1995, pp. 157-158)

Readers necessarily interpolate their own versions of the prosody in this transcript. Each invents a unique, biased version of what the conversation sounded like. While the time stamp approximates the duration of each utterance, we have no pitch or intonational information, or any measure of loudness. Without prosodic analysis, the transcript leaves room for a wide range of interpretations.

Segments, Boundaries and Chunks

While phrase contours show an overall shape and direction of intonational movement, other information is embedded in smaller segmented units with clear boundaries. These smaller 'meaning-bearing units' (Wennerstrom, 2001, p. 17) may be glides, agitations, shimmer and jitter (subtle, cycle-by-cycle F_0 changes in vocal intensity), pauses, and other elements of the 'rapidly changing spectral, intensity, temporal and tonal configuration' of speech (House, 1999, p. 17). Segments contain rhythmic elements of accent and stress that convey the relative importance of items, as well as whether a word or phrase has already been referred to in discourse (Warren, 1996). Segmental boundaries begin and end units of information.

An example of a beginning boundary is referred to as 'key'.[4] The key of a phrase refers to the pitch at the beginning of an utterance. A speaker's selection of key indicates to listeners information about what has been said immediately before and what may be spoken next. At ending boundaries, questions often end with an upward sweep to a higher pitch. Commands may end with an emphatic downward flourish. Wennerstrom (2001) describes ending boundaries as 'the pitch configurations at the ends of phrases, accompanied by a lengthening of the final syllables' (p. 20). Pitch boundaries may be high-rising, low-rising, partially falling, level, or low, all conveying different meanings and inferences in the context of an utterance. Pierrehumbert and Steele (1989), searching for categories of tone levels in small units of intonation, contend that English 'generates 28 nuclear configurations and 196 different contours for texts' (p. 183). With so many options to choose from, the prosodic speech signal is ever-changing. Beyond language and pronunciation differences, individual differences in articulation and vocal apparatus -- capacity of lungs, physical position of larynx, characteristic positions of lips and tongue during speech -- contribute to segmental and boundary variation. Some individual idiosyncratic variations are meaningful while others are not (Hart et al., 1990).

Segments with proscribed boundaries may also be described as perceptual 'chunks'. Chunking refers to the brain's preference for grouping items to facilitate recognition of patterns. Chunks may contain familiar intonational directions, such as the upward sweep of pitch that connotes questions. Listeners learn the repetitive patterns of a conversational partner and come to expect information to be grouped in predictable ways. Bradlow and Pisoni (1996) refer to this phenomenon as 'talker familiarity', whereby 'listeners learn to become sensitive to information in the acoustic signal about specific dynamic properties of the talker's vocal tract as an acoustic source' (p. 64). Hellier, Edworth, Weedon, Walters, and Adams (2002) manipulated acoustic parameters of urgency warnings in order to study acoustics in relation to semantics. In their experiment, a chunk of warning information contained specific parameters of loudness, pitch, intonational direction, duration, and rate of speech. Certain combinations of these elements conveyed and elicited the emotional content of a message; in this case, fear.

Paralinguistic Cues: Emotion

Paralanguage consists of expressive gradients of prosodic features such as loudness, duration, and pitch. Emotion is a paralinguistic (outside of language) cue which may be measured acoustically using these parameters. In an experiment that measured subjects' vocal responses in reward and punishment conditions, Bachorowski and Owren found that 'both positive and negative emotional states can be associated with increases in F_0' (1995, p. 223). In other words, the pitch of subjects' voices rose as emotion increased. The researchers also found gender differences, with females and males differing significantly in emotional intensity. Banse and Scherer (1996) used male and female actors to portray fourteen different emotions, and then asked subjects to identify intentions. Subjects were able to distinguish 'the existence of differential vocal profiles for a large number of emotions' (p. 630).[5]

Paralinguistic cues may convey emotion whether or not specific words are present. Lieberman and Michaels (1962) played recordings of modified speech to listeners who were asked to make judgments about the emotional content of what they heard. Eight types of randomly ordered emotional statements were heard in different presentations: with frequency and amplitude changes, in smoothed speech (lacking identifiable consonants), with pitch information only, in unprocessed ('normal') speech, and in monotone speech. Emotional content was recognizable in all presentations significantly more often than chance would predict. The emotional content of unprocessed speech with all normal acoustic cues present was recognized 85 per cent of the time. In monotone speech emotion was recognizable only 14 per cent of the time.[6]

Hellier et al. (2002) measured the acoustics of urgency warnings by playing recordings of actors reading in urgent, nonurgent, and monotone styles to subjects who rated the warnings. The researchers found that 'speakers were able to convey reliably different levels of urgency to listeners simply by being asked to do so' (p. 7). In contrast they found, as did Lieberman and Michaels (1962), that monotone speech was devoid of emotional content, lacking sufficient cues for processing. (Quiet whining voices likewise contained severely limited parsing information.) The Hellier et al. study indicates that the emotional intensity (measured acoustically) of an utterance is a significant part of its message.[7]

In summary, all elements of prosody combine to enhance mere words. Pitch changes form intonational contours that indicate specific intent, leading listeners to draw conclusions and collaborate in conversation. Segmented chunks of prosody enable the brain to process 'perceptually relevant variations in fundamental frequency used by the speaker to convey information' (House, 1999, p. 15). Prosody thus contains a significant portion of the message of human speech.

Speech Processing Considerations

Before moving to a specific discussion of prosody in aviation communications, let us consider some important points about how our brains and bodies process speech. For while we most often consider speaking to be a cognitive task mediated by the brain, we tend to overlook the body's participation in the production of speech. In reality, the body and brain are interdependent in the production and comprehension of speech.

Cognitive Processing

The cognitive events which combine to produce human speech (Lieberman, 2000) are mediated by an array of functions, from physiological to sociological to emotional. When speaking, an aviator's intonation may be a product of gender, motor skill, or fatigue (House, 1999; Lieberman, 2000; Lieberman, Kanki, and Protopapas, 1995). When listening, aviators' perceptions of intonation may be influenced by short-term memory capacity, cultural background, or a noisy environment (Loftus, 1988; Georgakopoulou and Goutsos, 1997; Warren, 1996). No single element determines how we say what we say, or how we hear what we hear.

Syntactic Processing Linguists disagree about whether the human brain houses genetic modules which facilitate language processing (Pinker, 1999), or if language develops using disparate parts of the brain in a kind of cooperative processing and learning venture (Lieberman, 2000; Tomasello, 1999). Putting aside these specific evolutionary biology controversies, the brain's language processor is assumed to be the array of cognitive resources contributing to perceiving, comprehending, and responding to language. After briefly describing the 'neural sorting process' (House, 1999) that allows the brain to decode and comprehend an utterance, we will consider how short term memory assists in the processing task.

House (1999) argues that a crucial component of syntactical processing is a pattern-matching function. The processor searches for familiar patterns, sorting information about the smallest units of pitch as well as the largest units of discourse such as sentences and paragraphs. While discerning individual prosodic items, the processor is also attending to average pitch, extreme endpoints, direction of intonation, and degree of slope. Gandour (1978) suggests that the just noticeable differences (JND) in F_0 (.3-.5 Hz at 120 Hz and 2.0 Hz when F_0 has a falling slope) allow for fine discrimination of prosodic cues. [8] The processor combines the small units of information into ever-larger thoughts and ideas to produce and comprehend (depending on whether the task is speaking or listening) phrases, sentences, paragraphs, and entire speech 'events' such as conversations, lectures, or sequences of aviation radio communications.

Stirling and Wales (1996) suggest three hypotheses for the way syntactical processors work to establish a single grammatical or semantic interpretation (to 'disambiguate' a message) of a spoken message. The hypotheses are the serial, parallel, and delay models. In the serial and parallel models, the processors 'assume a cumulative integration of any information which becomes available in parsing' (p. 194). The serial processor settles on one structure early in an utterance, while the parallel processor maintains all possible structures, holding all information as parallel possibilities, until most ambiguity is resolved. The delay model holds all information about the contents of an utterance until all ambiguity is resolved. All three models use a neural sorting process to search for cues and patterns leading to comprehension.

Whether serial, parallel, or delay, processors use available information from prosody - duration, pitch, loudness, sequence, and intonation - to decode (in linguistic terms, to parse) the meaning of an utterance. Syntactical processors may have 'frequency sweep detectors' (House, 1999, p. 15) that extract cues to intonational meaning. Such detectors search for common patterns in order to predict the outcome of a sentence. In syntax, such patterns include word order and familiar chunks of language. Intonational contours, key, and paralinguistic cues may all be included in a sentence and exploited as familiar predictive patterns (House, 1999).

Short-Term Memory The syntactic processor predicts sentence outcome by storing semantic, linguistic, and prosodic information in short-term memory as an utterance unfolds, relying on past experience to construct a reasonable expectation of how a sentence will end (Warren, 1996). There seems to be 'a cumulative integration of any information which becomes available in parsing' (Stirling and

Wales, 1996, p. 194), allowing listeners to use information from the first part of an utterance to more quickly draw conclusions about what will follow. Stirling and Wales cite evidence that more intense processing occurs at beginnings of intonational phrases than at endings. Stirling and Wales postulate that short term auditory memory processing capability fills up and goes to work, leaving the ends of phrases neglected for want of capacity. Length of an utterance may also be a factor, since auditory short term memory performance declines rapidly at about 15 seconds from the onset of new information (Loftus, Dark, and Williams, 1979). Short term memory performance benefits from the presence of chunked information, a prominent feature of prosody discussed above. Further, when memory load is high, performance decreases (Loftus et al.). As in so many instances, when workload increases, performance suffers.

For example, an unfamiliar accent may not only erode intelligibility, but also distract from other tasks proceeding simultaneously. A description of a runway incursion in the United States' National Aeronautics and Space Administration's (NASA) Aviation Safety Reporting System (2002b, p. 57) illustrates the problem:

> Attempted to get the ATIS before flying over the ranch, but could not understand it. The person that recorded it had a thick New England accent ... the same person ... told me that he had not cleared me to cross the active runway and that I had cut off a Dornier that made a go-around ... the controller's thick New England accent made him difficult to understand.

It is possible that this routine operation turned potentially dangerous because the pilot could not 'disambiguate' (to use a prosodic term) the spoken message from the controller. While short-term memory worked to decode the controller's message, other work was temporarily ignored. The pilot's flying obligations were temporarily relegated to an automatic function as the cognitive challenge of comprehending an unfamiliar regional accent soaked up processing capacity.

Talking as a Motor Skill

While we usually think of speech in cognitive or linguistic terms, talking is, in fact, a motor skill. The physical act of talking engages the vocal apparatus of breath, larynx, teeth, tongue and articulators. Further, talking is directly related to gesture. Lieberman (2000) argues that speech communication and bipedalism evolved at around the same time, employing adjacent brain structures in hominids (p. 151). As upright posture freed hominid hands, gesturing with hands during speech became an option. Speech and gesture evolved in tandem, with gesture becoming an integral part of expressive vocalization. The close connection between speech and gesture is well documented (Kendon, 1994; Iverson, 1998). A brief description of vocal physiology and gesture will provide a further frame of reference for comprehending the music of language.

Vocal Apparatus Before humans begin speaking, they first take a breath. The diaphragm muscle exerts upward pressure on inflated lungs, forcing air past the larynx and vocal cords. Muscles in the rib cage, upper body and neck regulate the flow of air. Vocal cords vibrate as air flows past them, and speech commences. The larynx regulates pitch; therefore the larynx is largely responsible for prosody.[9] According to Fox (2000), '...the various airways and cavities of the pharynx, mouth, and nose, and the associated muscles, especially those of the tongue acts as a kind of variable filter, modifying the airstream so as to produce the wide range of sounds required for speech' (p. 3). To simplify, breath supports the sound of a voice, while the lips, jaw, and tongue, interacting with the teeth, articulate language. The amount of individual variation in the sound of speech is significant, since the physiology of vocal apparatus varies from person to person.

Gesture In face-to-face communications, gesture is almost always present in all cultures. Instances in which gesture is absent are so rare that they serve only to probe the pervasive rules of gesture in communication studies. Gestures add emphasis to an utterance at the same time that they illustrate ideas by pointing, indicating size and quantity, or mitigating ideas. Gesture completes spoken communication by emphasizing and accenting important words and ideas in an utterance, becoming a crucial part of the environment of spoken language. Each person gestures in an idiosyncratic fashion, but there are common gestures across cultures. Hands chop the air for emphasis, open toward a listener in a giving motion, point to a person or thing that is the subject of discussion, and illustrate ideas by holding up a number of fingers or indicating that something may be high or low on a scale. Gestures precede the words they symbolize by about three seconds (Kendon, 1994), serving to literally pull words out of semantic memory.

Since prosody and other discourse studies by definition take the environment into account as a crucial component of discourse context, gesture should always be considered at some point in the discussion. In aviation, gesture makes its customary contributions to face-to-face communications, but in radio communications, it is largely absent (controllers are freer to gesture than pilots, whose hands are busy with tasks that usually prevent gesture, but we are not aware of studies that document controllers' tendency to gesture). The absence of gesture certainly contributes to speech with less intonational range, speech that tends towards monotone. Prosody of language is the focus of this chapter, but gesture can be thought of as physical prosody. Its absence affects the message.

Prosody in Aviation Communications

To return to our musical analogy, the music of every-day aviation speech ranges across several different 'styles'. Just as music may fall under popular, classical, or world genres, so different areas of aviation prosody may have distinct attributes and requirements. Radio communications or AIRSPEAK has a proscribed phraseology, order and manner of speaking, and often takes place in significant noise. Flight deck communications occur in a chain-of-command environment, where safety of flight is a paramount issue, and where assertiveness and mitigation issues are of prime concern (Linde, 1988). In an industry with lopsided gender balance, issues of power, inappropriate language, and harassment still permeate discourse (Sitler, Turney and Wulle, 1996). In a world where English is the recommended language of air traffic control, bilingual English speakers now outnumber monolingual speakers of the language (Jenkins, 2000), spawning fluency and intelligibility problems from flight deck to control tower.

In the next portion of this chapter, we will link prosody issues to aviation discourse and argue for an increased awareness and attention to the details of pitch, intonation, and the music of language. The discussion is necessarily broad here, so that different areas of aviation communication may be addressed. Issues of decoding and interpretation, expectation or subversion of spoken messages, prosody versus semantics, and cross-cultural miscommunication are prosodic themes recurring in all styles of aviation discourse. These issues are especially pertinent in the inclusive aviation workplace.

Pitch, Perturbations, and Gender

If, as Ohala (1983) and others argue, there is a cross-cultural universal frequency code of pitch, it has important implications for cross-gender communication. Turney (2002) found a significant number of males, often with ten years or more of experience, agreed with the statement, 'I have trouble understanding the female voice on the frequency', or 'I prefer male controllers during times of busy traffic' (p. 100). In the universal frequency code scheme, high-pitched voices are associated with smallness, intimacy, and lack of power. Males may have an instinctual reluctance, based in the frequency code, to rely on a high-pitched voice for instruction and control, especially during heavy traffic segments when safety of flight seems most at risk. Pitch and F_0 has been found to increase during times of high workload (Ruiz, Legros, and Guell, 1990), perhaps driving high-pitched voices of both genders even higher during rush hour. Ruiz et al. found that 'the time contours of the F_0 become more irregular and discontinuous in radio communications between pilots and ground staff when technical incidents occur. Sudden changes, or jumps, in the F_0 and rapid fluctuations from one syllable to the next can be observed' (p. 268). Brenner, Doherty, and Shipp (1994) also found F_0 increases during high workload. More research into this question could clarify the issue and guide training for controllers and pilots alike. Since every voice has a pitch range, training could include learning to exploit a wider range of frequencies as well as learning to expect a wider range of pitch.

There may be other explanations for Turney's finding that male pilots and controllers prefer speaking to other males on the radio. Since radio communications take place in an environment where white noise is a constant, masking of higher frequencies may be a factor. It is well established that pilots with many years of experience tend to have noise-induced hearing (NIHL) loss in the higher frequencies (Kent, Henning, von Gierke, Eng, and Tolan, 1986; Gawron, and Bock, 1990). With certain sounds in white noise difficult to hear even when hearing is normal (Sanders and McCormick, 1993; Studebaker, Taylor, and Sherbecoe, 1994), pilots and controllers with NIHL may struggle more with high-pitched voices. While datalink, improved headsets, and quieter engines may have a chance of reducing the incidence of NIHL in the future, aviation radio frequencies still carry a large number of transmissions. In some sectors there are as many as 400 transmissions in 50 minutes -- an average of eight per minute, and one transmission every 7.5 seconds (Yuditsky, 2003).

There is evidence that female voices have ample prosodic clarity and should be understood at least as well as males, if not better. In a study of indexical properties of speech perception, Bradlow and Pisoni (1996) found that women displayed 'fewer phonological reduction phenomena' (p. 69) such as faster rates of speech, diction errors, or generally sloppy speech -- all issues of prosodic segmentation and boundaries. Female speakers in Bradlow and Pisoni were the three most intelligible speakers, while males were the three least intelligible. Subjects in the Hellier et al. (2002) study of the perceived urgency of speech warnings found a female voice more convincing than a male voice. Zahn (1989) cites instances of female speakers being rated higher than males in 'aesthetic quality' (p. 61) of the linguistic content of speech.

Intonation, Contours, and Culture

How do intonation and its contours affect an inclusive aviation discourse? In this section we shall discuss mitigation and assertiveness in flight deck conversation, facing demeaning language at work, and cross-cultural language exchange.

Linde (1988) and Goguen, Linde, and Murphy (1986) have studied mitigation and assertiveness in aviation accidents and flight deck communication. Their excellent research has been influential, but has a serious drawback as discourse analysis. The research, like much textlinguistic work, is based on transcripts only, with no prosodic information available. Investigating the command-and-control speech act chain, Goguen et al. found that requests to superiors are often mitigated, 'a linguistic indication of indirectness and tentativeness in speech' (p. 1). Suggesting training for assertiveness, the researchers state that 'it should not be difficult to train subordinate crewmembers to use less mitigated language, termed "to be more assertive" in the NTSB reports' (p. 22). However, problematic lack of assertiveness is cited repeatedly in Crew Resource Management Issues in the NASA's Aviation Safety Reporting System Database. Statements such as 'I should have challenged the PIC' (2002a, p. 10), and 'The altitude bust would not have happened if I had been more assertive' (p. 4) appear in numerous reports. One captain, in evidence that mitigated language emanates from the left seat as well as the right, reported that hiding nervousness from a First Officer had caused a dangerous problem. Thus, while the assertiveness problem may have eased, it is clear that it has not been eliminated. And while the NASA self-reports are generally gender- and culture-blind, mitigation and assertiveness are important issues for members of minority cultures in the aviation environment.

Mitigation, while described in assertiveness training as a potential problem, may in fact be useful in many situations. Linde (1988) found that when crews used mitigated language in non-emergencies, they were able to productively discuss solutions to problems. Fischer and Orasanu (1999) have found that crews prefer shared responsibility models in flight deck communications. Fischer and Orasanu also found that females were more likely than males to include goal statements as a communication strategy. Such 'supportive statements' are not only 'politeness devices that serve to downgrade the effect of an utterance' (p. 4), but also provide context contributing to problem-solving and decision-making. Shared responsibility, supportive statements, and politeness devices are tactics of mitigation.

In some cultures, politeness may be mistaken for problematic mitigation. Stratachuk and Beneigh (2002) quote a South American First Officer flying for a United States carrier:

> I might tell the captain that I am going to warn the flight attendants to prepare for landing and many times they think I am asking them if I should do it ... it is only out of respect for his authority and respect for him as a crewmember that I constantly strive to keep him in the loop (p. 120).

This cultural confusion most likely stems from cross-cultural misunderstanding of politeness, but may also be linked to prosody. A United States captain may hear the intonational melody of questioning, while the Latino First Officer intends polite deference to authority. Instead of trying to stamp out mitigation in assertiveness training, we should determine when it is useful and when it is not, and train to use it appropriately.

Principles of prosody offer possible solutions. While discourse analysts may be able to list exactly which words to use to make speech more direct, prosody analysts may suggest ideal intonational patterns that give direct language its intentional force (in prosodic terms, 'illocutionary force'). Those with high-pitched voices could learn to exploit the lower range of a voice. Bilingual English speakers may learn when to avoid ending boundaries that sound like questions, while their monolingual crew mates learn the meanings for a wider range of prosodic contours.

In the aviation workplace, Turney has found sociological gender issues related to language (Sitler et al., 1996). One of these issues, facing demeaning language, may be remedied by consciously using prosodic techniques in conversation. Sitler et al. suggest that women devise strategies to deal with such workplace problems in order to 'confront negative attitudes directly and indicate lack of approval' (p. 339). This suggestion of *what* to do begs the question of *how* to do it. Proscribed language is one tool to use in demeaning or uncomfortable situations, but prosody is another. Not only the words used, but also the manner and expression, combine to create the desired message. Understanding that the pitch of one's voice is likely to rise under stress and high workload may help females regulate their voices.

Women and other members of cultural minorities who find themselves on the receiving end of demeaning or harassing speech may experience increased stress. Such scenarios are likely to trigger physical reactions that must be coped with at the same time one must think of the proper direct language to use. Brenner et al. (1994) found that heart rate increased as F_0, rate of speech, and loudness increased in high workload, stressful situations. Coping with a pounding heart, a suddenly louder, higher-pitched voice (with the negative connotation of 'shrill'), and a faster rate of speech make it more difficult to think of what to say, much less how to say it. Prosody awareness and training may be part of the solution.

In writing about cross-cultural issues in aviation, Ragan (2002) refers to the exchange function of language. Exchange is linguistic interaction, or 'language which refers to and acknowledges relationships, moderates directness, and expresses degrees of politeness' (p. 104). In AIRSPEAK, also called international Aviation English, the intonation of exchanges may be rooted in languages other than English. Bilingual speakers of English transfer some prosody from their first languages (Wennerstrom, 2000), as well as cultural impulses of politeness, directness, and other subtle interpersonal cues. Ragan calls for 'examining cockpit voice recorder evidence in a more sophisticated manner to include the personal, interactive exchange function of language use' (p. 110). Prosody should be integrated in the analysis as well. Transcripts from aviation accidents or training sessions could be analyzed for intonational content. Warren (1996) emphasizes that prosodic analysis reveals how speakers collaborate, providing superior disambiguation than syntactic structural analysis alone.

Johnny One Note and Rate of Speech

Two prosodic issues often emerge in aviation radio communications studies: monotone speech and rate of speech. The tendency in air traffic control to speak in either a strict monotone or a repetitive singsong pattern is common. Recall from studies by Lieberman and Michaels (1962) and Hellier et al. (2002) that monotone speech was stripped of so many prosodic cues as to become practically unintelligible. Rate of speech was difficult to control for in the design of Rantanen and McCarley's (2002) study of communication delays on controllers' vectoring performance. (Controllers' legendary ability to talk fast may confound scientists as well as pilots.) Monotone delivery and an excessive rate of speech are related.

Controllers spend their working hours issuing series of clearances that are remarkably similar. Depending on the position worked and the current weather, there may be little variation in successive clearances. For example, a Terminal Air Traffic Control Center (TRACON) controller in the United States is likely to spend a fair-weather rush hour shift vectoring all aircraft onto the exact same headings at the same or similar air speeds, with virtually no need for variation. Only the aircraft identification number differentiates one clearance from another. Speaking over a headset and usually sitting down, the controller has no eye contact with listeners, nor any need to gesture for the listener's sake. Repetition and lack of gesture tend to strip language of prosody. The resulting monotone delivery, turning controllers into Johnny One-Note, [10] is less intelligible than speech with a wider range of intonation. A variation on aviation monotone delivery is a repetitive singsong style, in which all clearances follow the same repetitive intonational pattern with a limited range of pitch. Whether monotone or sing-song, such clearances are more difficult to understand than speech with a natural range of prosodic cues, especially for bilingual speakers of English.

In crowded air space, the need for efficiency lends a sense of urgency to all radio communications. A fast rate of speech seems ingrained in aviation; indeed, quick responses and fast clearances are often necessary. But since it is easier to speak quickly within a limited prosodic range than to talk fast with greater pitch and intonational variation, a rapid rate of speech also tends to be monotone or sing-song. Articulation is degraded at high rates of speech (and also in monotone speech), robbing language of prosodic cues (Studebaker et al., 1994). Short-term memory may become more quickly overburdened with fast rates of speech, as the syntactical processor struggles to comprehend and retain a large amount of information in a short amount of time. Fast rates of speech may confound intelligibility for all listeners.

For both monotone delivery and rapid rate of speech, basic training in prosody issues could enhance communications training for both pilots and controllers. In recurrent training, attention to details of intonational range and change of pitch could improve both the delivery and comprehension of AIRSPEAK.

Language Fluency

An international level of fluency in AIRSPEAK is an urgent issue. The International Civil Aviation Organization is currently collaborating with several working groups to set standards for fluency in aviation English. The challenge is to find standards of mutual intelligibility while accepting the global reality that 'for the first time in the history of the English language, second language speakers outnumber those for whom it is the mother tongue, and interaction in English increasingly involves no first language speakers whatsoever' (Jenkins, 2000, p. i). Every day, a vast number of AIRSPEAK communications transpire among second language speakers. English and Aviation English as international languages are changing. New AIRSPEAK standards may require monolingual speakers of English to give ground in what they consider 'correct' usage, both in grammar, language, and prosody.

While waiting for new standards to arise -- and then to be implemented -- there are problems to be solved. Multilingual flight crews struggle to understand each other during critical phases of flight. Controllers at international hubs cope with a wide range of accents in the course of a day, sometimes narrowly averting disaster spawned by intelligibility problems.[11] Prosody plays a major role in language fluency. Awareness of prosody issues in fluency will promote intelligibility.

Along with comprehension, pronunciation, and grammar, language fluency requires acquisition of intonation. Wennerstrom (2000) points out that intonational variables in fluency include rate of speech, how often conversational 'repairs' (correction of misunderstandings) occur, type of hesitation phenomena, and 'interactive features of conversation management' (p. 103). These elements of fluency are contained in the pitch accents and boundary tones of prosody. In English, pitch differentiates important points in discourse that guide listeners' comprehension. Pitch is used in English to contrast new topics, or to refer backwards to older ones. When proper pitch guidance is missing, as when a novice speaker assigns equal pitch to every word, language becomes choppy, and meaning is obscured. Nonfluent speakers may resort to monotone delivery by assigning the same pitch and rhythm to all words. These strategies employ less variation in pitch contours as well, resulting in a flatter speech signal, with highs not as high and lows not as low as fluent speakers. Importantly for aviation, background noise obscures pitch and contour information.

The phenomenon called 'dysfluency' is a special prosodic challenge for nonfluent speakers. Dysfluencies are stumbles, misspeaks, and other non-meaningful units of speech such as 'um' and 'er'. Especially problematic are 'um' and 'er', which are verbal noises made while thinking of what to say next. Since nonfluent speakers spend a larger percentage of time thinking of how language should properly unfold, they tend to fall back on these 'thinking noises' more often than fluent speakers.[12] Repetitive use of 'um' almost always falls on the same heavily-accented pitch, pulling intonational contours toward monotone.

To be fair, though, monolingual speakers of English are hardly exempt from the 'um' habit. Training monolingual speakers of English to eliminate prosodic dysfluencies would assist bilingual speakers with English comprehension.

Reading and Intonation

Aviation professionals are often called upon to read aloud. Flight attendants read safety instructions to passengers, flight crews read checklist items to one another, controllers and flight service personnel read weather conditions and forecasts onto recordings such as Automatic Terminal Information Service (ATIS) or Flight Service Station phone lines. Reading well, with sufficient illocutionary force, is a difficult skill to acquire. We tend to take for granted that people who can read silently to themselves can read aloud if called upon, but there is a serious flaw in such reasoning. First, reading aloud tends to sound as if we are reading to ourselves, which makes listeners stop listening. Second, reading and talking are two different skills, employing different cognitive resources. Reading aloud is a hybrid skill, requiring a combination of public speaking fluency and individual literacy. Reading aloud almost always implies the absence of gesture, which strips language of expression. Prosody again helps unlock the secrets to fluent reading aloud; that is, reading that makes listeners pay attention and helps them remember the safety messages primary to the majority of aviation communications.

Three prosodic hazards of reading aloud are rate of speech, monotone and repetitive sing-song delivery, and lack of conversational cues. Rate of speech must be sufficiently slow to give listeners time to process the message. The pitfalls of monotone and repetitive delivery in reading are similar to the challenges faced by air traffic controllers who issue all clearances using the same intonation: it is simply easier for the brain and mouth to employ the same intonational contour over and over. A page of text may appear to be simply a succession of sentences (or safety warnings, or checklist items) to be gotten through in the easiest possible way. The reader defaults to a pattern that accomplishes the task of reading, leaving the task of communicating unfinished. Conversational cues are the prosodic elements that help listeners stay engaged. These cues occur naturally in fluent conversation, but are frequently absent in reading aloud. Natural conversation is characterized by contrasting high and low accented pitches, proper use of questioning or decisive phrase endings, and variations in loudness and duration of language.

Reading can be improved by training that devotes attention to prosodic details, and by practicing reading aloud. Southwest Airlines in the United States could be used as a model for how flight attendants read to passengers. Southwest's lighthearted attitude combined with stern safety instructions often strikes just the right balance. In any event, the task of reading aloud should not be left to chance on the assumption that everyone can do it.

Summary

The music of human speech conveys information crucial to the spoken message. Moving pitches form intonational contours containing crucial segments of information. Emotional cues are embedded in prosody. Cognitive processing of prosody takes place in short-term memory. Efficient processing depends on speakers' abilities to speak clearly and on listeners' abilities to hear. Variables in comprehension include the relative noise of the environment, individual differences in vocal apparatus, the presence or absence of gesture, and the cultural differences present in any given exchange. The brain's syntactical processor searches for familiar patterns that may predict the outcome of a sentence. Real-time syntactic processing depends on short-term memory capacity.

Certain prosodic challenges exist in aviation. In a field dominated by males, higher pitched female voices may be harder to hear for pilots with noise-induced hearing loss. There may be a cross-cultural tendency to equate lower pitched male voices with power and authority, leaving females at a disadvantage in a chain-of-command industry. Intonational contours may contribute to problematic mitigation among flight deck crews. Intonational contours in a multicultural workplace may cause confusion and misunderstandings. Monotone speech, common in radio communications, exhibits fewer prosodic cues and is difficult to understand. Standards of fluency in AIRSPEAK include acquisition of appropriate English prosody. Aviation professionals who must read safety information to passengers and crew must read with proper prosodic emphasis in order to be understood.

The science of prosody reveals a great deal about the music of everyday aviation communications. In the inclusive aviation workplace, prosody may reveal differences, but also function as a tool to bridge culture and gender biases. The pitch of voices, contours of speech patterns, and emotional cues in prosody could add a 'third dimension' to communications studies. Prosodic measurements should be included in aviation communications research.

Notes

1   Modern vocoders are used, among other things, to compress digitized speech signals into lower bandwidths in hopes of increasing air traffic control radio channel capacity. La Due, Sollenberger, Belanger, and Heinze (2002) studied the effectiveness of digitized speech signals from two different types of vocoders in en route and terminal transmissions. Their study compared speaker gender and background noise and found no intelligibility preferences for either sex, and no significant effects of background noise on the digital signal. However, 'natural' analog radio transmissions were rated more intelligible than vocoder-compressed speech. Compressing radio transmission signals removes a degree of the naturally occurring prosody of human speech.

2   While some of these disciplines do not directly invoke prosody in research, they raise prosodic issues time and again, usually stopping short of acknowledging any prosodic role in discourse. Bowers and Jentsch (2002) studied sequential communication patterns in teams to find effective speech content for high-performing crews. They used such classifications as 'uncertainty statements', 'action statements', 'responses', and 'acknowledgments', all of which may also be identified with prosodic features that render the statements more or less understandable. Linde (1988) likewise has studied transcripts of communications in aviation accidents, searching for effective sequences of communication. While Linde's in-depth analysis teases out much detail of mitigation and assertiveness, it too begs the question of how the music of communication affects the message, and further, how aviation professionals might train to achieve the optimum musical patterns. Drew (1992) offers extensive analysis of conversations in institutional settings which detail sequences, focus, social action, context, and goals. Here again, application of the principles of prosody could reveal the crucial information contained in the sound beneath the words, adding 'expression and intent to the code of language' (Hart et al., 1990, p. 3).

3   In 'tone languages' such as Chinese, pitch does have lexical meaning in addition to paralinguistic meaning. Lexical meaning in tone languages often follows frequency code patterns, with words denoting smallness residing at high pitches, and words for largeness occurring at lower pitches (Ohala, 1983).

4   The key of a purely musical phrase likewise conveys information that guides listeners' understanding of a composition. A minor key may sound sad, while a major key often conveys happiness. Key may be relatively high or low, or contain 'sharp' or 'flat' tones. Mozart was fond of writing love songs in A major, a key he considered suitably romantic.

5   Banse and Scherer (1996) used the following emotions to test for classification: hot anger, cold anger, panic, anxiety, despair, sadness, elation, happiness, interest, boredom, shame, pride, disgust, and contempt.

6   Lieberman and Michaels (1962) used boredom, confidentiality, doubt, fear, happiness, objective questioning, objective statement, and pompous statement as the emotions in their study of F_0 and loudness in emotion.

7   Hellier et al. (2002) found an increasing degree of urgency in these words, in this order: 'note' (least urgent), 'warning', 'caution', 'danger', and 'deadly' (most urgent). All words used in the study were 'deadly', 'danger', 'warning', 'caution', 'risky', 'no', 'hazard', 'attention', 'beware', and 'note'.

8   Human voices usually employ a pitch range encompassing about 100 Hz (Gandour, 1978). Ability to discriminate subtle changes (JND) in F_0 means that clumsy articulation or non-fluent prosody can rob the speech signal of important processing cues.

9   Human male larynxes descend at puberty, forcing the voice lower and louder than female voices. According to Ohala's (1983) frequency code, low-pitched voices imply the speaker is large, 'aggressive, assertive, self-confident, dominant, self-sufficient, etc. The meaning of high pitch in addition to small is nonthreatening, submissive, subordinate, in need of the receiver's cooperation and good will, etc' (p. 8). Thus may gender differences in vocal apparatus serve to color, confuse, or contradict a spoken message.

10   The song from *Babes in Arms* by Richard Rogers and Lorenz Hart (1937), begins with the line: 'Johnny could only sing one note and the note he sang was this: Ah!' Ironically, the song is filled with melodic leaps and rhythmic syncopations. Pilots and controllers take heed.

11   In NASA's Aviation Safety Reporting System CRM database, a First Officer reported an altitude bust while flying with a captain who had 'a poor understanding of English. In my opinion, fluency in English would have either resolved this problem or greatly reduced the time to sort out the problem' (p. 16). In January, 2002, in Anchorage, Alaska, a China Airlines A340 with 237 passengers took off on taxiway 24 instead of runway 32, leaving the impressions of its main gear in a 2-foot high snow bank twenty feet from the end of the taxiway (Croft, 2002). AIRSPEAK fluency coupled with fatigue may be contributing factors in this incident.

12   Dysfluencies afflict fluent speakers as well, sometimes to the great distress of listeners. The use of 'um' follows the same monotonous intonational pattern whether used by nonfluent speakers as time to think, or as a verbal habit by fluent speakers.

References

Bachorowski, J. and Owren, M.J. (1995). 'Vocal Expression of Emotion: Acoustic Properties of Speech Are Associated with Emotional Intensity and Context', *Psychological Science, 6* (4), 219-224.

Banse, R. and Scherer, K.R. (1996). 'Acoustic Profiles in Vocal Emotion Expression', *Journal of Personality and Social Psychology, 70* (3), 614-636.

Bolinger, D. (1972). 'Around the Edge of Language: Intonation', in D. Bolinger (ed.), *Intonation: Selected Readings*, Hammondsworth, UK: Penguin, pp. 19-29.

Bolinger, D. (1989). 'The Universality of Affect and a Review of Symbols', in D. Bolinger, *Intonation and Its Uses: Melody and Grammar in Discourse*, Stanford University Press, pp. 1-5.

Bowers, C.A. and Jentsch, F. (2002). 'Using Communications Analysis to Understand Team Development: An Example', *Proceedings of the Human Factors and Ergonomics Society*, 295-297.

Bradlow, A.R., Nygaard, L.C. and Pisoni, D.B. (1996). 'Indexical and Linguistic Attributes in Speech Perception: A Review of Some Recent Findings', in B. Kanki and O.V. Prinzo (eds.), *Methods and Metrics of Voice Communications*, pp. 61-70, DOT/FAA/AM-96-10.

Brenner, M., Doherty, E.T, and Shipp, T. (1994, January). 'Speech Measures Indicating Workload Demand', *Aviation, Space, and Environmental Medicine*, 21-26.

Chang, N.T. (1958). 'Tones and Intonation in the Chengtu Dialect', in D. Bolinger (ed.), *Intonation: Selected Readings*, Penguin, CITY, pp. 391-413.

Croft, J. (2002, February 4). 'China Airlines Take-off Blunder Investigated', *Aviation Week and Space Technology*, 48.

Drew, P. and Heritage, J. (1992). 'Analyzing Talk at Work: an Introduction', P. Drew and J. Heritage (eds.), *Talk at Work*, Cambridge University Press, pp. 3-65.

Fischer, U. and Orasanu, J. (1999). 'Cultural Diversity and Crew Communications', *Proceedings of the 50th Astronautical Congress in Amsterdam*, American Institute of Astronautics, Inc.

Fox, A. (2000). *Prosodic Features and Prosodic Structure: The Phonology of Suprasegmentals*, Oxford.

Gandour, J.T. (1978). 'The Perception of Tone', in V.A. Fromkin (ed.), *Tone: A Linguistic Survey*, New York: Academic Press, pp. 41-76.

Gawron, V.J. and Bock, D.H. (1990, August). 'In search of an Inherent Ordering of Vowel Phonemes, or Do Pilots Hear Like Engineers Do?', *Aviation, Space, and Environmental Medicine*, 758-760.

Georgakopoulou, A. and Goutsos, D. (1997). *Discourse Analysis*, Edinburgh: University Press.

Gregory, R.L. (ed.) (1997). *The Oxford Companion to the Mind*, New York: Oxford.

Goguen, J., Linde, C., and Murphy, M. (1986). *Crew Communications as a Factor in Aviation Accidents*, Ames Research Center, Moffett Field: National Aeronautics and Space Administration.

Hart, J., Collier, R., and Cohen, A. (1990). *A Perceptual Study of Intonation: An Experimental-Phonetic Approach to Speech Melody*, Cambridge.

Hellier, E., Edworthy, J., Weedon, B., Walters, K., and Adams, A. (2002). 'The Perceived Urgency of Speech Warnings: Semantics Versus Acoustics', *Human Factors*, *44* (1), 2-17.

House, D. (1999). *Tonal Perception in Speech*, Sweden: Lund University Press,

Iverson, J. (1998). 'Gesture When There Is No Visual Model', Iverson and Goldin-Meadow (eds.), *The Nature and Functions of Gesture in Children's Communication*, San Francisco: Jossey-Bass, pp. 89-116.

Kendon, A. (1994). 'Do Gestures Communicate?', in A. Kendon (ed.), *Research on Language and Social Interaction*, Hillsdale, New Jersey: Erlbaum.

Kent, S.J., Henning, E., von Gierke, Eng, D., and Tolan, G.D. (1986 April). 'Analysis of the Potential Association between Noise-Induced Hearing Loss and Cardiovascular Disease in USAF Aircrew Members', *Aviation, Space, and Environmental Medicine*, 348-360.

Jenkins, J. (2000). *The Phonology of English as an International Language*, Oxford: Clarenden.

La Due, J., Sollenberger, R., Belanger, B., and Heinze, A. (2002). *Human Factors Evaluation of Vocoders for Air traffic Control Environments Phase I: Field Evaluation*, Atlantic City, NJ: Federal Aviation Administration William J. Hughes Technical Center, DOT/FAA/CT-TN97/11.

Lieberman, P. (2000). *Human Language and Our Reptilian Brain: The Subcortical Bases of Speech, Syntax, and Thought*, Boston: Harvard.

Lieberman, P., Kanki, B.G., and Protopapas, A. (1995). 'Speech Production and Cognitive Decrements on Mt. Everest', *Aviation, Space, and Environmental Medicine*, 857-864, 66.

Lieberman, P. and Michaels, S. (1962). 'Some Aspects of Fundamental Frequency and Envelope Amplitude as Related to the Emotional Content of Speech', in D. Bolinger (ed.) *Intonation and Its Uses: Melody and Grammar in Discourse*, Stanford University Press, pp. 235-248.

Linde, C. (1988). 'The Quantitative study of Communicative Success: Politeness and Accidents in Aviation Discourse', *Language in Society*, *17*, 375-399.

Loftus, E. (1988). *Memory: Surprising New Insights into How We Remember and Why We Forget*, New York: Ardsley.

Loftus, G., Dark, V.J. and Williams, D. (1979). 'Short-Term Memory Factors in Ground Controller/Pilot Communication', *Human Factors*, *21* (2), 169-181.

National Aeronautics and Space Administration (2002a). *Cockpit Resource Management (CRM) Issues*, Aviation Safety Reporting System Database Report Set, December.

National Aeronautics and Space Administration (2002b). *Pilot-Controller Communications*, Moffett Field, California: Aviation Safety Reporting System Database Report Set, December.

National Transportation Safety Board (1995). *Aircraft Accident Report: Flight into Terrain During Missed Approach, USAir Flight 1016, DC-9-31, N954VJ*, NTSB/AAR-95/03, Washington, D.C.: U.S. Government Printing Office.

Ohala, J.J. (1983). 'Cross-Language Use of Pitch: An Ethnological View', *Phonetica*, *40*, 1-18.

Pierrehumbert, J.B. and Steele, S.A. (1989). 'Categories of Tonal Alignment in English', *Phonetica*, *46*, 181-196.

Pinker, S. (1999). *Words and Rules*, New York: Basic Books.

Ragan, P. (2002). 'Deadly Misunderstandings: Language and Culture in the Cockpit', in *Proceedings of the Aviation Communications Conference*, Arizona State University and Embry-Riddle Aeronautical University, 103-113.

Rantanen, E.M., McCarley, J.S. and Xu, X. (2002). 'The Impact of Communication Delays on Air Traffic Controllers' Vectoring Performance', *Proceedings of the Human Factors and Ergonomics Society*, 56-60.

Rodgers, R. and Hart, L. (1937). 'Johnny One Note', *Babes in Arms*, New York: Chappell.

Ruiz, R., Legros, C., and Guell, A. (1990, March), 'Voice Analysis to Predict the Psychological or Physical State of a Speaker', *Aviation, Space, and Environmental Medicine*.

Sanders, M.S. and McCormick, E.J. (1993). *Human Factors in Engineering and Design*, New York: McGraw-Hill.

Sekuler, R. and Blake, R. (1994). *Perception*, New York: McGraw-Hill.

Sitler, R., Turney, M.A. and Wulle, B. (1996). 'Attitudes reflective of gender-based issues in the aviation and transportation workplace', in *Applied Aviation Psychology: Achievement, Change and Challenge, Proceedings of the Third Australian Aviation Psychology Symposium*, Aldershot: Avebury.

Stirling, L. and Wales, R. (1996). 'Does Prosody Support or Direct Sentence Processing?', in P. Warren (ed.), *Prosody and Parsing, A Special Issue of Language and Cognitive Processes*, Psychology Press, Erlbaum, 11(1/2), pp. 193-212.

Stratachuk, R. and Beneigh, T. (2002). 'Communication and Airline Safety in the Multicultural Crew Environment', *Proceedings of the Aviation Communications Conference*, Embry-Riddle Aeronautical University, 115-125.

Studebaker, G.A., Taylor, R. and Sherbecoe, R.L. (1994, April). 'The Effect of noise Spectrum on Speech Recognition Performance-Intensity Functions', *Journal of Speech and Hearing Research*, *37*, 430-448.

Tomasello, M. (1999). *The Cultural Origins of Human Cognition*, Boston: Harvard.

Turney, M.A. (2002). 'Gender Factors in Pilot-Controller Communications', in *Proceedings of the Aviation Communications Conference*, Embry-Riddle Aeronautical University, 98-102.

Warren, P. (1996). 'Prosody and Parsing: An Introduction,' in P. Warren (ed.), *Prosody and Parsing, A Special Issue of Language and Cognitive Processes*, Psychology Press, Hove, 11(1/2), pp. 1-16.

Wennerstrom, A. (2000). 'The Role of Intonation in Second Language Fluency', in H. Riggenbach (ed.), *Perspectives on Fluency*, Ann Arbor, MI: University of Michigan Press, pp. 102-127.

Wennerstrom, A. (2001). *The Music of Everyday Speech: Prosody and Discourse Analysis*, New York: Oxford.

Yuditsky, T. (2003). Number of transmissions per hour in high workload TRACONS, Federal Aviation Administration Hughes Human Factors Laboratory, Newark, NJ, personal correspondence.

Zahn, C. J. (1989). 'The Bases for Differing Evaluations of Male and Female Speech: March, pp. 59-74.

Chapter 12

Nonverbal Cues 'Speak' Volumes

Mary Ann Turney

Introduction

Nonverbal signals are another way to convey messages of inclusion or exclusion, thus supporting or rejecting diversity. Before we developed speech, it is likely that humans depended heavily on nonverbal communication. However, we often forget that the impact of such communication continues. In spite of the sophistication, subtlety, and flexibility of speech, many of us still convey important messages through nonverbal communication. Body language can sometimes be clear and overt and easily interpreted; at other times, it is quite subtle and hard to 'read' (Raudsepp, 1993). It is these subtle forms of nonverbal communication that can be misunderstood particularly among diverse individuals where initial trust has not yet been established.

Nonverbal communication is reported to reveal what a person really is thinking and feeling. Some experts believe that this form of communication is more important than speech. They estimate that only seven percent of a communication's power lies in words as such, yet fully 55 percent lies in body language. The main factors involved in nonverbal communication include physical space, facial expression, eye contact, posture, gestures, and appearance. (Raudsepp, 1993; Thompson, 1996).

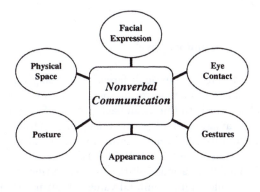

Figure 12.1 Factors related to nonverbal communication

Eye contact is one of our most expressive nonverbal cues; another is physical space. Body posture and position also convey meaning, as does facial expression. Taking an elbow to guide someone, an arm pat, a head nod, a hand gesture – even our foot movements convey messages to others. Cross-cultural nonverbal cues will continue to influence cooperation and collaboration and there is no quick method for learning the meaning of these multiple nonverbal cues. Nevertheless, sincerity and a genuine respect for varying codes of behavior take us a long way to success and mutual acceptance.

Functions of Nonverbal Communication

Nonverbal communication can function as a language in itself. It can 'speak' volumes to those who learn how to 'read' the signals. Birdwhistell (1970) suggests that only about a third of the social meaning of a conversation is communicated by the actual words spoken; the rest is communicated by watching people's actions (Reid & Hammersley, 2000). Reid and Hammersley describe the role of nonverbal communication as an augmentation or replacement for verbal communication. Nonverbal communications convey emotional information about what people feel and how they are relating to us. Our impressions are largely based on nonverbal information. We gather impressions of people by the way they smile or make eye contact, or lean forward to indicate they are listening to us. We make judgments based on nonverbal signals that suggest such desires as a wish to speak, or feelings like unhappiness, uncertainty or nervousness. Many people develop less skill in deceiving others nonverbally than they develop in deceiving others verbally. 'Leakage' is a term that defines a situation in which people accidentally reveal their true feelings through nonverbal signals that they cannot control. These 'leakage' signals can consist of foot movement, sighs, arms folded, etc. (Reid & Hammersley, 2000).

Physical Space and Comfort Level

Hall and Hall (2001) found a basic difference between people of varying ethnic and national backgrounds in their sense of space and how they handle their personal space. People of northern European background – Scandinavian, Swiss, English, German – tend to avoid much physical contact. In contrast, people whose heritage is Italian, Spanish, Russian, French, Latin American and Middle Eastern like close personal contact (Hall & Hall, 2001; Reid & Hammersley, 2000).

E.G. Hall found that various cultures have strict rules about physical space and distance and these rules signify cultural values. In many Anglo cultures, a distance of 0.5 to 1 meter is appropriate for informal conversations and as much as 3 meters can be involved in more formal exchanges. In the Arab world and in Latin America, such distances are much shorter. In Chinese culture those distances are larger, but Chinese people can tolerate smaller distances in non-conversational situations, such as crowded shops and restaurants (Gallois & Callan, 1997).

Although we frequently neglect to think about it, 'space parameters are perceived and distances are selected not by vision alone, but with all the senses.' The ears identify auditory space; the skin identifies thermal space and kinesthetic space is perceived with the muscles of the body. Similarly, the nose perceives olfactory space. It is the individual culture that, in a sense, 'programs' what sensory space information is agreeable and what is disagreeable. Culture is always a factor.

Body language is learned, just as is spoken language. We observe and imitate those around us as we grow up. National, ethnic, and class behavior patterns are learned early in childhood and tend to continue throughout life (Hall & Hall, 2001).

An Interesting Contrast

Rules about touch vary among cultures. For British and Americans, a light touch on another person's arm or back can carry great impact in meaning. Latin American, southern European and Arab cultures, however, take little notice of light touches. On the other hand, the latter groups notice the absence of touch and interpret it as coldness or even hostility (Gallois & Callan, 1997).

American and European men believe that direct eye contact is a sign of personal integrity and straightforwardness. The Japanese norm, however, is that subordinates avert their gaze after briefly returning eye contact with a supervisor. Japanese executives talk about aggressive American and European men and interpret their direct gaze as a form of defiance against authority (Hamada, 1996).

With regard to space in the workplace, Hamada (1996) relates the reactions of American businessmen in a Japanese business located in the United States, an operation in which the office space was modeled after the Tokyo headquarters. The office space was open to 'encourage interpersonal communication and the corporate spirit of teamwork' (p. 163). American and European managers didn't care for this open setting and indicated a need to hold meetings in a private space. They felt demeaned as managers to be forced to operate in this open office space. They complained about noise levels and lack of privacy.

Examining issues of physical contact, Hamada's study looked at differences between Japanese and American men in the company. Different attitudes toward body movement and touching surfaced. Japanese men held other men by the arm and slapped others on the back as a friendly congratulatory gesture and sometimes casually leaned on one another. One Japanese engineer, who was also a martial arts champion, said that touching was a positive thing and intensified feelings of connection with co-workers. European and American male engineers became very upset about body contact in the business setting. Whenever one of the Japanese managers touched one of the Anglo managers, the Anglo's shoulders were observed to tighten, his body to stiffen, and his facial expression turn angry. Ultimately, a physical fight broke out between a Japanese and an American engineer.

Cultural Differences in Facial Expressions

A study of facial expressions among cultures suggests that expressions of fear, anger, surprise, disgust, and happiness tend to be universal. However, Mandal et al (2001) found that negative emotions were least distinctly identifiable in Japanese faces, followed by Indian and North American faces. Male facial expressions were more distinctly identifiable than those of females in the study. This was true of expressions of happiness, particularly among Japanese and Indian men, but not true among men in the North American culture (Mandal et al, 2001).

Gallois and Callan (1997) found that the smile on the face of a Japanese businessman does not necessarily convey joy; in fact, smiling in Japan is often an indication of nervousness, social discomfort, and occasionally sorrow. In collectivist cultures such as Japan's, expressing strong emotions in public, especially negative feelings, is often suppressed in order to preserve harmony. Thus, Chinese and Japanese people can be thought to be inscrutable to Western Europeans (Gallois & Callan, 1997).

Adler (2002) states that many Indian people look down when acknowledging authority, 'a behavior many European and North Americans misinterpret as signaling a lack of trustworthiness.' The result is that team members fail to develop sufficient trust in their Indian colleagues to delegate or share responsibilities appropriately (Adler 2002, p. 142).

Eye Contact, Body Movement, Teamwork, and Power

American blacks greet each other with eye contact even when they don't know one another, but are simply passing by. Some believe that the behavior of American whites regarding eye contact gives the impression that a person isn't even there or doesn't exist. Whites in America, however, tend to avoid eye contact with *anyone* in the street (Hall & Hall, 2001).

Physical proximity has been reported to have some affect on how individuals work together. Actual or perceived distance can weaken the way in which people engage together in tasks (Burgoon, et al, 2002). These findings seem to be important in considering the flight deck environment, where physical proximity is held relatively constant, but emotional proximity may vary considerably.

A number of studies have reported that gender has a significant effect on many nonverbal behaviors displayed in conversation. Some differences included touch, facial expression, posture, proximity, vocalics, and visual gaze (Bente, Donaghy, and Suwelack, 1998). Eye contact studies using computer simulation paradigms indicate that men 'stare or ignore,' while women 'avert eyes or watch' (p. 14). Recent thinking, however, suggests that nonverbal behavior should be studied not individually, but in context, since context variables can cause gender differences to disappear or change. For example, people change their observed behavior if a situation is perceived to be uncomfortable rather than neutral or positive; the degree of intimacy also affects nonverbal behavior.

Bente, Donaghy, and Suwelack (1998) studied the body movement and visual behavior of 20 men and 20 women (ages 20-35) engaged in mixed-sex paired interactions in Cologne, Germany. Variables that were considered included the sex of the subjects, partner familiarity, and the visual attention of the partner. Analysis revealed significant gender differences in frequency and duration of body movement and visual attention. Interestingly, the experimental situation was akin to the aviation flight deck in that subject pairs were placed in low chairs in close proximity. Results of the study point to gender differences in nonverbal behavior patterns in both familiar and unfamiliar pairs. Men generally showed more body movement, but only when participants were familiar. In the unfamiliar situation, body movement of both males and females was about the same.

In gaze behavior, clear differences were also found. Men broke eye contact more often. Women sustained eye contact longer. Women's eye contact was found to frequently adjust to the needs of male partners. Men often looked away while women were speaking, but women seldom looked away while men were talking. Significant differences also were noted in the way movement and gaze were temporally related. Women were more reactive to the gaze of men and 'women were more likely to interrupt their movement when the male partner looked away' (Bente, Donaghy, and Suwelack, 1998, p. 54). In a French study by Gueguen and Jacob, women were reported to be more influenced than men by eye contact, glances, and/or smiles (Gueguen & Jacob, 2002).

Another study related to eye contact and teamwork by Whitelock and Scanlon (1998) found that women look at the partner more when working on a problem in pairs in relation to pairs of men or mixed-gender groups. Women also exhibited more mutual gesturing – a sign of cooperation and maintenance of the collaborative process. Results concluded that women use eye contact more than men when working in teams.

Power Base

Results of a U.S. study done at the University of Colorado by Aguinis and Henle (2001) on nonverbal behavior and female employee's power bases indicate that women face a 'Catch 22' situation regarding eye contact behavior and perception of power. The study revealed gender differences in how nonverbal behavior affects perceptions of power. When men engaged in direct eye contact, they received high credibility and power ratings. When women engaged in similar direct eye contact, they were rated as having negative (coercive) power.

Facial expression was also examined. When females had relaxed facial expressions (as opposed to tense expressions), results suggested perceptions of lower power and when they had nervous facial expressions, they were perceived as having higher power. The authors suggest that if women choose to behave according to their organizational role expectations, they may violate gender role expectations and be perceived negatively. If their nonverbal behavior meets gender role expectations and they avoid direct eye contact, they may not be perceived as effective in terms of organizational roles. Study subjects, both men and women, revealed differences in perceptions of a man and a woman engaging in the same types of nonverbal behavior. According to the authors, 'the present findings extend predictions of the social role model to the relationship between nonverbal behavior and power perceptions' (Aguinis & Henle, 2001, p. 547).

Silent Messages

Albert Mehrabian suggests that actions override words. Thus silent messages may reinforce our words or contradict them. Either way, they are more potent than the words we speak and when there is inconsistency, our credibility crumbles, because most people will believe the nonverbal. Thus, learning how to read and send the right messages is essential in a workplace where diversity is welcomed (Raudsepp, 1993).

Summary

Nonverbal messages are an important way to convey meaning. These 'messages' often reveal what a person is really feeling. Our relationships with those around us are affected by nonverbal behaviors such as smiles, eye contact, space parameters, and the like. Rules concerning nonverbal behaviors vary with cultures. What one person considers polite may be offensive to another. Studies show that gender and culture affect how individuals work together and how power is perceived. Since nonverbal communication can be viewed as a 'cultural event' (Guerrero, De Vito & Hecht, 1999), and actions communicate more than words, it makes sense to consider cultural context and how our nonverbal messages are interpreted.

References

Adler, N.J. (2002). *International Dimensions of Organizational Behavior*, Fourth Edition, South-Western.

Aguinis, H. and Henle, C.A. (2001). 'Effects of Nonverbal Behavior on Perceptions of a Female Employee's Power Bases', *Journal of Social Psychology, 141*(4), 537-549.

Bente, G., Donaghy, W.C. and Suwelack, D. (1998). 'Sex Differences in Body Movement and Visual Attention: An Integrated Analysis of Movement and Gaze in Mixed-Sex Dyads', *Journal of Nonverbal Behavior, 22*(1), 31-58.

Burgoon, J.K., Buller, D.B. and Woodall, W.G. (2002). *Nonverbal Communications: The Unspoken Dialogue*, NY: McGraw-Hill.

Dovido, J.F., Kawakani, K. and Gaertner, S.L. (2002). 'Implicit and Explicit Prejudice and Interracial Interaction', *Journal of Personality and Social Psychology, 82*(1), 62-68.

Gueguen, N. and Jacob, C. (2002). 'Direct Look Versus Evasive Glance and Compliance with Request', *Journal of Social Psychology, 142* (3), 393-96.

Guerrero, L.K., De Vito, J.A. and Hecht, M.L. (eds.) (1999). *The Nonverbal Communication Reader*, IL: Waveland Press.

Hall, E.T. and Hall, M.R. (2001). 'The Sounds of Silence', in J.M. Henslin (ed.) *Down to Earth Sociology: Introductory Readings*, New York: The Free Press.

Hamada, T. (1996). 'Unwrapping Euro-American Masculinity in a Japanese Multinational Corporation', in C. Cheng (ed.) *Masculinities in Organizations*, Thousand Oaks, CA: Sage Publications.

Mandal, M.K., Harizuka, S., Bhushan, B., Mishra, R.C. (2001). 'Cultural Variation in Hemifacial Asymmetry of Emotion Expressions', *British Journal of Social Psychology*, *40*, 385-98.

Raudsepp, E. (1993, Sept 24). 'Body Language Speaks Louder Than Words', *Machine Design*, *65*, 85-88.

Reid, M. and Hammersley, R. (2000). *Communicating Successfully in Groups: A Practical Guide for the Workplace*, London: Routledge.

Thompson, R. (1996). 'Actions Speak Louder Than Words', in J. Billsberry (ed.) *The Effective Manager: Perspectives and Illustrations*, pp. 276-286.

Whitelock, D. and Scanlon E. (1998). 'The Roles of Gaze, Gestures, and Gender in CSC', *Journal of Computer Assisted Learning, 14*(2), 158-165.

Chapter 13

Protocols, Rank, and Social Status Influence Communication

Mary Ann Turney

Introduction

In studies on levels of group cultures, Schein (1992) stated that 'culture defines what to pay attention to, what things mean, how to react emotionally to what is going on, and what actions to take in various kinds of situations' (Schein, 1992, p. 23). In considering 'what to pay attention to,' a mark of the aviation industry culture has been the importance of protocols, rank and status.

Historically, the captain in charge of a commercial airliner had high status and authority. These individuals were generally looked upon by most societies as superior in rank both by position and by gender (since nearly all were males). The correct protocol required that their actions and decisions were not to be questioned. Communication between aircraft captains and their support crews became formalized and crews were expected to communicate in the most deferential manner, or, under some 'commanders' to remain silent unless asked a direct question.

An incident recorded by the Aviation Safety Reporting System (ASRS) reflects the problem such protocol can create. A Beech Jet 400 operated by a corporation was involved in a runway incursion at Burlington, Vermont (BVT) in 2001. Excerpts from the FO's (First Officer's) report follow:

> I believe a major contributing factor to this incident was poor CRM. The PIC fails to use proper CRM when you fly with him. There is no mistake that he is the PIC. He is also the Chief Pilot and aside from jeopardizing your job, there is no one to bring your complaints to. He makes all of the decisions on his own with little or no input from the other pilots and is offended if you question him.[1]

The tradition of absolute authority and deferential communication has changed to some degree due to status-related accidents and more than two decades of crew resource management (CRM) re-training in communication techniques. The challenge ahead, however, remains the reconciliation of the remnants of this traditional paradigm with the complexity of the modern aircraft – a complexity which is supplanting the single leader with a crew or team approach to flight management and which is further supplanting national male-only crews with multi-national, mixed gender crew teams.

The new paradigm will likely evolve more rapidly now that the flight crew is essentially sealed off from the cabin crew as a result of security concerns, thus requiring that cabin crew make all decisions related to flight safety.

Another view of the protocol problem is evident in the circumstances of a runway incursion accident that occurred in Detroit, Michigan in 1990. The flight was the Captain's first after an extended medical leave. He was faced with unfamiliar procedures, manuals and checklists. Although the FO was relatively new to airline operations, he had exaggerated his military experiences and rank when sharing his background with the Captain.

The Captain may have been overly impressed with the FO's capabilities and knowledge of Detroit operations, since the FO had indicated that he was familiar with these operations. Consider an excerpt from the dialogue between the Captain and the FO taken from the cockpit voice recorder (CVR):

> Captain: Okay, Jim, you just watch and make sure I go the right way
> FO: Just kinda stay on the ramp here
> Captain: Okay
> Captain: Until the yellow line I guess huh?
> Captain: That fog is pretty bad here
> FO: I'll be broken-hearted if we don't get back
> FO: Hey it looks like it's goin' zero zero out there
> (Later)
> FO: Guess we turn left here
> Captain: Left turn or right turn?
> FO: Yeah, well this is the inner here. We're still goin' for Oscar [taxiway intersection]
> Captain: So a left turn
> FO: Near as I can tell. Man I can't see [expletive] out here
> Captain: Yeah Man this is …
> FO: That's still the inner through that way
> Captain: Okay
> FO: Go that way
> Captain: Okay
> FO: There's Oscar 6 right here
> Captain: Okay, so what do we do here?
> (Shortly after)
> FO: Yeah this is Oscar 6
> Captain: We gotta be below minimums
> FO: Oh yeah. I think they'll tell us
> Captain: Six hundred feet. Now we can see six hundred feet. Think so?
> FO: Naw. I don't think we got six hundred feet

(Shortly after)

FO: Okay I think we might have missed Oscar 6. See a sign here that says ah the arrows to Oscar 5. Think we're on Foxtrot now

(Shortly after)

Captain: This, this a right turn, Jim?

FO: That's the runway

Captain: Okay, we're goin' right over here then

FO: Yeah, that way. Well, wait a minute. Oh (expletive) this, oh, ah. I think we're on ah, Xray [taxiway] here now

Captain: Give him a call and tell him that, ah...

FO: Yeah, this is nine. We're facing one six zero yeah. Cleared to cross it

Captain: When I cross this which way do I go? Right?

FO: Yeah

Captain: This, this is the active runway here, isn't it?

After several minutes of additional confusion, the DC-9 taxied onto the active runway and a collision occurred with a B-727 in the process of taking off.

It appears that there was a role-reversal between the Captain, and the FO. There seemed to be a loss of situation awareness, yet the Captain relied on the FO to tell him their exact location in a dense fog. It may be that adding to the confusion was the protocol that inhibited the Captain from asking directly 'where are we exactly?' and the FO from telling the Captain that he was not sure until they had inadvertently taxied onto the active runway. The result was a collision resulting in 8 fatalities.

This chapter provides a look at research findings relating to protocol, social rank, and status as significant variables affecting the quality and characteristics of communications among individuals of differing status and rank.

Social Rank

Fournier, Moskowitz, and Zuroff (2002) suggested the following as a test of responses to social rank:

> Picture yourself in a one-up position; you are a senior executive responsible for a corporate work team ... A subordinate attacks, criticizing you for a recent decision. Your standing in the eyes of your supervisees is now potentially in jeopardy. What do you do? An extensive range of behavior is at your disposal. Nevertheless, one might expect that certain kinds of behavior would be more typical given your high-ranking position.

> Now picture yourself in the one-down position; you are a junior executive assigned to a corporate work team ... Your supervisor attacks, criticizing you for your recent performance. Your standing

in the eyes of your superior is now potentially in jeopardy. What do you do? Although a range of behavior is once more at your disposal, one might again expect that certain kinds of behavior would be more typical given your low-ranking position (Fournier, Moskowitz, and Zuroff, 2002, 425).

Theorists predict that social rank guides communication strategies used in situations like those described above. However, social rank is a complexity that is frequently guided by external cues such as dominant or subordinate social roles or ranks, or by internal cues, such as dominant or subordinate personality traits.

External Cues

Fournier, Moskowitz, and Zuroff (2002) measured appraisals of threat by asking subjects (randomly selected from industry) to rate the extent to which they felt criticized by another.   Because physical struggles for social rank are relatively rare, people tend to assert social rank through criticism or condescension, which Moskowitz (1994) defines as a form of 'hostile dominance' (Moskowitz, 1994 as cited in Fournier, Moskowitz, & Zuroff, 2002). This study examined the effects of rank on communication in workplaces where individuals were hierarchically organized into supervisor and subordinate positions. Variables considered were perceived criticism, tendencies to use sarcasm, threats, agreeableness and inferiority. It was hypothesized that perceived criticism or condescension would trigger an individual's response 'contingent on his or her rank relationship to the potential adversary' (Fournier, Moskowitz, & Zuroff, p. 426). Appraisals of threat from a subordinate were found to produce retaliation in the form of sarcasm (quarrelsomeness), whereas appraisals of threat from a superior were found to keep the individual from expressing his or her opinions and complying with the supervisor (submissiveness).

These findings were not unlike behaviors observed among flight deck crews where authoritative captains stifled opinions of First Officers and, in some cases, additional crew members by employing sarcasm.   Furthermore, some cultures revealed protocols that restricted supporting members of flight crews from expressing opinions at all.

Internal Cues

Another finding from the work of Fournier, Moskowitz, and Zuroff (2002) revealed that the presence of dominant or subordinate personalities was found to affect whether responses to criticism would be submissiveness or quarrelsomeness. The study examined completed records of interactions over a 20-day period. Participants filled out forms (records) with information that included their appraisals of threat (criticism) and their internal rank and standing (inferiority level). The forms also asked for information pertaining to their behavior relative to each   of   four   measures   of   an   interpersonal   matrix   (submissiveness, quarrelsomeness, dominance, agreeableness) which they were given (Fournier, Moskowitz, & Zuroff, p. 426).

Data were analyzed using mixed linear modeling, taking into account that events are nested within participants and are unbalanced across participants. Results indicated that external rank influences internal rank perceptions and these internal states affect an individual's communication responses. Perceptions of threat or criticism were found to predict either hostility or submission, depending on the rank of the individual being criticized. The study concluded that 'individuals who felt more inferior tended to quarrel more frequently with subordinates and to submit more frequently to superiors' in situations where threat was perceived to exist (Fournier, Moskowitz, & Zuroff, p. 430). In positions of power, these individuals tended to become tyrannical, escalating without provocation to preserve their rank.

These results are reminiscent of findings from early CRM investigations in which individual captains were found to be tyrannical in controlling flight deck communication protocols by means of rank. Other kinds of more subtle rank-related issues persist on today's flight decks. In 2001, China Airlines stopped hiring military pilots over the age of 40 due to the problem of military rank overriding airline rank on the flight deck. If two former military pilots were flying together and one made a mistake, the other, if he were of lower rank in the military, would not say anything about the error even if he were captain of the flight (Dennis, 2001).

Forms of Address and Terms of Reference

Dickey (1997) found that people alter their speech patterns to fit the person they are addressing and the audience. Results from a study of Americans and Europeans ranging in age from 20-75 years indicated that the person being addressed will always affect the speaker's language choice. This may involve choosing to address a person by a formal title or a first name; it may involve use of nicknames, or formal and informal use of the pronoun 'you,' which has more formal options in several languages. Alteration of speech patterns may take many different forms depending on age, status, relationships, and so forth.

Dickey's results revealed that although Accommodation Theory accounts for people altering speech patterns to fit the addressee, such alterations can take different forms. Some speakers bring their speech patterns closer to those of the addressee (convergence) while others emphasize differences in their speech patterns (divergence). The term 'convergence' implies that each person has a standard usage of his/her own and departs from that under certain circumstances.

Accommodation seems to involve shifts in speech style based on non-linguistic characteristics of the addressee. For example, it was observed that when there was greater need for a speaker to gain social approval, the speech pattern showed a greater degree of convergence. In this study the identity of the addressee always had some effect on what language the speaker chose to use (Dickey, 1997).

These findings may suggest that differences in rank among aircrews will affect the language choices of individuals within those crews. The effects may be convergence, i.e., speakers bringing their speech pattern closer to that of the person being addressed, or the effects may be divergence, i.e., the speech pattern is deliberately chosen to differ from that of the person being addressed.

Cultural Protocol and Commissive speech

The modern workplace seems to have replaced traditional directive speech with more commissive speech in which individuals are proactive in committing themselves to activities rather than being ordered to do things (Bilbow, 2002).

In a study of different cultural groups in a large multinational airline corporation in Hong Kong, Bilbow (2002) found that culturally based protocols seemed to influence commissive speech acts of Chinese and Westerners. Commissive speech acts is a term used to include both *offers* and *promises*. *Offers* are uninitiated or spontaneous commitments to 'do something' while *promises* are responses to 'do something' after a suggestion has been made.

After analyzing eleven video-recorded meetings (15 hours), the study results indicated no difference in the number of commissive speech acts between the two cultural groups. However, although the Chinese participated equally in obligating themselves to future action, there were statistically significant differences in the circumstances and directness with which the speech acts were spoken. Western commissive speech took the form of *offers* most frequently, while Chinese speakers generally opted to make *promises* in response to suggestions. Bilbow suggests that this may be the result of the 'predisposition' of Chinese speakers to follow a protocol not to initiate conversation, but to require that responses be explicitly sought. Another factor, according to Bilbow, may be the Chinese speakers' perception of linguistic weakness among native-speakers since English is the language of the corporate culture.

Given the reality of differences among multi-national cultures in what is acceptable protocol, it is evident that the potential for misinterpretation of these differences exists. If the demonstration of willingness of a team member to participate is measured by a protocol such as commissive speech acts, and some groups appear unwilling to actively take on commitments, these groups can be labeled as not team players and this may have negative consequences in how they are perceived by the group (Bilbow, 2002).

Status

Status and Communication on the Flight Deck

Since the flight deck of commercial airliners was identified as a culture highly influenced by status and authority, Palmer, Lack, and Lynch (1995) studied how speech acts were used to define task roles and reveal status-based conflicts. Status generalization theory predicted that 'status exercises authority and control consistently and non-consciously even when status characteristics have no direct association with the task at hand' (Bergerf et al, 1972; Torrance, 1969 as cited in Palmer, Lack, & Lynch, 1995, p. 86). Research studies related to this theory found that high-status individuals assume high-authority roles, thus controlling task-based interactions. But what happens when temporary task demands require low-status individuals to assume high authority?

Palmer, Lack, and Lynch's (1995) study of 44 commercial airline pilot volunteers examined this question. The study considered 'performative speech acts' that were used to define roles and reveal conflicts between authority and status during 39 simulated flights. During these scenarios the transfer of authority was accomplished through speech acts, such as 'I have the airplane' and 'You have the airplane.' These speech acts were termed 'performative' as they are not meant to be true or false, but meant to signal a change in task and relationship between the pilots. It was asserted in the study that by initiating a transfer of flying task, a pilot asserts force on crew to accept a redefinition of roles.

There were 137 transfers of pilot control across 22 crews. In 94%, an initiation and acknowledgement were present. Captains were found to initiate more transfers than first officers. Eight times captains exhibited status-based control by taking over the pilot flying task without performative exchanges found in the other transfers of flying task. In these cases, ambiguity resulted and three times this led to potentially problematic situations in which both pilots were simultaneously manipulating flight controls.

The communication styles during the transfer of flight controls were more indicative of status relationships. Use of mitigated commands demonstrated evidence that the effects of status could be reduced when authority roles were transferred. A direct command style was the sole domain of high-status individuals, but a more polite, less forceful command style was used when a crew member of lower status, such as a First Officer, assumed the higher authority role of manipulating the flight controls. Lower-status crew members increased the number of direct commands when assuming the high-authority role of pilot flying, but the increase was small and First Officers never used direct commands to initiate transfers when in pilot-not-flying (PNF) positions (Palmer, Lack, & Lynch, 1995).

Weick's (1990) Tenerife disaster analysis considered communication in an organizational context. Weick stated that 'Communication dominated by hierarchy activates a different mindset regarding what is and is not communicated and different dynamics regarding who initiates on whom. . . In the cockpit where there is a clear hierarchy . . . it is likely that attempts to create interaction among equals is more complex, less well-learned, and dropped more quickly in favor of hierarchical communication when stress increases' (Weick, 1990, p. 585). When communications are affected by hierarchical tendencies, however, results include potential miscommunication and such behaviors as 'gate-keeping, summarization, changing emphasis within a message, withholding, and changing the nature of the information' (Stohl & Redding, 1987 as cited in Weick, 1990).

Gender Status and Communication

Dovidio et al (1988) studied sex differences in five power-related speaking behaviors. The five power behaviors were: (1) amount of speech, (2) number of speech initiations, (3) rate of gesturing, (4) looking while speaking and (5) looking while listening. Men were found to demonstrate higher levels of power-related behavior, particularly when the task was considered to be a masculine task, such as manipulating the controls of an airplane (Dovidio et al, 1998 as cited in Sitler, 2001). Hulit and Howard (1993) and Tannen (1994) measured interruptions in conversations between males and females. They found that men tended to interrupt both male and female speakers more than women.

Carli's (1999) study of gender and interpersonal power examined patterns of verbal disagreement. Carli found that male subjects increased their disagreements to a greater extent with female peers who were not in agreement with them than with males who disagreed with them. Results suggested that as long as women were agreeable, men used pleasant verbiage, but when women were too direct and resistant to their ideas, men responded more directly and aggressively than they did with other men. The study concluded that men are more persuaded by a man using direct, aggressive verbiage than by a woman using such strategy (Carli, 1999).

Sitler (2001) reported that women's speech tends to be generally less direct than that of men. However, Sitler cited an interesting finding from Linde's study of 'black box' recordings of cockpit conversations. Linde found that crews who used the most indirect speech seemed to function better than other crews. In these crews, captains were less likely to ignore hints from subordinate crew members. As part of Linde's study of talk among cockpit crews in flight simulations, retired but still active pilots observed and rated the performances of the simulation crews. The crews they judged top in performance had a higher rate of mitigation than crews they judged to be poor. Linde concluded that every utterance functions on two levels - the prepositional (what it says) and the relational (what it implies about the speakers' relationships) - crews that attend to the relational level will be better crews (Sitler, 2001).

Robinson and Smith-Lovin (2001) distinguished between cohesion-building humorous utterances that tend to solidify the group and differentiating humorous utterances that tend to define individuals as distinct from the group. Study results suggested that women and low participators used more cohesion-building humor while higher status people (men and high participators) used more differentiating humor.

Summary

Status generalization theory predicts that 'status exercises authority and control consistently and non-consciously even when status characteristics have no direct association with the task at hand' (Bergerf et al, 1972; Torrance, 1969 as cited in Palmer, Lack, & Lynch, 1995, p. 86). Thus, protocol, social rank, and status are variables that affect the characteristics and the quality of our communications.

However, these variables are complex and are sometimes molded by external cues such as social roles, and at other times are molded by internal personality characteristics and perceptions.

The influence of status on communication has been well documented and may alter what is said and what is heard. When communications are affected by hierarchical tendencies, results include a number of potential miscues. Considering the differences among multi-national cultures in what is acceptable protocol, great potential for misinterpretation and misinformation exists. Some recent studies suggest that less hierarchical language, such as that used by women, results in effective crew interaction and coordination.

Note

1 ASRS report number ACN 529903.

References

Bilbow, G.T. (2002). 'Commissive Speech Act Use in Intercultural Business Meetings', *IRAL, 40*, 287-303.

Carli, L.L. (1999). 'Gender, Interpersonal Power, and Social Influence', *Journal of Social Issues, 55*(1), 81-99.

Dennis, W. (2001). 'Asian Carriers Embark on Self-Improvement Course', *Aviation Week and Space Technology, 154* (12), p. 110.

Dickey, E. (1997). 'Forms of Address and Terms of Reference', *Journal of Linguistics, 33*, 255-274.

Dovidio, J.F., Heltman, K.B., Brown, C.E., Ellyson, S.L., and Keating, C.F. (1988, October). 'Power Displays between Women and Men in Discussions of Gender-Linked Tasks: A Multi-Channel Study', *Journal of Personality and Social Psychology*, 580-587.

Fournier, M.A., Moskowitz, D.S., and Zuroff, D.C. (2002). 'Social Rank Strategies in Hierarchical Relationships', *Journal of Personality and Social Psychology, 83*(2), 425-433.

Hulit, H.M. and Howard, M.R. (1993). *Born to Talk*. New York: Macmillan.

National Transportation Safety Board (1995). *Aircraft Accident Report: Runway Incusion, Northwest Flights 1482 and 299J*, 5416B, NTSB/AAR-91/05, U.S. Government Printing Office, Washington, D.C.

Palmer, M.T., Lack, A.M. and Lynch, J.C. (1995, March). 'Communication Conflicts of Status and Authority in Dyadic, Task-Based Interactions: Status Generalization in Airplane Cockpits', *Journal of Language and Social Psychology, 14*(1-2). 85-101.

Robinson, D.T. and Smith-Lovin, L. (2001). 'Getting a Laugh: Gender, Status, and Humor in Task Discussions', *Social Forces, 80* (1), 123-158.

Schein, E.H. (1992). *Organizational Culture and Leadership (Second edition)*. San Francisco: Jossey-Bass.

Sitler, R. (2002, March). 'Gender Communications in the Cockpit', *Proceedings of the Aviation Communications Conference*. Phoenix, AZ: Embry-Riddle Aeronautical University.

Tannen, D. (1994). *Talking from 9 to 5: How Women's and Men's Conversational Styles Affect Who Gets Heard, Who Gets Credit, and What Gets Done at Work*, New York: William Morrow.

Weick, K.E. (1990). The Vulnerable System: An Analysis of the Tenerife Air Disaster', *Journal of Management, 16*, 571-593.

PART III

ENVIRONMENT

Chapter 14

'Who Are You Calling a Safety Threat?' A Debate on Safety in Mono-Cultural Versus Multi-Cultural Cockpits

Ashleigh Merritt and Surendra Ratwatte

Introduction

This paper takes the form of a debate: on the one side, multi-cultural cockpits are argued to be less safe because of language and cultural problems, and different standards and backgrounds. These differences contribute to greater uncertainty and hesitation, which can pose a serious threat to safety. The opposing view argues that mixed-nationality cockpits are no less safe than mono-cultural cockpits, indeed they may be safer, because of the increased compliance with SOP's, and greater reliance on crew resource management principles such as more precise communication and more cross-checking. Data from mono- and multi-cultural airlines will be used to support both arguments.

Commercial aviation is undergoing a boom phase, and will continue to do so, well into the next century. More people are flying, more planes are being built to meet the demand, and more airlines are looking for pilots to fill their expanding needs. More and more, pilots from around the world are being recruited to fill the experience gap – the question is, 'do these mixed-culture crews pose a threat to safety'?

The argument that multicultural crews pose a safety threat will be presented by Dr. Merritt, a researcher who studies culture in aviation. The argument that multicultural crews do not pose a safety threat will be presented by Captain Ratwatte, a pilot at Emirates Airlines who has flown in a multicultural environment for practically his entire career. These opposing views will be reconciled in the conclusion.

Mixed Culture Crews Can be a Safety Threat

The Aerospace Crew Research Project at The University of Texas at Austin has undertaken an extensive study to establish the relationship between national culture and pilots' work values and attitudes (Helmreich & Merritt, 1998; Merritt, 1998, 2000; Sherman, Helmreich, & Merritt, 1997). The survey-based research with 10,000 pilots from 25 airlines in 18 countries has highlighted both the similarities and the differences amongst pilots of different cultures.

There was an almost universal endorsement by pilots of the importance of communication and teamwork; however, the expression of these concepts varied cross-culturally. For example, pilots from Australia, New Zealand, and Ireland were the most assertive and direct in their communication style, while the pilots of Japan and Korea employed a more formal communication style premised on greater concern for harmony and face-saving. Similarly, while more than 85% of pilots in every country disagreed with the command statement that captains who encouraged crewmember questions were weak leaders, the level of endorsement of the statement 'Junior crewmembers should only question the actions of the captain when the safety of flight is threatened' ranged from as little as 9% in one country with egalitarian, low power distance values, to 71% in the country with the most hierarchical orientation. In other words, while there was general endorsement of some CRM concepts (communication, teamwork, and effective leadership), subtle differences emerged when more specific behaviors were rated. This is a common finding in cross-cultural research - the leadership research, for example, shows that while an effective leader is universally described as someone dedicated to both task and relationship issues, the actual behavioral manifestation of these values varies widely across cultures (Smith & Peterson, 1988). I believe this phenomenon accounts for the illusion of cultural similarity in the aviation world - pilots everywhere value safety and high professional codes, but how those codes are enacted is indeed a function of culture.

The strongest cross-cultural differences in our study were observed in the areas of command styles, as mentioned, and tolerance for rules and set procedures. For example, agreement with the item 'Written procedures are required for all in-flight situations' ranged from 16% to 84% across the 18 countries. Other, more idiosyncratic differences which were observed in the data were: Brazilian pilots ranked advancement to high level jobs as their most important work value, while Taiwanese pilots ranked it second to last in a list of 17 work values (consider the implications for employee motivation); American pilots were the only group where less than 50% agreed that senior staff deserve extra benefits and privileges (consider the implications for command interactions); Korean pilots report greater shame when they make a mistake in front of other crewmembers (recall the Korean pilots who chose to stay in their burning cockpit after crashing); Filipino pilots view their airline as being like a large family, and favor a more benign, paternalistic command style (this applies to captains as well as management); Taiwanese pilots show the strongest preference for rules and set routines (consider the level of proceduralization and adherence!); and Anglo pilots (from Australia, British Hong Kong, Ireland, New Zealand, and the USA) were united in ranking sufficient time away from the job for personal or family life as their number one work value (consider the implications for organizational commitment versus personal concerns) (Merritt, 1996). This sampler of differences is designed to highlight the subtle and not-so-subtle differences between pilots in their attitudes toward leadership, communication, and preference for rules.

Given that these differences exist, it is not difficult to imagine the confusion that some mixed-culture crews must experience. Putting an overly assertive, egalitarian-minded first officer with a hierarchically minded captain who expects deference could be very disruptive. Similarly, a pilot who was trained to operate the automation 'by the book' could be frustrated with a co-pilot who prefers to disengage the automation, and exercise some personal discretion with the flight. Consider these comments taken from a survey of pilots working for a multi-national airline in the Middle East. Their frustrations included:

- Cultures where the captain is treated as a god and he himself treats others with modest disdain. Creates friction with crewmembers from other cultures.
- When customs dictate there is only one captain and he is not to be questioned - occasionally non-standard procedure required and there is marked inability of independent thought and over-reliance on the captain.
- When there is a cultural reluctance to advise a more senior person of an observed mistake.
- Some nationalities have a cultural background that does not foster self-criticism! Errors made by them are often covered up.
- Dealing with problems encountered with crews whose culture fears loss of face.

These comments, primarily from Anglo-Western pilots who favor low power distance and open discussion in the cockpit, indicate real sources of friction with other nationalities. Another serious frustration derives from not knowing the other crewmember's flight experience and training background. Interestingly, comments from some European and Asian pilots point to the ethnocentric assumptions of some Anglo-Western pilots regarding their own 'superior' flying skills. As one pilot commented 'it is sad that most every other nationality is ready to acknowledge the need to alter their behavior to compensate, but some Anglos do not'. Such an attitude can be difficult to tolerate, and does not encourage teamwork.

Add language to the above differences and the level of confusion and resultant hesitation intensifies. Some native English speakers at the Middle Eastern airline said that it requires greater effort and concentration to ensure no confusion exists and that the time spent ensuring understanding can be at the expense of aircraft monitoring. Meanwhile some non-native speakers of English commented that English speakers do not speak distinctly. Clearly, there is a huge difference between the normative mandate that English be the language of the cockpit, and the reality of pilots speaking in other than their first language - a very high level of linguistic proficiency is needed before one can communicate freely, openly, and without hesitation. The following concerns (translated into English) were voiced by Chinese pilots who work with a minority of expatriate captains in their airline.

- Because communication is difficult, it is easy to misunderstand each other in emergency situations.
- In an emergency situation crew coordination became slower due to the communication.
- Under an emergency, there is big trouble for communication.
- The most frustrating thing is if there is an emergency situation. Communication will be a big problem.
- There is no problem under normal situations, but the communication speed would be a problem under emergency.

These are honest concerns for safety under emergency conditions. And let's not forget religion, politics, economics, humor, and history. The average dinner party can barely survive these differences - what hope does the multi-cultural cockpit have! Pilots have commented that relationships on duty are not as relaxed as with members of the same nationality because of customs conflict, and that long flights can be oppressive because of language barriers, and different senses of humor. Social separation post flight, based on rank or cultural group, also makes it difficult to establish a team spirit or group identity. A study of civilian aircraft concluded that safe cockpits are characterized by open communication, good fellowship and helpfulness (Redding & Ogilvie, 1984). Multinational crews appear to be seriously compromised in both regards - language barriers and cultural differences are inhibiting the open communication and team fellowship needed for safe flying. In summary, cultural differences, variations in aviation experience and background, and linguistic difficulties can all lead to uncertainty and hesitation at best, and frustration, resentment, and paranoia at worse. These behaviors can be hazardous in time-pressure situations, which is why I argue that multi-cultural cockpits can pose a serious safety threat.

Mixed-Culture Crews Are no More a Threat to Safety Than Mono-Cultural Crews - In Fact They May be Safer!

America may well claim to be the birthplace of aviation, and Americans certainly dominate the aviation industry, both as manufacturers and operators. Yet, not even the USA can claim to have the ideal attributes for the operation of complex multi-crew aircraft.

When I started my airline career, the company I worked for had many expatriate captains. They were a motley crew, mainly British, but with a handful of Americans, Europeans, Australians and Indians among them. Some of them, much more than others, were a real pleasure to fly with. Not merely relying on a good knowledge of the airplane and their own flying skills to carry the day, they had other talents that were hard to pin down. They had the ability to make everyone [no matter what his or her background or position] feel important, never talked down to anyone and constantly asked for and considered the opinions of the entire crew. We were all made to feel like important members of the team, no matter how young or inexperienced we were. It was only later that I realized this holistic approach to safety could be quantified. It is what we called CRM, before the shrinks had managed to reduce it to an industry.

I do not agree with my colleague's argument that multi-cultural crews pose a safety threat for several reasons - in fact I believe that in many ways multi-cultural cockpits are safer and more efficient. But let me begin by asking the fundamental question 'Is there even such a thing as a purely mono-cultural crew'? National culture apart, aren't we ignoring corporate and occupational cultures? Many airlines these days are the products of mergers, while the pilots themselves may well have come from less successful companies. How does this all tie together in the cockpit? For example, take two well known Texas based US airlines. One is that phenomenally successful major domestic carrier, well known for its cohesive nature and *joie de vivre*, the other a huge international company staffed with pilots from many different airlines that have long since disappeared. I have friends in both companies and know that they have very different organizational cultures despite their geographical proximity. Add to this the size of your country and 'commuting' lifestyle of many US pilots, where the crew could easily live in different parts of America. Cultures within the US differ widely from coast to coast. [Try telling a New Yorker he is culturally the same as a Texas cowhand or a West Coast surfer and see what reaction you get.] Whither cultural commonality now?

Definitions aside, there is absolutely no statistical evidence to support an assumption that a multi-cultural cockpit is any less safe than a mono-cultural one. While accidents tend to be geographically specific, they are *not* culturally specific. Of the three major accidents in Central/South America last year for instance, only one was a Latin American airline. The others were a North American carrier and a European one. The poor safety record in South America can be accounted for by a combination of high mountains, poor infrastructure and relatively crowded skies. Culture plays very little part in any of this. Neither Boeing, ICAO, ISASI, IATA, or the NTSB have yet to identify expatriate pilots as a threat to safety!

CRM as 'a way of life' is a controversial concept, especially in highly individualistic societies. Remember that at this symposium we are preaching to the converted. As my distinguished colleague is well aware, despite the demonstrated value of CRM, there are many 'boomerangs' out there, pilots who pay lip-service to the discipline but proceed to ignore it on the line. Safe within the confines of one's own national culture, this is an easy slope to slide down. When working as an expatriate, though, this is another luxury that is not available. Every day is spent in a foreign culture. It becomes necessary to use the principles of CRM all the time, not just to pass a check-ride. So, in effect, provided the principles are presented in a convincing manner, for many of us CRM becomes a useful tool in coping with life in a strange land. What works in the cockpit, seems to also work in Flight Operations, other departments of the company, and in fact, almost anywhere we have to deal with people on a daily basis. It starts to become routine, for the unspoken assumptions and agreements that one makes so effortlessly in one's own culture, are no longer an option. Every statement has to be considered carefully - there are employees from over 70 nationalities within my company and it is all too easy to offend. This is not to say that we do not have our problem employees, just that those who stay with the company learn to adjust, some sooner than others.

Complacency and broad assumptions should have no place in any cockpit. The varied mix of people we fly with and the fact that English is a second language for many of them, makes it vital that the thought process be articulated very clearly. Clear, concise verbalization of intent and requirements must take place and be undertaken 'by the book'. This leads to a high degree of SOPs being used, as it is otherwise all too easy to get confused. Our pilots are forced to cross-check constantly, in order to confirm that what was discussed is what is being done. After a while this becomes natural, a definite plus for safety. As airlines in the USA struggle with issues of complacency, poor checklist usage, and slipping adherence to SOP's (Hines, in press), they might do well to consider the most commonly cited statement of the Chinese pilots who work with expatriates: '...all will be well if everyone follows SOP's'.

That ephemeral quality known as 'the professional pilot culture' ensures that all pilots, regardless of their backgrounds, work to the highest standards. Ours is a calling with perhaps the highest degree of self-selection in the world. Anybody who has had to jump through as many hoops, be poked and prodded as often, and lose as many nights' sleep, must be highly motivated. Safety, even more than a smooth landing or an active sex life, is what pilots really desire. A boringly smooth and uneventful flight is what pilots crave, no matter where they come from or what language they speak.

And let's not forget religion, politics, humor and history. Surprisingly, many pilots share a similar sense of humor, though the jokes are not exactly 'Politically Correct'. Even politics crops up, and can be an eye-opener. Having Islam explained by a committed and articulate Muslim whom one respects as a competent professional, helps to clarify many misconceptions. But, what do pilots from different cultures talk about most? The same thing that pilots from the same culture talk about - aviation! It becomes easily the dominant topic, which can greatly enhance a new recruit's learning curve. We have pilots who have flown to just about every major airport in the world, including those in the former USSR and mainland China. Some of their insights and experiences are promulgated through company publications or policies. Even more of it is shared in the conversations that take place in the cockpit during those long night flights. This valuable exchange of knowledge cannot be quantified, nor can it be easily formalized. The likelihood of such a barter taking place, however, is much greater in a multi-cultural airline due to the paucity of neutral topics, and also the variety of experiences between the pilots. 'Local knowledge' is invaluable, and is much easier to unearth in a company that recruits from all over the world.

Regardless of the country of origin, any international flight by its very definition, is a multi-cultural experience. In CRM, the more one practices the principles and techniques of the discipline, the more adept one becomes. So too, a crew well versed in dealing with many cultures and accents within the cockpit, is better positioned to cope with a variety of such inputs from outside. Anyone who has heard an American pilot trying to cope with rapid-fire instructions from Paris ATC in *franglais,* will know what I'm talking about. Quite often another pilot will intercede and translate the instructions, much to the relief of everyone else.

There is also a darker side to being an expatriate. Pilots who fly in their native countries enjoy a degree of union representation probably unmatched in other professions. This protection is not usually available to the expatriate. The only safeguards we have is for the organization to lay down the boundaries and procedures very clearly, and for the individual to interpret them conservatively. While this may occasionally make for an inefficient operation, it certainly ensures a safe one.

These then, are the strengths of flying in a multi-cultural environment. Communication, both within and without the flight deck, tends to be clearer and more standardized. Pilots tend to be more adaptable to different accents and methods of doing things. There is a greater reservoir of experience to draw from, and a wider dissemination of this knowledge due to aviation being sometimes the only common interest. CRM becomes the linchpin that holds all this together, rather than just a passing fad.

Resolution

Given the evidence from both sides, can there be a resolution of this issue? We believe so. First, one fact that has emerged is that perhaps there is no such thing as a truly mono-cultural cockpit, that all cockpits are a blend of national, regional, organizational and occupational sub-cultures. Equally so, it is the blend of cultures that ultimately determines the airline's strengths and weaknesses, such that no two airlines share the same concerns. For the airline based in East Asia, where local pilots are the majority and expatriate pilots are the minority, language is the most fundamental barrier to safe operations. In Emirates Airlines, where expatriate pilots are the majority, but management is still local, then the expats tend to form their own culture bonded by their common experiences as 'outsiders'.

Second, both arguments acknowledge the importance of culture in the cockpit. While one side argues that cultural differences can be problematic, the other side states that cultural awareness, flexibility and a 'best practices' approach can introduce safeguards into the system which enhance efficiency, as well as safety.

Finally, both arguments suggest that the same qualities that make a good pilot anywhere also make a good multi-cultural pilot, anywhere. The best pilots are not only technically competent, but they are also aware and respectful of their fellow crewmembers, they show a healthy respect for SOP's and other organizational policies, they utilize CRM strategies as a means of managing various cockpit activities, they are dedicated to safe and professional practice, and they will go the extra distance to ensure that a high level of safety is maintained. By comparison, a pilot who performs poorly in his/her own country, perhaps a boomeranger with poor acceptance of CRM concepts, may perform even more poorly or more rigidly as an expatriate pilot in a foreign environment.

Recommendations

The following safety recommendations were written specifically for multi-cultural airlines. However, if one can accept that every airline is in fact 'multi-cultural' then many of the suggestions can be seen as applicable to all operators.

We believe there are several ways in which a multi-cultural airline can promote safety. The first is to set clear organizational standards and policies that eliminate previous cultural assumptions and explicate all the organization's goals and procedures. A pilot from Pakistan can then work effectively with one from Papua New Guinea, because both can expect to see their performance standards mirrored by the other.

Training is the second tool for enhancing safety. When asked how Emirates could maintain or improve its current safety record, the answer from pilots was 'Train, train, train'. LOFT in particular becomes a powerful means of rehearsing the company standards and procedures. Indeed more training time may be needed to ensure that all pilots, regardless of background, perform to the company standard during normal *and* abnormal conditions, with sufficient remedial training offered as required. Emergency procedures training could focus on greater co-ordination of cockpit and cabin. CRM and situation awareness (SA) debriefings should be considered an integral part of recurrent training, and emphasis placed on their value in an organization committed to diversity.

Two other forms of non-technical training could also be considered. Intercultural awareness training could be provided to expatriate pilots, their families, *and* the host nationals. This training, before and after arrival in the new country, will facilitate quicker adaptation to the new environment, stronger co-operation (and less defensiveness) amongst the pilots, and more effective long-term performance of the company.

Language training may also be necessary. English is the official language of aviation and its practice should be mandated, however, language training is not just for the non-native speaker of English. Anglo pilots, who have been arbitrarily granted the linguistic advantage, should be taught how to communicate simply, slowly, and precisely with non-Anglo personnel as required. All pilots should strive for open and unambiguous communication in the cockpit - one pilot's struggle to be precise in his second or third language should be matched by another pilot's willingness to listen closely and respond simply, without condescension or colloquialisms.

The third area in which a multi-cultural airline can enhance its safety prospects is through recruitment. Pilots should be selected not only for their technical competence but also for their potential to be interculturally effective. If we define an expatriate's effectiveness as a combination of on-the-job performance, personal and family adjustment, and length of stay with the company, then the best predictors are openness, flexibility, patience, maturity, stability, self-confidence, perseverance, problem-solving, tolerance, professional commitment, and initiative (Kealey, 1996). These qualities ensure that a pilot's technical competence is demonstrated in a culturally sensitive manner, ensuring optimal performance and exchange of skills.

Conclusion

If we have not been too obscure, then the resolution and recommendations for safety should reveal our true agenda in writing this paper. We believe that *culture can be a problem in the cockpit, but only if its influence goes unacknowledged.* As a result, a well-managed multi-cultural cockpit is as safe as any other well-managed cockpit, although some of the safety concerns may differ. Therefore, in any airline, it is Management's role not only to define and then recruit the best pilots, but also to diagnose the strengths and weaknesses of the operation, and design organizationally-appropriate, culturally-sensitive interventions which will optimize the safety and performance of all its employees. All airlines should strive for a safety culture to which their members can subscribe.

Postscript, 2003

This paper was originally written for an aviation conference in 1997. At the time the authors were interested in presenting two sides of an argument about culture. Since then Dr. Merritt has worked in France for 2 years and returned to the USA, and Captain Ratwatte has been promoted from flying the line to the position of Manager, Human Factors, at Emirates Airlines. When asked to contribute this paper to the current volume, we asked ourselves, 'What has changed since we wrote the paper 6 years ago?'

(Merritt) In many ways, the topic of culture in aviation has not progressed beyond this point. There may be pragmatic reasons for this lack of progress associated with the logistic difficulties of organizing cross-cultural research. There may also be political reasons in as much as some members of the dominant culture in aviation may have a vested interest in maintaining the status quo, i.e, encouraging unquestioned acceptance of and assimilation into the dominant model of aviation practices (Merritt, 2003). However, this view may be changing. The International Civil Aviation Organization (ICAO) intends to publish in 2004 a Human Factors Digest—'Cross-cultural Factors in Aviation Safety'--that presents the safety case underpinning culture and aviation. With the official support of ICAO, cultural issues may finally draw greater attention.

(Ratwatte) While little has changed in the academic arena regarding culture, the world has been shocked and destabilized by cultural forces. September 11, 2001 ushered in a new era of ethnocentrism prompted by fear of the unknown. The world's differences have been exaggerated and polarized, not reduced as some might hope. How has this affected aviation?

- The atmosphere of tolerance, impartiality and pluralism, qualities that were the most admired characteristics of western society, are under threat. The current US Administration is unashamedly jingoistic and this attitude has even infected the press. Anyone who watched the Iraqi war on Fox TV will know what I am talking about. Since airline pilots are not known to be very liberal at the best of times, how long before this attitude insinuates its way into the flightdeck as well?

- Many individuals of visible minorities (i.e. non-white, including myself) are not wholly comfortable traveling around the US anymore. This is not mere prejudice. When the US will not issue 'crew visas' to pilots wishing to take delivery of new aircraft from the sole surviving American manufacturer because of their religion and (possibly) appearance, there is something wrong. Even long term legal residents of the US who are from certain areas of the world feel under threat to the extent that many have left the country (Wall Street Journal, Nov. 2002).

- Certainties have been questioned. The industry is shaky and leading airlines (salary wise) are almost bankrupt.

- Given the state of the airlines in the West, there is now a global oversupply of pilots. The urgent need to train local nationals in the absence of other sources of pilots does not exist. Added to this is the fact that flying airplanes is a profession that is not so attractive anymore. Travel is not what it used to be and pilots are not the respected figures they once were.

- As a result of the world schism, training appears to be more difficult than it used to be. Overtly western behaviors are not readily accepted by non-western pilots. Sometimes, when the individuals or the company are secure enough there is outright rejection. In other cases, lip-service is given to these concepts in order to conclude the training, followed soon thereafter by reversion to manners they are more comfortable with.

- The flightdeck was one place where this writer (among others) found a haven of peace and understanding. What mattered was whether one could fly an airplane or not. Politics were left on the ground along with your personal problems – or such was the myth that the pilot fraternity subscribed to. It has been proven to be wrong on both counts, to the detriment of the profession and society in general.

It is our hope that cultural differences may one day be acknowledged, explored, and accepted in a way that promotes greater aviation safety and prosperity.

References

Helmreich, R.L., and Merritt, A.C. (1998). *Culture at Work in Aviation and Medicine: National, Organizational, and Professional Influences.* (Paperback edition 2001) Aldershot: Ashgate.

Hines, W.E. (1998). 'Flight Crew Performance in Standard and Advanced Technology Aircraft', in *Proceedings of the Ninth International Symposium on Aviation Psychology*, Columbus OH: Ohio State University.

Kealey, D. (1996). 'The Challenge of International Personnel Selection, in D. Landis and R. Bhagat (Eds.), *Handbook of Intercultural Training* (2nd. Ed.) London: Sage.

Merritt, A.C. (1996). *National Culture and Work Attitudes in Commercial Aviation: A Cross-Cultural Investigation.* Unpublished doctoral dissertation, University of Texas at Austin.

Merritt, A.C. (2000). 'Culture in the Cockpit: Do Hofstede's Dimensions Replicate'? *Journal of Cross-Cultural Psychology, 31*, 283-301.

Merritt, A.C. (2003). 'Aviation Safety: Dominant and Minority Culture Obligations', in *Proceedings of the Twelfth International Symposium on Aviation Psychology*, Columbus, OH: Ohio State University.

Redding, S.G., and Ogilvie, J.G. (1984). 'Cultural Effects on Cockpit Communications in Civilian Aircraft', *Flight Safety Foundation Conference, Zurich.* Washington: Flight Safety Foundation.

Sherman, P.J., Helmreich, R.L., and Merritt, A.C. (1997). 'National culture and Flightdeck Automation: Results of a Multi-National Survey', *International Journal of Aviation Psychology, 7* (4), 311-29.

Smith, P.B., and Peterson, M.F. (1988). *Leadership, Organizations, and Culture.* London: Sage.

Chapter 15

Inclusive Versus Exclusive Strategies in Aviation Training

Mary Ann Turney, Irene Henley, Mary Niemczyk, William K. McCurry

Introduction

Successful training and education programs focus on the varying instructional needs of diverse students. Important differences related to learning exist universally and have broad implications in the aviation industry, an industry that must compete for the talent of the increasingly diverse worldwide workforce. The ability to address cross-cultural, racioethnic, and gender differences is essential in making aviation education and training more inclusive. The increased use of computer-based instruction and distance learning technologies are key factors in developing aviation programs applicable to a multicultural environment. Guidelines for Inclusive Course/Model Development provide specific focus for inclusive strategies and offer the training organization an opportunity to define and create learning and training environments that are inclusive.

Diverse Learners

One of the challenges for aviation educators and trainers is to meet the learning needs of their diverse students in the development and delivery of programs. Both individually and collectively, learners are of a heterogeneous nature – they may come from many different ethnic backgrounds, may be from different socio-economic groups, may be men or women, and may come from various geographical areas. These multiple factors have an impact on the nature and extent of both their access to education and training and its relevance to their needs. Similarly, the broader social and cultural context has a significant impact on the experiences of learners in gaining access to and enjoying a productive learning experience.

Flannery (1994) suggests that 'learning theories based on individualism and autonomy reflect values and attributes that are primarily Western, white, middle-class, and male.... [However], individualism is not equally valued by all groups even within our [American] society. For example, the value orientations and learning processes of persons of non-European cultural background ... tend to be based on communal and collective values' (p. 22). Hayes and Colin (1994) point out that both formal and informal curricula can promote racist and sexist beliefs. Implicitly or explicitly, training programs are susceptible to the exclusion of certain groups of people because of how we conceptualise the learner.

Exclusion in aviation educational contexts can be seen at many levels. It can occur in the ways in which the notion of the 'learner' is generalized and embedded in learning theory. For example, if we assume that learners are individualistic, goal-oriented, and competitive, we limit methodology to support only this type of learner and exacerbate the tokenism effect on other learners who do not fit the paradigm. In this way, we limit access to some individuals and decrease the available talent pool of learners.

Learning Style and Orientation

In developing training programs that avoid exclusive strategies, it is important to look at how individual students learn and why they succeed. Classroom instructors, for example, must be aware of the need to present information in ways that satisfy a variety of learning styles. Although lecture or textual presentations are somewhat effective for learners who have little knowledge of the subject area, facilitation is more effective for learners who need to be engaged in setting goals and using previous knowledge and experience. From the literature on adult learners, we know that adult learners are practical and seek application of their knowledge. They are responsive to action-oriented learning and when they see a need for learning something, they are resourceful (Karp, Turney & McCurry, 1999). In addition, if a new skill is learned but there is no immediate opportunity for its use, the skill or knowledge will fade (Zemke & Zemke, 1995). Continual review and recurrent learning are therefore essential.

Gender Differences

According to the Society for Neuroscience (1998), clear evidence exists regarding brain functional differences between women and men. Shaywitz (1995) was first able to demonstrate the functional differences between the brains of men and women. Her study showed 'actual differences in the parts of the brain used when men and women were thinking and coming up with the same answers' [1] With magnetic resonance images of a man's brain and a women's brain, Shaywitz was able to demonstrate clearly that in decoding words, men use a small area on one side of the brain, whereas women use areas on both sides of the brain simultaneously. A number of researchers suggested that women perform differently from men on spatial tasks. For example, women are more rapid at identifying matching items, a skill called perceptual speed (Kimura, 1992). In summary, 'regardless of the specific underlying neuropsychological interpretation, left hippocampal activity in men and right frontoparietal activity in women reflect the gender-specific recruitments that differentiate male from female subjects' (Gron, Wunderlich, Spitzer, et al, 2000).

About ten years ago, Tannen (1990) elicited surprise when she stated that women's and men's learning preferences are different. Her research revealed that men prefer debate-like situations in which they pursue knowledge by ritual opposition, while women like to share and learn by interacting in a collaborative manner. Years earlier, Gilligan's (1982) research found that authoritative systems were more important to men in defining relationships than to women and Belenky, Clinchy, Goldberger and Tarule (1986) contended that women value affiliation and acceptance more then do men. Women were also found to be more participatory than men in their learning styles (Emanuel & Potter, 1992). Thus, women seek collaborative and cooperative learning environments (Turney, Sitler, & Wulle, 1996).

Sitler's extensive study (1999) on flight training of women suggested that confidence was a significant factor in women's learning. Stuart's in-depth study (1999) of 27 women pilots, revealed that 'women's need for explanations [during flight training] may be an issue of confidence. It may be that a woman is so afraid of doing something wrong in an airplane that she wants to know all that she can possibly know about why she is doing something, so she will not make a mistake. Knowing all about something builds her confidence' (p.49).

Competition Issue

Student achievement is not only driven by potential, but also by motivation - how students feel about what they are learning (Inglehart, Brown & Vida, 1994, p. 311). For example, women do not persist in undergraduate concentrations like medicine as well as men. This leads to the question of whether competitive career fields may have a different appeal to male and female students and, as a result, may affect persistence rates for men and women differently.

Reactions to competition are based on the differing appraisal processes of women and men. The more either group values competition, the better the members will perform. However, 'when men and women look at a competitive environment, they focus on different aspects' (Inglehart, Brown & Vida, 1994, p. 317). Men focus more on the challenge of the situation. Women focus more on the person-related issues. In fact, women were found to avoid conversations or get-togethers when they perceive the environment to be competitive.

The relationships between competition and performance were tested with a group of 534 subjects (330 male and 204 female) who were in their second year in an AB-MD (medical) program at the University of Michigan. Factor analyses were done on four competition measures including students' own values of competition, their evaluations of the faculty values, and their evaluation of the competitive tone of the school environment (Inglehart, Brown and Vida, 1994, p. 321).

For women, the more competitive they perceived the environment to be, the less well they performed because they appeared to focus more on personal and relational issues, whereas the more men perceived the environments as competitive, the better they performed apparently because they focused more on the achievement-related aspects of competition.

New Methods, New Technology

Student-centered learning. Student-centered learning is a recent re-focus in education that allows learners to process information more completely and use their knowledge more effectively as new situations occur. Student-centered learning is adaptable to individual differences in learning styles, culture, and gender. This methodology offers the student decision-making opportunities, develops problem-solving strategies, and allows learners to process information through self-discovery. Thus learners are able to use their knowledge more effectively as new situations occur.

When students become adept at addressing their uniqueness and examining content at multiple levels of complexity, understanding is deepened and student retention is increased. Student-centered approaches involve connecting knowledge with context. Individuals who discover what information is needed to solve a specific real-world problem uniquely determine meaning. Through Internet technology, students can be provided with learning environments of unprecedented power and potential for authentic situated problem solving. It is the solving of authentic problems that provides evidence that there is true understanding. (Land, & Hannafin, 1996).

Computer-based instruction and distance education. Computer-based instruction and distance learning have the potential to provide students with the support necessary to meet their individual needs and achieve their individual learning goals (Winecki, 1999). If computer-based instruction is well designed, it can meet the challenge of supporting success among students of widely varying backgrounds, cultures, and needs. Too often, instructional designers and curriculum developers have become enamored of the latest technologies without dealing with the underlying issues, such as learner characteristics and needs, the influence of instructional media upon the learning process and the active role of the student in that learning process (Sherry, 1996).

Software ease of use, for example, is critical to promoting success in computer-assisted instruction. If the students continually need help in overcoming obstacles in the software, they will quickly become frustrated (Heinich, Molenda, Russell, & Smaldino, 1998).

The role of the students changes significantly in a computer-based learning course or in a distance education situation. No longer are students in a passive role of note-taking during lectures, but are now active and responsible for their learning. They are expected to construct their own knowledge by working individually, with other students, and interactively with instructors. Students need preparation to make the transition to more active technology-based learning environments (Twigg, 1999). This is especially true for student populations whose previous experience involved only passive learning and unquestioning agreement with the instructor-authority figure.

How best to assist students with strategies for learning is another important consideration in a computer-based learning setting. These strategies include how to organize time, tools, and materials to complete tasks. Students need to be acquainted with concepts such as time budgeting, delayed gratification, and scheduled self-reinforcement. They need to know how to estimate the length of time a task will take to complete and how to create a suitable working environment with minimal distractions (Cates, 1991).

Several studies focusing on distance learning have found that learners in this environment had trouble distinguishing important features and facts from unimportant or extraneous ones. Students need help in learning to recognize the distinction. Not only must they be able to identify the relevant from the irrelevant, but they must also understand what characteristics distinguish the two. If we do not teach this to our students, we can expect many unsuccessful learners to continue to focus on extraneous content and we can expect many more teaching experiences where we wonder how on earth students could have missed the point (Cates, 1991).

Many instructors were themselves good students who learned easily. Consciously, or unconsciously, they picked up the 'tricks of the trade,' the techniques that learners use to handle and retain greater amounts of information or to pass examinations. Such instructors may tend to believe, therefore, that their students know these same techniques or will easily adapt to what is required. Such assumptions are reminiscent of early flight instructor methods of 'do as I do' or 'watch me and do it the same way.' Today, however, educators need to assist students to understand how to employ a wide range of learning strategies (Cates, 1991). This assistance is particularly critical when the instructor is not physically present, or when the instructor is creating a learning module that will reach students through computer-based instruction or distance learning.

Inclusive Strategies

There are distinct strategies that can be implemented to improve the access of all learners to education. Golding, Volkoff and Ferrier (1997) summarise strategies for improving access, participation, and outcomes for identified groups. A number of writers have addressed the issues of ensuring that curriculum is more inclusive. 'Inclusivity in the curriculum requires dealing with at least some of the differences among people based on the factors of race, ethnicity, economic class, gender, age, ability/disability, sexual orientation, and so on' (Tisdell, 1995, p. 13 cited in Merriam & Caffarella, 1999, pp. 343-344). Within the aviation context, Turney (1995) recommends ways in which Crew Resource Management (CRM) training can be improved by taking into consideration gender-related differences in both learning and leadership styles.

The following guidelines have been adapted from draft guidelines developed by TAFE (Training and Further Education) NSW (New South Wales) (1997) to assist course/module writers and curriculum developers in preparing inclusive curricula. The intent is to provide a checklist and examples to help ensure that programs are inclusive of all groups of learners. The checklist provided in the Addendum to this chapter includes specific questions listed under 'key components of developing a course/module:'

1. Title and Description
2. Planning, Content and Choice of Materials (Anecdotal, examples)
3. Language and Delivery (visual aids)
4. Assessment Methodology

[See Addendum for specific guidelines]

Organizational Support

The culture and value system of an organization is a key influence on the development of training programs that are inclusive - and thus on students' learning. Cox and Beale (1997) define inclusivity as 'creating a climate in which the potential advantages of diversity for organizational or group performance are maximized while the potential disadvantages are minimized' (p. 2). The literature on mergers and acquisitions provides some examples of factors that affect acculturation. One of these is the degree to which the organization values diversity and adapts its functions to that end. 'Organizations which do not place a high value on diversity will tend to impose pressure on all members to conform to a single system of existing organizational norms and values' (Cox & Beale, 1997, p. 208). But as the workforce becomes more culturally diverse with mergers and joint ventures, organizations that have traditionally been monocultural need to shift toward a multicultural environment in which inclusive strategies are the norm.

Note

1 'Men and women use brain differently, study discovers', *New York Times*, February 16, 1995.

References

Belenky, M., Clinchy, B., Goldberger, J. and Tarule, J. (1986). *Women's Ways of Knowing: The Development of Self, Voice, and Mind*, New York: Basic Books.

Cates, W.M. (1991). 'What We Need to Teach Students before They Work on Computer-Assisted Instruction: Lessons Gleaned from CAI Failures', *International Journal of Instructional Media, 18* (2), 129-140.

Cox, T. and Beale, R. (1997). *Developing Competency to Manage Diversity.* San Francisco, CA: Berrett-Koehler.

Emanuel, R.C. and Potter, W.J. (1992). 'Do Students' Style Preferences Differ by Grade Level, Orientation toward College, and Academic Major'? *Research in Higher Education, 33,* 395-414.

Flannery, D.D. (1994). 'Changing Dominant Understandings of Adults as Learners', in E. Hayes and S.A.J. Colin III (eds.), *Confronting racism and sexism,* San Francisco: Jossey-Bass, pp. 17-26.

Gilligan, C. (1982). *In a Different Voice,* Cambridge, MA: Harvard University Press.

Golding, B., Volkoff, V. and Ferrier, F. (1997). *Stocktake of Equity Reports and Literature in Vocational Education and Training,* Brisbane: Australian National Training Authority.

Gron, G., Wunderlich, M., Spitzer, et al. (2000, April). 'Brain Activation during Human Navigation: Gender-Different Neural Networks as Substrate of Performance', *Nature Neuroscience 3* (4), 404-408.

Hayes, E. and Colin, S.A.J. III. (1994). 'Racism and Sexism in the United States: Fundamental Issues', in E. Hayes and S.A.J. Colin III (eds.), *Confronting Racism and Sexism,* San Francisco: Jossey-Bass, pp. 5-16.

Heinich, R., Molenda, M., Russell, J.D. and Smaldino, S. (1998). 'Computers', in *Instructional Media and Technologies for Learning,* Prentice Hall, pp. 199-219.

Inglehart, M, Brown, D.R. and Vida, M. (1994). 'Competition, Achievement, and Gender: A Stress Theoretical Analysis,' in P.R. Pintrich, D. R Brown, and C. E Weinstein, (eds.) *Student Motivation, Cognition, and Learning,* Matawah, NJ: Erlbaum.

Karp, R., Turney, M.A. and McCurry, W. (1999). 'Learning Style Theory and Aviation Education', *Proceedings of the Tenth Annual International Symposium on Aviation Psychology,* Columbus, OH: Ohio State University.

Kimura, D. (1992, September). 'Sex Differences in the Brain', *Scientific American,* 119-125.

Land, S.M. and Hannafin, M.J. (1996). 'Student-Centered Learning Environments: Foundations, Assumptions, and Implications', ERIC document: ED 397810.

Merriam, S.B. and Cafarrella, R.S. (1999). *Learning in adulthood — A comprehensive guide,* San Francisco: Jossey-Bass.

Pintrich, P.R. (1995). 'Understanding Self-Regulated Learning', in P.R. Pintrich (ed.), *Understanding Self-Regulated Learning,* San Francisco, CA: Jossey-Bass, pp. 10-11.

Sherry, L. (1996). Issues in Distance Learning, *International Journal of Educational Telecommunications, 1* (4), 337-365.

Sitler, R. (1999). 'The Cockpit Classroom: Women's Perceptions of Learning to Fly and Implications for Flight Curriculum and Instruction', *Proceedings of the Tenth Annual International Symposium on Aviation Psychology,* Columbus, OH: Ohio State University.

Stuart, R. (1999). 'Gender Differences in the Cockpit', *New Zealand Wings.*

TAFE NSW (1997). *Draft Guidelines for Inclusive and Key Competency-rich Curriculum/Module Development,* Sydney, Australia: TAFE, NSW.

Tannen, D. (1990). *You Just Don't Understand: Women and Men in Conversation*. New York: Ballentine Books.

Turney, M.A. (1995). 'Women's Learning and Leadership Styles: Impact on CRM', in N. McDonald, N. Johnston and R. Fuller (eds.), *Applications of Psychology to the Aviation System: Proceedings of the 21st Conference of the European Association for Aviation Psychology (EAAP)*, Aldershot, UK: Avebury, pp. 262-268.

Turney, M.A., Sitler, R. and Wulle, B. (1996). 'Attitudes Reflective of Gender-Based Issues in the Aviation and Transportation Workplace', in B.J. Hayward and A.R. Lowe (eds.), *Applied Aviation Psychology: Achievement Change and Challenge*, Aldershot, UK: Avebury, pp.332-342.

Twigg, C. (1999). 'Improving Learning and Reducing Costs: Re-Designing Large-Enrollment Courses', available: www.center.rpi.edu/PewSym/mono1.html.

Visser, L. and Visser, Y. (2000, February). 'Integrated Cognitive and Affective Student Support in Distance Education', Paper presented at the *Association of Educational Communications and Technology Conference* Long Beach, California.

Winiecki, D.J. (1999). 'Preparing Students for Asynchronous Computer-Mediated Coursework: Design and Delivery of a "distance education bootcamp"', *Proceedings of the 15th Annual Conference on Distance Learning and Teaching*, Madison, WI.

Zemke, R. and Zemke, S. (1995, June). 'Adult Learning: What Do We Know for Sure'? *Training, 32*, 31-40.

Guidelines for Inclusive Course/ Module Development

Course/module Component

1. Title
Does the title imply that the needs of a diverse range of students will be addressed or does it refer to an issue that is relevant to one particular cultural group?

2. Course development
Is the course being developed to meet industry and market needs?   Is the course being reviewed regularly?

3. Course outcome
Has there been an attempt to identify course outcomes beyond a statement about the occupational classification?   Have higher level competencies been included (e.g., critical thinking, reflection on performance, etc.)?

4. Course/ Module purpose
Does the description of the course/module purpose set up barriers to students from different backgrounds?   Does the course/ module purpose position the learner as an active participant rather than a passive receiver of learning?

5. Relationship to competency standards
Do the competency standards being used relate to a diverse range of students?   Do the competency standards relate to higher-level competencies (problem solving, task management, etc.)?

6. Content
Can content include processes as well as knowledge outcomes?

Does the content reflect the learning needs and particular instructional delivery modes of a diverse range of students?

Does the content have the flexibility to be adapted to meet specific interests or particular groups of students?

7. Assessment strategy

Could the assessment strategy limit the possibility for some groups of students to demonstrate a grasp of the course/ module purpose?

Have you provided ways for students to be more active participants in both learning and assessment strategies?

Have you recommended that assessment tasks integrate knowledge, problem solving, and task management in relevant contexts (i.e., use a holistic/ integrated assessment approach)?

8. Curriculum outcomes

Do the outcomes reflect the needs of students from a diverse range of backgrounds?

Is there appropriate integration of the curriculum outcomes?

9. Assessment criteria

Do assessment criteria clearly state what is expected of and achievable for all students?

Do the assessment criteria focus on the process as well as the products of an activity?

10. Conditions

Will the learning and assessment conditions make it difficult for some students to complete learning and assessment activities?

Are materials required to complete assessments accessible and useable by all students including those from equity groups?
Are authentic contexts listed?

Have you suggested any support mechanisms to maximise curriculum outcomes?

Are assessment guidelines written in clear, plain English so that trainers can use them or so that self-assessment is a possibility?

Are students given a choice of appropriate assessment methods?

Are assessment methods appropriate to the module purpose and learning outcomes?

Have you checked that the assessment tasks are not assessing skills other than those listed in the curriculum outcomes?

Have you identified language, literacy or numeracy skills required to complete the module and to participate in the anticipated diversity of workplace activities?

11. Delivery

Have you suggested a wide range of teaching strategies?

Have you prescribed a range of delivery modes?

Is a range of learning and assessment tasks and appropriate contexts recommended?

Is a positive learning environment being fostered?

12. Language

Have you listed the key terminology and/or jargon that all students should be able to use and understand in this module?

Have you avoided using language which identifies one particular group of people, or which is sexist or racist and excludes some students

Is the language and are the references/texts required to complete the course/module appropriate to the level of the course?

Chapter 16

Ergonomics and Diversity

Patricia C. Fitzgerald

Introduction

The study of ergonomics in aviation environments has received a great deal of attention in the last few decades. Military and commercial aircraft flight decks have become more technologically complex, necessitating an increase in research efforts to ensure safe operation. All aircraft design benefits indirectly from this work. With the exception of some advanced instrumentation, however, most training aircraft have undergone little change in the past 40 years.

Because women are now flying a variety of military aircraft, flight deck design is under greater scrutiny. Researchers and military officials are revisiting the ergonomic criteria used in design specifications. As the workforce becomes more diverse, this issue is gaining importance. One way to explore what specific factors are relevant to the future aviation workforce is an assessment of the ergonomics of training aircraft.

The Study

After conducting interviews with pilots flying training aircraft, it was apparent that many experience a variety of ergonomic difficulties in the aircraft in which they train. Shorter individuals often require devices to aid in reaching instruments and controls. Sighting over the instrument panel can also pose problems. For larger aviators, fitting in the aircraft seat is often an issue. Therefore, one goal of this exploratory study was to identify the ergonomic impediments that are encountered by pilots who are smaller, and larger than average. A further objective was to determine which non-standard devices are most commonly used to compensate for ergonomic issues.

Ergonomic Issues

While the study of ergonomic issues in aircraft began prior to World War I, it has received considerably more attention in recent decades (Meister, 1999). In a review of the history of measurement in aviation systems, Meister (1999) stated that early efforts focused on controls, instruments, and simulators. According to Edwards (1995), ergonomics was a major focus of the 1975 IATA Technology Conference. Among the issues discussed were instrument layout and design, crew factors, and 'the importance of well-designed pilots' seats to provide proper support' (p. 566). As technology advanced, however, many of the questions turned from ergonomic issues to complex systems and the effects of faster flight (Edwards, 1995; Meister, 1999).

Technological advances dictate that current research efforts investigate a wide range of topics. For example, studies have elaborated on the criteria for the design of flight decks (Buratto, 1997), new design concepts that focus on the central role of humans in the flight environment (Schutte, 1997), and new training aircraft flight deck designs that utilize technological improvements for controls and instrumentation (Roscoe, 2002). While these research efforts are required, it is imperative to include the variety of body types that accompany the increasingly diverse talent pool.

Anthropometry

The application of anthropometrics in aviation began in 1937 (Meister, 1999). Anthropometry is the study of the physical characteristics of the human body (Sanders & McCormick, 1993). Static dimensions are taken when the body is in a fixed position, and are used in the design of the things people use; a good example in the aviation environment is headsets. Another application of this science concerns the physical characteristics of the body. In their analysis of recent data, Sanders and McCormick (1993) compared the physical dimensions of U.S. males and females. In many of the measures, the 5th percentile for men was roughly equivalent to the 50th percentile for women. They also compared civilian Japanese males to U.S. Air Force black and white males, and found a similar disparity.

Dynamic dimensions are another measure taken when the body is in action (Sanders & McCormick, 1993). An example in the aviation setting would be reaching for the fuel selector valve. This action is not simply a function of arm length because shoulder, back, and hand movements likely contribute to the completion of the task. When possible, both types of anthropometric data should be used in the design of things. Since limits for design specifications are set based on the typical people for whom the object is designed (Sanders & McCormick, 1993), and the pilot population has traditionally been white male, aircraft design has primarily focused on the anthropometric data of this population.

Military and Commercial Flight Deck Design

In research on flight deck design in military and commercial aircraft, Weber (1997) investigated the anthropometric specifications that are used in development. Weber's study found that the original design for the Joint Primary Aircraft Training System (JPATS) suggested a minimum sitting height of 34 inches, the 5th percentile dimension for males. With this standard, at least 50 percent of the eligible females would not fit in the aircraft. After a great deal of debate, the Air Force recommended reducing the standard to 32.8 inches. While this revision served to accommodate more women and smaller men, many are still excluded. However, a reduction to 31 inches would include about 82 percent of the female population.

Weber (1997) contends that political pressure to make more opportunities available to females in the military contributes, in part, to the changes in the specifications. In the commercial sector, however, profit motives are more likely to drive development. Nevertheless, anthropometric data used by the military form the basis for commercial specifications. The minimum measurement is set at the 25th percentile military female, and the maximum is the 95th percentile military male. As Weber states (1997), the commercial pilot population is likely different from the military population. Data on the anthropometrics of a much more diverse population need to be gathered to accurately project the ergonomic requirements of the future commercial pilot population.

Training Aircraft Flight Deck Design

While a great deal of literature concerning the design of training aircraft exists, little research has been conducted to assess the ergonomic implications for pilots who are smaller or larger than average. In a study of gender differences on the flight deck, however, Stuart (as cited in Sitler, 1998) reports that 16 of the 27 female survey respondents experience problems fitting in the training aircraft they fly. Reaching the rudder pedals and brakes is difficult for some pilots when the seat does not move forward enough. For others, the control yoke is too close to the body when the seat can be advanced enough to reach the rudder pedals. Sitler (1994) states that women tend to use both hands to flare when landing, especially when transitioning to twin-engine aircraft. Stuart (as cited in Sitler, 1998) suggests that positioning the seat closer to facilitate reaching the rudder pedals may account for this finding. In this case, the smaller pilot is closer to the control column, shortening the range of arm movement. These findings clearly indicate that further research is required to identify the limits imposed by flight deck design.

Other Considerations

With the changes that are taking place in the workforce, and the changes that are anticipated in the future, further research on the design specifications of aircraft flight decks must be conducted. For instance, Sheard, Pethybridge, Wright, and McMillan (1996) report that a significant number of the helicopter aircrew they surveyed experienced back pain. While the discomfort was not debilitating, the researchers state that the pain may distract the pilot and have a negative effect on flying. The authors suggest a redesign of the seat to minimize the incidence of back pain. Until this is done, however, they recommend the use of supplemental lumbar support.

The current designs of aircraft flight decks also limit career opportunities for smaller than average men and women (Davey & Davidson, 2000; Weber, 1997).

Davey and Davidson (2000) interviewed pilots from an international airline in Europe and found that the minimum height requirement was 5 feet, 3.5 inches. The authors recommended that the airline lower the restriction and push for flight deck designs that accommodate smaller individuals. Weber (1997) reports that, despite the adjustable seats, some smaller pilots have difficulties operating controls and reaching rudder pedals. During manual operations, these factors may be of greater concern.

As these studies indicate, there is increasing interest in redesigning military and commercial aircraft flight decks to accommodate smaller individuals. The extent to which this needs to be addressed for training aircraft requires consideration. Similarly, ergonomic factors for larger than average pilots must also be addressed.

Methods

Few studies address the issues concerning pilot size in training aircraft. This exploratory study was designed to obtain information from pilots in regard to the ergonomic problems that they experience in training aircraft.

Participants

Fifty-one students in the Arizona State University flight program participated in the study. Twenty-four percent were flight instructors, 41% indicated that they had a commercial certificate, and 57% reported that they had an instrument rating. Private pilots comprised 84% of the sample. The remaining 16% did not respond to this item, or wrote in that they were student pilots. Heights ranged from 60" (5'0") to 79" (6'7"). While females comprise only 6% of certificated pilots nationwide, the study sample included 18% women.

Materials

To develop the questionnaire for this study, flight instructors and general aviation pilots were interviewed to gain insight regarding ergonomic problems experienced in training aircraft. Interviewees discussed issues with reaching controls, instruments, and switches. Figure 16.1 contains a list of items included on the questionnaire. Participants rated their comfort level performing the function on a Likert scale ranging from 1 (*very uncomfortable*) to 5 (*very comfortable*). An open-ended item was also included, and participants were requested to provide comments relating to other flight deck design issues that they had experienced.

1.	Fully deflecting the rudder
2.	Reaching the flap switch/lever
3.	Reaching the fuel selector valve
4.	Reaching the gear switch
5.	Reaching the manual gear mechanism
6.	Reaching the air vents
7.	Reaching gauges on the opposite side of the cockpit
8.	Seeing over the instrument panel

Figure 16.1 Items rated on a 5-point Likert scale to assess level of comfort performing each function

In addition, the devices that pilots use to help compensate for comfort issues were included. To reach rudder pedals, and to see over the instrument panel, shorter pilots often use supplemental cushions. Other devices included rudder and seat belt extensions. Participants responded about their uses of these items, and were asked to specify any other devices they use in an open-ended item.

Finally, respondents were requested to indicate their gender, height, weight range, and aviation certificates and ratings held.

Design and Procedures

Pilots in three aviation classes volunteered to complete the questionnaire. Two of the classes consisted of students in the upper division of the program. The third class contained a mixture of students from all undergraduate grade levels. The students were informed that the survey concerned training aircraft flight deck ergonomics, and that participation was voluntary. Most participants completed the questionnaire in fewer than five minutes.

Results

Frequencies were calculated for the variables under study. In response to the Likert scale items, 27 (53%) of the participants reported that they experience some level of discomfort performing at least one function in training aircraft. Reaching the fuel selector valve (29%) and the manual gear mechanism (27%) were the most frequently cited problems. Twenty-two percent found reaching the air vents to be uncomfortable. Seeing over the panel, and reaching gages on the opposite side of the panel, posed some difficulty for 20% of the respondents. Discomfort was also reported in fully deflecting the rudder (16%), reaching the gear switch (10%), and reaching the flap switch (8%).

Six participants reported that they were neutral or comfortable executing the functions listed on the survey, but they related the problems they experience in the comments section. The heights of these subjects ranged from 6'0" to 6'7". Two participants cited difficulties performing slips, and two others reported that the yoke hits their knees or kneeboard. The other two pilots stated that lack of headroom is an issue. The 6'7" pilot also referred to the back strain resulting from the need to recline the seat.

The remaining 18 subjects responded that they are comfortable in the aircraft. It is interesting to note, however, that 13 of them range in height from 5'8" to 6'0". To gain a clearer understanding of the heights that fit best in training aircraft, the responses from the total sample were broken down by height ranges (see Figure 16.2). Twenty-nine (57%) of the pilots that completed the survey are in the 5'8" to 6'0" category. In addition to the 13 pilots that do not experience problems, seven indicated that reaching the manual gear crank was the only difficulty they encountered. The remaining nine pilots rated multiple functions as uncomfortable.

Twenty percent of the sample ranged from 5'0" to 5'7". Six students indicated at least three areas of discomfort. One participant reported one function that was

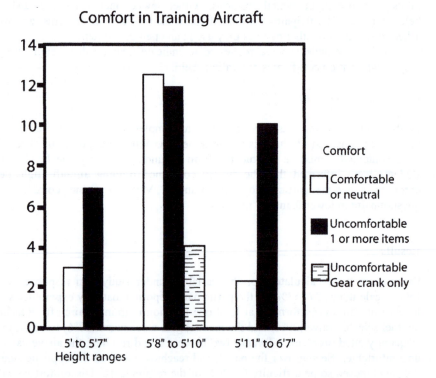

Figure 16.2 Participant reports of comfort level in training aircraft

uncomfortable, and the remaining three reported no problems. The most common issue, experienced by 50% of this group, was difficulty seeing over the instrument panel. Four of the students identified problems in reaching gages on the opposite side of the panel and reaching the fuel selector valve.

The survey also included items to determine the extent to which non-standard devices are utilized to compensate for ergonomic issues. Seat cushions are used by 16% of the students. Four percent use a back cushion, and one person reported the use of a seat belt extension.

Finally, Pearson Product Moment Correlations were performed. As would be expected, height and sighting over the instrument panel yielded a low positive relationship (r=.287), that was significant at the .05 level. Significant results were not found for the other functions included on the survey. This is likely due to the fact that participants at both ends of the height range indicated discomfort.

Discussion

The results indicate that there are, indeed, ergonomic issues in training aircraft. Contrary to expectations, few of the pilots use supplemental devices. A larger sample size may yield different results. The lack of support may also be explained by the variety of adjustments that may be made to the seat. Future efforts should attempt to include a greater number of shorter participants to obtain a clearer picture of the non-standard devices that pilots use in training aircraft.

It was also expected that shorter pilots would report the greatest number of problems. The number of subjects in this category was small, but the results indicate that a large proportion of these respondents encountered multiple reaching difficulties. In some cases, making an adjustment to compensate for one difficulty introduces a different problem. This is illustrated well by the following comment made by a 5'7" male:

I have a problem. In order to push the rudder pedal full deflection, I have to move the seat all the way forward. This is a problem because I also have to raise the seat. When I have a kneeboard on my lap I am unable to move full deflection of the ailerons. I could lower my seat, but I would not be able to see over the panel completely.

The results support the expectation that taller pilots also experience problems in the aircraft. Several of the taller pilots indicated that they were very comfortable with all the items on the questionnaire, but they wrote in some comments about issues that they have in the when flying. One 6'7" pilot stated that, to see clearly, he needs to recline the seat, which puts a strain on his back. A 6'5" pilot wrote this comment:

For us lengthier folks, slips become rather difficult. When you push one rudder all the way in, your other knee comes up and interferes with the yoke. It makes it almost impossible, but if you angle your legs just right it is manageable.

A 6'4" pilot had a similar issue and made the following observation:

When doing a slip, I feel like I barely fit in the cockpit. I have to use the side of my foot and my knee is smashed on the wall. If anything, I'm too big, or the cockpit is too small.

Pilots ranging in height from 5'8" to 6'0" comprised the largest sub-set of the sample. While more than half of them noted that at least one function was uncomfortable, many referred only to reaching the manual gear crank. Because the crank is sometimes located behind the seat, it is difficult for many pilots to reach. Furthermore, none of the participants in the other groups singled out this item. When they reported discomfort in reaching the gear crank, they also indicated other functions that posed difficulty.

While more data need to be collected to draw a firm conclusion, these results suggest that people between 5'8" and 6'0" are the most comfortable in training aircraft. While this group reported the fewest instances of discomfort, they did indicate some difficulties. Overall, 65% of the respondents reported at least one uncomfortable function in handling training aircraft. Further studies are needed to address these issues.

Recommendations for Further Studies

This study was limited to students in the aviation program at one university in the United States, and it is likely that all of the participants fly the same low-wing four seated aircraft. The results of the study, therefore, may not be generalized to training aircraft as a whole. In addition, the subjects were all university undergraduates. Their experiences may not be representative of the diverse pilot training community. To gain a better understanding of the ergonomic issues, the study should be expanded to include pilots of various ages, and a wider sample of aircraft types.

Further studies should include anthropometric measurements. In their study concerning automobile interiors, Chaffin, Faraway, Zhang, and Woolley (2000) found stature and age had significant effects on reach motion postures. A smaller effect was found for gender. Studying similar dynamic dimensions in the aircraft is necessary to accommodate various aircraft users. Furthermore, the only measurement used in this study was the self-reported height of the subjects. Other static variables, such as sitting height, are relevant to the functions addressed in this study, and need to be assessed to provide reasonable recommendations to manufacturers.

Pilot fatigue, especially during flights of long duration, is another consideration. As Hitchcock (1999) states, errors are more likely when the pilot is fatigued. This factor may take on added importance when the pilot is not comfortable in the airplane. Future research should include an analysis of this possibility.

Summary

This chapter explored ergonomic issues associated with greater diversity in the physical size of the future pilot workforce. Results of a study of university aviation students confirmed that current training aircraft have design deficiencies that are uncomfortable for a variety of pilots. While the pilots of median height range appear to be the most comfortable, a majority of the respondents reported ergonomic difficulties. The United States Air Force is accommodating a larger number of pilot candidates by using a greater range of anthropometric measures in the design of the JPATS trainer. To facilitate the inclusion of a diverse pool of candidates in aviation careers, this practice is recommended for the development of all training aircraft.

References

Buratto, F. (1997). 'Elaboration of Ergonomic Criteria for Flight Deck Design', *Proceedings of the Ninth International Symposium on Aviation Psychology*, Columbus, OH, 837-842.

Chaffin, B.C., Faraway, J.J., Zhang, X. and Woolley, C. (2000). 'Stature, Age, and Gender Effects on Reach Motion Postures', *Human Factors*, *42*(3), 408-420.

Davey, C.L. and Davidson, M.J. (2000). 'The Right of Passage? The Experiences of Female Pilots in Commercial Aviation', *Feminism and Psychology*, *10*(2), 195-225.

Edwards, E. (1995). 'Aviation Ergonomics: Whence and Whither?', *Ergonomics*, *38*(3), 565-569.

Hitchcock, L. (1999). 'Pilot performance', in D.J. Garland, J.A. Wise and V.D. Hopkin (eds.), *Handbook of Aviation Human Factors*, Mahwah, NJ: Erlbaum, pp. 311-326.

Meister, D. (1999). 'Measurement in Aviation Systems', in D.J. Garland, J.A. Wise and V.D. Hopkin (eds.), *Handbook of Aviation Human Factors*, Mahwah, NJ: Erlbaum, pp. 257-276.

Roscoe, S.N. (2001). 'Ergonomics: Designing the Job of Flying an Airplane', *The International Journal of Aviation Psychology*, *12*(4), 331-339.

Sanders, M.S. and McCormick, E.J. (1993). *Human Factors in Engineering and Design* (7th ed.), New York: McGraw-Hill.

Schutte, P.C. (1997). 'Wings: A new Paradigm in Human-Centered Design', *Proceedings of the Ninth International Symposium on Aviation Psychology*, Columbus, OH, 865-871.

Sheard, S.C., Pethybridge, R.J., Wright, J.M. and McMillan, G.H.G. (1996). 'Back Pain in Aircrew – An Initial Survey', *Aviation, Space, and Environmental Medicine*, *67*(5), 474-477.

Sitler, R.L. (1994). 'Gender Differences in Learning to Fly', *Proceedings of the Fifth Annual International Women in Aviation Conference*, Lake Buena Vista, FL.

Sitler, R.L. (1998). 'The Cockpit Classroom: Women's Perceptions of Learning to Fly and Implications for Flight Curriculum and Instruction', *Dissertation Abstracts International*, *59*, 07A.

Weber, R.N. (1997). 'Manufacturing Gender in Commercial and Military Cockpit Design', *Science, Technology, and Human Values, 22*(2), 235-253.

Chapter 17

Clash of Subcultures in On-Gate Communication

Christy Armentrout-Brazee and Marifran Mattson

'Coming up with good processes that *should* work isn't the problem ... the problem's in the implementation.'
- Senior Maintenance Manager of a major airline

Introduction

In the wake of events that have occurred over recent months, the airlines have found themselves facing increased organizational tensions and greater competitive challenges than they have seen in the last several decades. Even before September 11, 2001, however, airlines recognized that passengers and those responsible for making their travel decisions were being offered a wider array of flying choices than ever before. For example, when Southwest was successful by offering low-cost fares with no-frill services, United Airlines followed suit by offering their own versions of this strategy called 'Shuttle by United.' On a more personal level, airlines have also been trying to devise strategies to draw customers away from their competitors. Redeeming the frequent flyer miles customers have with other airlines is one such method. Another factor that can either improve or reduce the competitiveness of an airline is the ability of organizational members from various groups within the organization to work together productively. Unlike many industries, in most airlines several different unions represent various employee groups (i.e., flight attendants, pilots, maintenance technicians, customer service agents). As a result, the ways in which organizational members view the actions of these different groups within the organization, or subcultures as they will be referred to in this article, are often filtered or limited by their affiliations within their own subculture. Individuals fail to recognize the impact that they have on other groups' members or the ways they are impacted upon. This leads members of different subcultures to feel and even act antagonistically toward each other rather than working toward their shared overall organizational goals.

This chapter discusses a project developed and carried out by Purdue University researchers with the goal to create a competitive edge for one airline's operation by reducing the number of deferred cabin items. This would improve the condition of the cabin, as well as minimizing the number of items on the deferred list carried over from station to station along an aircraft's daily flight schedule. Prior to the start of the project, members of the organization identified communication among the stakeholders in the process was the key factor limiting the efficient and effective correction of defects in the cabin. In other words, organizational members were unable to efficiently and effectively communicate with each other to improve the flying conditions of passengers in the aircrafts' cabins. The goal of this paper is to describe the central role of communication in the emergence and maintenance of organizational subcultures.

The Underlying Factor: Communication Among Subcultures

To address this issue, the organization wanted to develop a communication strategy to improve the passing on of information between flight attendants, pilots, and maintenance technicians located at the airport gate. The idea was to reduce the number of deferred items on aircraft at the gates in a manner that would still allow for on-time departures. However, after job shadowing and conducting a number of interviews and observations with pilots, flight attendants, and maintenance technicians, the problem was found to run much deeper than what the project originators had envisioned. Rather than the project requiring only the addressing of such issues as what information was needed, who had that information, who needed to receive the information, and at what time was the information needed during the aircraft's visit, researchers found that the biases held by members of the subcultures played equally important roles. Therefore, in working on this project, the researchers were able to view a microcosm of the workplace in which the clashing of these subcultures was apparent. Furthermore, this research provided the opportunity for those involved to better recognize and understand the impact these dysfunctional relationships had on the communication of vital information within the on-gate process.

During the first part of the project, researchers conducted a series of interviews and observations with flight attendants, pilots, and maintenance technicians as they did their regular aircraft servicing routines when the aircraft were parked at the gates at four different airports. Over a period of approximately six weeks, the researchers were able to develop a fairly clear understanding of the processes that individuals used in order to report aircraft cabin defects. Typical defects included such items as reading lights that did not work, seat cushions that had been soiled, seats that did not recline properly, coffee makers that were identified as being inoperative, or galley carts that did not function properly. In the ideal case, the flight attendant would report the defect to the pilot in a standardized manner and the pilot would then report the item to the gate maintenance technician prior to or promptly after aircraft arrived at the gate. In this way, the maintenance technician would have time to assess the problem and address it if possible without causing the next flight to take a delay. Problems with this process became apparent to management when items on aircraft deferred lists that should have been fixed were not and when airworthiness items were causing costly delays to the airline. In both cases, these factors were not conducive to creating the kind of flying experience the airline insisted on providing to their flying customers.

Organizational Culture and Communication

Organizational culture is neither a thing owned by an organization nor a disparate part of an organization that can be labeled or controlled. Furthermore, it is not a monolithic form that is designed by management to be soaked up and enacted by the rest of the employees. Instead, it is a dynamic facet of all the interaction that occurs within that organization and among its members. Clifford Geertz (1973) argued that, 'man is an animal suspended in webs of significance he himself has spun... culture [is] those webs' (p. 5). As such, an organization's culture both constructs and is constructed by the communication that goes on among its members. 'As webs, cultures are spun continuously as people within the social system interact with one another and create their own rules and norms' (Daniels, Spiker, & Papa, 1997, p. 203). Another way of stating this is that organizational culture is the way things are done around here (Martin, Feldman, Hatch, & Sitkin, 1983). Individuals within an organizational environment interact and behave in certain ways based on the beliefs and values shared among their peers. When the behaviors, beliefs, and values are in keeping with those of the group, they are reinforced and encouraged to continue. However, when individuals act or speak in terms that do not reflect the culture of the group, they typically are not endorsed by their peers and may even threaten to be excluded from interactions with members of the group. Therefore, the culture of an organization is not a static form, but instead lives and either grows or withers based upon the sorts of interactions that occur among organizational members.

Another characteristic of organizational cultures that demonstrates they are not monolithic forms is that these cultures are not entities in and of themselves. Rather, they can be understood as being composed of multiple subcultures. While the subcultures share common features of the culture itself, they have their own features that set them apart from each other. For example, the organizational culture of a university may be understood as the aggregation of the many subcultures that exist among the university's schools (i.e., School of Liberal Arts, School of Engineering, School of Technology). Furthermore, one can identify sub-subcultures within these schools by looking more closely at the types of interactions that are carried on among members of particular departments (i.e., Department of Aviation Technology, Department of Graphic Technology, Department of Computer Technology). When applied to an airline organization, it is the various employee groups or subcultures that make up the overall organization's culture. While the top management and owners of the organization impact the organization's culture, their impact is limited and heavily influenced by the organization's subcultures (Conrad & Poole, 1998; Daniels, Spiker, & Papa,

1997). Over time, certain artifacts, rites, and rituals emerge as having special importance or meaning to those within the subculture. For example, members of the flight attendant subculture would have very different understandings of having oversized luggage brought to the gate than would a member of ramp service. While the ramp service person would likely view the item as a bother that they will have to attend to before they complete the loading of passenger baggage, it is probably more representative to flight attendants of the impending confrontation that they will be forced to have with the bag's owner before boarding is complete. Of key interest to this project are the ways in which biases held by members of the flight attendant, pilot, and gate maintenance technician subcultures involved in the on-gate process interfere with the interactions and completion of tasks required to fix cabin defects. The next section describes a series of specific examples where the overall organizational goal of providing the best flying experience to the airline's customers was eclipsed as a result of biases held by members of one subculture toward another. While there are many generalizations forwarded in the next sections and, of course, there are exceptions to the rules, these biases represent the feelings that the majority of individuals from each of the subcultures expressed during the course of the research. Furthermore, members of the subcultures expressed these perceptions as representing their subcultures rather than as their own personal views.

Sure, Jot it on a Cocktail Napkin

Awareness of cabin defects typically occurred in one of two ways. First, a flight attendant might become aware of a defect as she or he performed her normal work routine. An example of this could be finding a coffee pot that did not work correctly. Second, she or he could be made aware of the defect by having a passenger bring it to her or his attention. For example, a passenger might find that the audio system does not work and he or she cannot hear the movie from his or her seat's system. The existing process for passing this information to maintenance had the flight attendant who discovered the defect make a note of it and pass this on to the head flight attendant. Using a diagram of the aircraft to describe the location of the defect and a set of codes that indicated the type of problem, the head flight attendant would then fill out a form including all pertinent information. This information would then be passed on to the pilot who would note the defect in the aircraft's logbook which the gate maintenance technician was required to review and address if possible prior to releasing the aircraft for its next trip.

Although seemingly simple, this process was rarely smooth. One problem that came up often was that defect information was transferred to the relevant parties late in the flight. The end of a flight is very busy for both the pilots and the flight attendants. Often passengers would not tell the flight attendants of the defects until the end of the flight or after arrival. Other times, flight attendants would be busy completing their services and clean up such that they would not have the chance to relay information forward to the head flight attendant. In addition, as the time left in the flight grew shorter, it was often likely that information would be less than complete or accurate.

Another factor that impacted this reporting process was that often information about a defect would be noted on whatever was available to the flight attendant at the time of the report. As the heading of this section indicates, it was noted by all three groups that this commonly would be a cocktail napkin that would eventually be forwarded up to the pilots. As so much of what pilots have been trained to do is based in following procedures and doing things by the book, getting the information via a cocktail napkin was often seen as less than adequate. In talking to gate maintenance technicians, they had similar feelings about the use of napkins for passing on defect information, but it was based more on their perceptions that the flight attendants just didn't think it was important to provide the information to them in a professional manner. At least some of the technicians saw this as a slight being made against them by the flight attendants and stated that if they didn't get the information on the form it was not their responsibility to 'bust their butts' making up for it.

Further, the information on the napkins was often very general and of little help in determining the nature or location of the problem. Several of these napkins were shown to researchers. In one case, for example, a napkin read, 'reading light out above one of the seats toward the back of the coach section.' In other words, for the gate maintenance technician to even find the location of the defect would take a significant amount of time before actually fixing it. In another example, a flight attendant on a Boeing 747-400 had written 'coffee maker inop' and forwarded on to the pilot. There were more than 15 coffee makers spread throughout the aircraft's many galleys. In both these cases it was a pilot who showed the researchers the napkins, and in both cases the pilots had chosen to ignore the information and not log it in their aircraft's logbook. In both cases, the defective items were seen as cosmetic issues and were perceived by the pilots to have no relation to the airworthiness of the aircraft. In another case discussed with the researchers where an airworthiness defect issue was passed forward on a napkin both the pilot and the gate maintenance technician made sure that they tracked down the flight attendant and had him personally show them the defect to ensure it was properly addressed.

Adding another wrinkle to this scenario, the diagrams, codes, and forms that were supposed to be used to identify exactly what was defective and where in the cabin it was located were regularly inaccurate in their depictions of the actual aircraft in use. These diagrams were supposed to represent the particular configuration of the aircraft in service and have corresponding codes for use on the report form. In this way, these items would allow for an effective and efficient means of representing the information needed to the gate maintenance technician. Although it was unclear if the wide use of cocktail napkins instead of the forms was a reaction to the difficulty posed in trying to use the diagrams, codes, and forms, it was clear that at least part of the group chose not to follow the procedure. Furthermore, after having several opportunities to have head flight attendants point out the problems with the procedure, one of the researchers clearly recognized how the form procedure could introduce more problems for the gate maintenance technician than the cocktail napkin. It should be noted that most flight attendants involved in this research project went to great lengths to write down the information that, in their minds, fulfilled their responsibilities for reporting defects. In most cases, both the flight attendants and the pilots agreed that the flight attendants made sure to have all the necessary information included. However, the very fact that the information was located on the napkin rather than the form was enough for some pilots and gate maintenance technicians to disregard defects they deemed to be cosmetic in nature.

It's Not Worth Bringing Up

While talking with pilots during the project, either while their aircraft was parked at the gate or while jumpseating between stations, it was discovered that many of the pilots saw themselves as gatekeepers of information about the aircraft between the flight attendants and the gate maintenance technicians. In other words, often the pilots of an aircraft saw it as their responsibility to determine what information did or did not warrant being passed on to either the gate maintenance technician or others, such as individuals located in the operations center. As discussed above, in some cases pilots would make the choice not to note defects in the cabin when they were not airworthiness items because they felt the information was not clear or was incomplete. In other cases, pilots made a judgment call that because either there was a short turn-time for the aircraft or the particular station was not likely to have the parts or tools required to fix the defect they would put off reporting the defect until they reached the next station or the aircraft had completed its schedule for the day.

One reason for these decisions hinged upon the pilots' concerns that if the gate maintenance technicians tried to apply a fix, it could take longer than expected and compromise an on-time departure. Regardless of whether or not this is a good way of judging actual airline performance, various members of the media report on-time departure statistics that can have an impact upon such important customers to an airline as business passengers. Typically these passengers pay more for their tickets than leisure customers, but in return they also view their time as a precious commodity that should be protected. Furthermore, they want to be assured that they will make it to their connecting flights. On-time performance is one measure perceived to be a good indicator of these factors, and as such, it is closely tracked throughout airline organizations.

Another reason that pilots might decide not to complete the process of writing up the defect was that there was no code appropriate or applicable to the particular problem. In walking one of the researchers through the process of logging a defect in the codebook, one pilot explained that he always went back and checked the codes listed by flight attendants to be sure they were correct. He explained, 'The gals don't mess up all the time, but enough that it's worth a once-over.' The other pilot also pointed out that because the codes were very general and miss many of the things that can go wrong with a cabin item, it was often up to the flight attendant to choose the code she or he felt most closely represented the problem. If the information was received soon enough before the end of a flight, the pilots were often able to relay the information ahead using the ACARS system. The gate maintenance technician was then able to pull up information about the flight and the aircraft prior to its arrival and gather whatever tools or parts would be necessary to fix the problem. However, after the flight enters into its descent the pilots tended to be too busy to spend time logging cosmetic defect items.

A third reason that explains why a defect that was identified might not be forwarded also had to do with time. In cases where the pilots felt that there was not enough information to correctly identify the defect or they were unsure of the accuracy of its description, they may have disregarded the information to keep the gate maintenance technician from preparing to address the defect incorrectly. A gate maintenance technician described the frustration he felt when he got to the aircraft ready to address the defect only to find that it required something else entirely from what was indicated by the codebook. Not only did this reinforce tensions among members of the different cultural groups, but it also could lead to the fix taking a longer amount of time because the gate maintenance technician now had to remove what was brought originally into the aircraft and replace it with the correct items. Therefore, it was reported by pilots that there were cases where rather than have the gate maintenance technician take the time setting up to do a fix that likely wouldn't be what was needed, they waited until they arrived at the gate and mentioned the item if they thought of it.

The 'Honey-Do Effect'

With these biases held toward the flight attendants, it was interesting to discover the routines they had developed to get defects in the cabins fixed rather than deferred. An interesting interaction was observed between members of the gate maintenance technician and flight attendant subcultures described as the 'honey-do effect.' Although several gate maintenance technicians brought up the issue, a number of flight attendants also recognized the term and its use. When an aircraft was parked at the gate, it was the procedure at this airline that a gate maintenance technician boarded the aircraft, went to the cockpit, and checked the logbook. In some cases, if the flight crew was still onboard, the maintenance technician would also check to see if there was anything else unusual or noteworthy besides what was listed in the logbook. On two occasions while job-shadowing with a gate maintenance technician, one of the researchers was encouraged by the technician to move quickly through the cabin where the flight attendants were preparing for their next flight and go directly to the cockpit. The researcher was dressed in a pair of maintenance technician's coveralls so as to stand out less in the work environment and the gate maintenance technicians cautioned that if she did not move quickly she would receive the 'honey do effect.' The technician explained that often if a flight attendant saw a gate maintenance technician on the aircraft, she or he would ask them to fix something for them. In other words, the flight attendants would say something like, 'Honey, could you do this?' For example, a flight attendant might say, 'Honey, could you take a look at the coffee pot in the forward galley for me?'

A second possibility which was encountered involved a flight attendant on another aircraft who asked, 'Honey, I can't get the movie to run in the economy cabin. Could you have someone take a look at it before we begin boarding?' In the latter case, the gate maintenance technician called on his radio to request that someone bring some tools and take a look at the video system.

On the surface, this interaction might appear to work sufficiently well, the biases operating just below the surface work against the organization's overriding goals of customer satisfaction and reduced deferred item lists on the aircraft. The gate maintenance technicians who were part of the research project explained that they felt like the flight attendants were belittling them by addressing them in this manner. They felt that if there was a problem, then the flight attendants should follow procedures and not expect the gate maintenance technicians to drop what they were doing to deal with cosmetic items in the galley. Several of the gate maintenance technicians said they believed that the flight attendants saw them as grease monkeys and of lesser status because they worked mostly outside of the aircraft. In other words, having the flight attendants address them in the manner they did during the 'honey-do effect' reinforced the negative perceptions held by many maintenance technicians in the industry that they are seen as a lower class of employees because their work is largely hands-on.

Furthermore, the flight attendants that talked about the 'honey-do effect' with one of the researchers stated that they, too, would prefer not having to try to catch a gate maintenance technician as he or she walked through the cabin. They stated that if they did not, however, go to these lengths sometimes, they would never have the defective items in the cabins addressed by a gate maintenance technician. They also stated that they felt that having to go to this extra step of either seeking out or cornering them on the aircraft made flight attendants appear like less than the flying professionals they were. For example, if a flight attendant had not had the opportunity to check her or his galley or check to see that the video system was running, there was a concern that there might not be another chance at getting a gate maintenance technician on board to look it over. Therefore, at times, when flight attendants suspected something in the cabin was defective they would seek assistance early from the gate maintenance technician. One explanation for this was that it was not uncommon for members of the outgoing flight attendant crew to relay information about what they considered to be serious defects in the cabin to the incoming crew for the next flight. Again, in such cases, both the flight attendants and gate maintenance technicians pointed out that the information was often vague or incomplete, only further complicating the situation.

It's Only Because They Don't Have to Deal With the Customer

It was the perception, and in some ways the reality, that members of the three subcultures had different goals in mind for the flight. Of course, they all shared the overriding concern that safety be maintained at the highest level to ensure that no one was hurt and no damage was done to the aircraft. Beyond that, however, there were differences. The mandate placed upon pilots and maintenance technicians first and foremost is to maintain and operate the aircraft in a manner that will not bring harm to anyone or anything. This mandate was put in place by the FAA to make certain that at no time the safety of the customer, crew, or aircraft be compromised for a non-safety reason. At the same time, the flight attendants are also faced with the mandate to provide a safe and pleasant experience for the passengers so as to encourage customers to book future flights with the airline. Therefore, the differences in organizational expectations for members of these three subcultures were strongly affected by the ways in which their work experiences were tied to the relative satisfaction of the flying customers. On one occasion, a researcher was accompanying a gate maintenance technician through the terminal where several people were waiting for a transcontinental flight that had been delayed more than three hours. He leaned over to the researcher and made the statement, 'Boy I'm glad I don't have to climb on a plane and spend the next four hours with those people.' Therefore, the experience that flight attendants have while doing their jobs is heavily influenced by the level of satisfaction the customers experience both before and during a flight. On the other hand, both the pilots and the maintenance technicians work apart from the customers and therefore, may be less likely to take passenger satisfaction into account when determining which defects can or cannot be addressed at the gate.

Because of this difference between the working experiences of members of these three groups, there was a definite perception on the part of many flight attendants that their needs for having the cabin in full working order went unrecognized or ignored. They perceived a general failure on the part of pilots and gate maintenance technicians to understand how having such seemingly cosmetic items as an inoperative video screen in a business class seat or having a broken coffee pot in the main cabin can impact their ability to provide the kind of service customers expect.

Communication Strategies to Address These Issues

As with being a member of any culture, when one is on the inside it is very difficult to 'see' the different views or biases perceived by various subcultures (Pacanowsky & Trujillo, 1995). One often does not realize or recognize the affect that one's culture has upon her or his behaviors or beliefs until someone from outside the group points them out. For this reason, organizational members from the various subcultures could benefit from being exposed to the values, beliefs, and rationales used by their counterparts to explain why they do their work in the ways they do. In this way, they also may better recognize how their lack of awareness regarding the impact of the actions of others and one's own actions impact upon each other. Furthermore, organizational members may begin to understand how the biases within each subculture and those held toward the other groups are at the heart of many of the biases that lead to the issues described above.

One major factor that was identified as a contributor to the misconceptions between the three groups involved the small amount of cross-functional training that occurred in both the initial and recurrent training sessions for members of each of the three groups. It was reported that at no time in their trainings were pilots or maintenance technicians placed in a room with experienced flight attendants in order to learn more about their job and the work they do. Scarcely better, at this particular airline, new flight attendants attended at least seven weeks of initial training where they were given a wealth of information about carrying out their safety and service-related duties. During this period, there was one hour-long session in which several experienced pilots were brought into the classroom to briefly describe how the roles of the flight crews and flight attendants intertwined. In general, however, flight attendants viewed this session, like much of the rest of their training, as the pilots' opportunity to explain what the flight attendants should do to help them in their jobs with little reciprocation. Rather than having the one-sided discussion or ignoring the need for this type of interaction, it was proposed that each group should receive familiarity training in order to learn more about what each group contributes toward creating and maintaining a safe and pleasant travel experience for the airline's customers. For example, after talking with a maintenance manager at one of the airline's hub stations, he thought it would be a great idea to bring in several gate maintenance technicians to the flight attendant training sessions to give them a general explanation of what they do during the turn of an aircraft and answer questions the flight attendants might have. While this had not yet been implemented as a standardized part of the flight attendant training schedule, there was still an interest and some unofficial sessions had been held at the flight attendant domicile at that particular hub. If this same sort of interaction could be accomplished prior to the informal indoctrination that occurs as one learns the ropes of the job on the job, it might be possible to begin recreating the long-standing negative relations that exist between these groups.

Along the same lines, several flight attendants talked about how when they worked at other airlines they had been required to spend part or a whole shift job-shadowing with a gate maintenance technician and how beneficial it was for them to see the technicians actually performing their duties. Likewise, gate maintenance technicians job-shadowed a flight attendant to gain a better understanding of the duties flight attendants are expected to perform. Even better than the interaction among these individuals during training sessions outside their work environments, by job-shadowing the individuals were able to understand both the opportunities and the constraints that members of the other groups encountered. Therefore, it was possible for these individuals to develop empathy toward their counterparts and better understand how their actions could impact upon the abilities or ease with which other groups' members could accomplish their tasks. In other words, experiences like these encouraged the individuals to consider how their actions or failures to act could impact upon members of the other groups' abilities to carry out their functions to the best of their ability. Again, by taking the perspective of the other people affected by one's decisions and understanding the constraints faced by each group's members, more accurate or more forgiving attributions were developed to try to explain the decisions and actions taken by individuals from other groups.

While training is one means of breaking down the barriers that keep members of the different subcultures from interacting effectively, there are other factors that the organization could address that could reduce the tensions described above. For example, one way in which members of these groups differentiated their status to the organization was related to the amount, type, and timeliness of information given to the groups. It was the perception among organizational members that pilots were given more information in a more timely manner than either maintenance technicians or flight attendants, with flight attendants receiving the least. Individuals who knew people in the different groups talked about how they received information at different times or got different information altogether from their counterparts in the other groups. One flight attendant was married to a pilot and she said her husband would tell her things about the organization he received and she would then tell it to her peers, as that was the only way they perceived they could remain well informed. At this airline there was no single means of communicating a message to all employees that was sure to reach everyone. There were a variety of means used by the various groups, but there was little coordination among the messages that were sent out through those channels. This was a more complicated recommendation than it might first appear as neither flight attendants nor pilots have a set schedule of when they will be in their domiciles or receiving their email. Furthermore, not all flight attendants had email or knew how to use it in order to stay informed during their trips. However, if the airline wanted to assure members of all three groups that they were not viewed differently and should work together rather than maintaining their separation in status it would have needed to find ways to better ensure that the same messages and the same information were shared among all organizational members.

A second factor that the organization could have improved would be ensuring that the charts and codebooks located in the aircraft were accurate and as complete as possible. Much of the frustration that was generated by having inaccurate or incomplete information was not the result of laziness or lack of concern for the person who would need to address the defect as was often assumed. As mentioned earlier, when faced with inaccurate or incomplete information to pass on to the next party, the individuals reporting the defect often did the best they could with the options presented to them. If the organization, or at the very least the individuals who managed the reporting system, developed a better way to identify locations and the codes to assign for various problems, it is possible that those who received the information might have been less suspicious of what they were told and more likely to recognize the true intent of the information provider. By not having a working system in place, the organization was setting up members from these three groups to fall back on the negative attributions and pre-existing biases to explain system failures rather than recognizing that it was a system failure that allowed incorrect or inaccurate information to be used.

Summary

Effective communication among organizational subcultures in airline operational work settings is a key factor in determining the successfulness of airlines and their ability to produce the quality of product that will allow them to remain competitive in today's aviation marketplace. In a project with one of Purdue's airline partners, researchers sought to improve the system in place for on-gate communication process. On-gate communication referred to the sharing of information about aircraft cabin defects with the gate maintenance technicians so as to reduce the number of items carried on an aircraft's deferred item list. Through a series of interviews, observations, and job-shadowing experiences, a number of factors presented themselves as contributors to lack of timely or effective communication. However, as the project progressed it became clear that many of the problems that led to this situation were caused by the biases and poor interaction that was derived in large part from the difference in the subculture of the three main groups involved in the process. These included the flight attendants, pilots, and gate maintenance technicians. Each group had its own way of understanding their jobs and the jobs of their peers in the other groups, as well as specific practices and routines that had been developed to carry out interactions with other groups' members. In the issues brought up in the paper, poor communication was often due to a lack of shared perspective among different groups' members and negative intentions attributed to individuals' behaviors based on their memberships in the other subcultures. Several strategies were described to improve the interaction among and between members of these groups. One strategy was to develop and implement awareness training for members of the groups to heighten their knowledge of both how they impact and are impacted upon by the actions taken by members of the other groups. A second strategy involved creating a job-shadowing program where members of the groups would spend parts of their shift accompanying a member of another group as they went through their normal work routine. The last strategy was for the organization to ensure that it does not encourage or enable the biases between subcultures by creating organizational processes and tools that are inaccurate or unfriendly for those who must rely upon them to complete their job tasks. By addressing the conflicts and conflicting views among the subcultures of these three workgroups, the organization may better be able to create working environments in which problematic issues like the on-gate communication process function in a more successful and effective manner.

References

Conrad, C. and Poole, M.S. (1998). *Strategic Organizational Communication: Into the Twenty-First Century*, San Diego, CA: Harcourt Brace College Publishers.

Daniels, T.D., Spiker, B.K. and Papa, M.J. (1997). *Perspectives on Organizational Communication*, 4th ed. Madison, WI: Brown and Benchmark Publishers.

Geertz, C. (1973). *The Interpretation of Cultures*. New York: Basic Books.

Martin, J., Feldman, J., Hatch, M.J., and Sitkin, S.B. (1983). 'The Uniqueness Paradox in Organizational Stories', *Administrative Science Quarterly, 28*, 438-453.

Pacanowsky, M.E. and Trujillo, N. (1983). 'Organizational Communication as Cultural Performance', in K.E. Hutchison (ed.), *Readings in Organizational Communication*. Dubuque, IA: Wm. C. Brown Publishers, pp. 100-121.

Pacanowsky, M.E. and Trujillo, N. (1995). 'Communication and Organizational Cultures', in S.R. Corman, S.P. Banks, C.R. Bantz, M.E. Mayer (eds.), *Foundations of Organizational Communication: A Reader*. New York: Longman Publishers USA. pp. 160-171.

Schein, E. (1990). 'Organizational Culture', *American Psychologist*, 45(2), pp. 109-119.

Chapter 18

Making Everyone Part of the Team: A Model

Merrill R. Karp and Mary Ann Turney

Introduction

As the aviation workforce becomes more diverse, i.e., more multi-national and multi-cultural, aviation education and training institutions should re-examine the structure and organization of the aviation knowledge transfer process. This chapter presents an aviation education model that incorporates the authors' research on a number of factors that influence the success of aviation education efforts. The resulting model combines data-driven and literature-supported enhancements to aviation education to address how to assure successful learning within a diverse workforce. The model includes faculty and peer group interventions, as well as implications of adult learning, in-depth theory, and curriculum that addresses all learning styles, immediate application after the classroom experience, group learning, and mentor involvement. In addition to aviation, this model has the potential for application in any high technology aviation environment, including air carrier training and military training. Investing in enhancements for curriculum delivery formats should have a high payoff in increased retention of a diverse workforce.

Review of the Literature

A key component for developing a Diverse Workforce model was to examine the relevant literature (Figure 18.1) to determine how people learn and what educational enhancements could be incorporated to retain students in collegiate aviation programs (Karp, et al, 2002b).

Women's and Men's Learning Characteristics

The literature reflects a wide spectrum of individual characteristics that differ among individual learners as well as differences that exist between men and women as unique groups. These learning characteristics should be examined when developing a model to understand how both women and men learn. Contrasting the learning characteristics of the two genders further underscores the issues that must be considered in the construction of a knowledge transfer process (Emanuel & Potter, 1992; Machado, 1994; Turney, 1995; Stuart, 1999; Tannen, 1990; Weiss, 1993):

1.   Women most frequently like to share and learn by interacting with each other, while men often prefer debate-like situations in which they pursue knowledge.
2.   Men tend to be more independent while women often are very participatory in their learning.
3.   Women often find mentors more important in learning than do men.
4.   Authoritative systems and status are not as important to women as to men.
5.   Women value affiliation and acceptance more than men do.
6.   Male language is more direct and female language contains greater imagery.
7.   Men tend to dispel knowledge while women tend to seek consensus.
8.   Women often display uncertainty or hesitancy in speech, even when they are sure of themselves, while men tend to be more absolute and confident.
9.   Women may be slower to gain confidence than men.
10.   While men are likely to exchange information to establish status, women talk to exchange information and to establish cohesion.
11.   Women tend to consider family concerns and an aviation career more than men do.
12.   Women need to understand a subject thoroughly before proceeding during their training, while men tend to prefer the trial and error method of flight training.
13.   Men are more competitive and women are more collaborative.

Student Focus

While the term 'adult learner' is often thought to only include persons seventeen or older who are not enrolled full-time in high school or college, the term adult learner in its broadest sense applies to every adult participating in organized education (Cross, 1979). In adult-focused aviation education, the extensive amount of technical material that must be covered for the course, and the limited time available in the classroom, requires that every moment of educator-learner exposure be maximized. Aviation educators must motivate the learners, assure that the learners fully understand the importance of each component in the learning process, and then facilitate the students' progress (Knowles, 1980).

Breaking participants into small learning groups to exercise new skills and knowledge in relative safety is critical to understanding and retention. Participants in an adult learning process are normally hesitant to try out new knowledge and skills in front of others. Small 'praxis' teams that practice and reflect can overcome the reluctance to risk (Zemke & Zemke, 1995).

Adult Learning

As discussed in Chapter 4, adults require an in-depth understanding of materials they are learning. They see a need to have the skill to apply recently acquired knowledge to new situations. This requires a detailed comprehension of the *why and when*, and not just the *what*. In line with the adult education model, goals for learning objectives and the methods for knowledge transfer and evaluation are important details for the educator to explain, in order to assure a 'buy-in' by the learners as to the level of effort that will be required by the students and evaluated by the instructor (Karp, et al, 2002b).

Learning Style Theory

Learning style theory, that is, the way people learn best, is a critical consideration in delivering aviation academic programs. One model that makes sense for pilot training suggests that there are three recognized primary, or dominant, learning styles: First, *visual learners*, who learn best by reading or looking at pictures. Second, *auditory, or aural, learners*, who learn best by listening. And third, *hands-on, tactile, or kinesthetic learners*, who need to use their hands or whole body to learn (Filipczak, 1995). If knowledge transfer is to take place for both women and men in the classroom, then all of these dominant learning styles should be addressed in the academic environment (Filipczak, 1995).

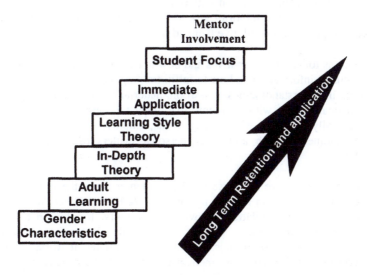

Figure 18.1 Review of literature and methodology across a broad range of educational areas

Immediate Application

If the learners acquire a new skill or knowledge, but then have no opportunity to use it or are delayed in using it, the skill or knowledge will fade. Immediate application of acquired knowledge is critical for adult learning and reinforcement to take place (Zemke & Zemke, 1995).

A valuable tool to assist in hands-on learning, in connection with the classroom, is computer-based learning. With the increased access to computer-based tutoring programs, students are moving away from passive reception of information to more active engagement in the acquisition of knowledge (Kozma & Johnston, 1991).

Group Learning

Learning in small groups or teams allows students to gain information from their peers as well as the instructor. It works well in the aviation training environment as it can be easily combined with immediate application methodology (Karp, et al, 2002b). Group learning includes cooperative, collaborative, and observational learning as described in Chapter 4.

Mentor Involvement

Mentoring has been identified as an important component of the training process, particularly for women and minority groups. Students seek to meet faculty and other interested people who will give them advice on:

1.   Options for career alternatives and how to best pursue those choices.
2.   Accurate information on how to fulfill training requirements.
3.   Help in understanding how classroom material relates to the real world.
4.   Practical advice with problems that impact progress and performance, especially problems with money, loans, employment, time conflicts and management, health and other personal matters (Seymour & Hewitt, 1997).

While students should have a diverse faculty to mentor them, the single strongest *need* expressed by women in a study by Seymour & Hewitt (1997) was the need for a personal, supportive relationship with their faculty. In addition to faculty, sources for practical mentors, or role models, can also be professionals in the student's family or circle of friends, people they encounter at work, school, or during internships. Experienced women in the student's field make particularly good mentors. In Seymour & Hewitt's study, women expressed the desire to meet other women who had been able to balance their professional, family, social and personal lives.

Research

The review of the literature provided a rich backdrop against which to conduct interviews, focus groups, and to conduct a survey among aviation students. The analysis of the follow-on research resulted in some interesting revelations. Results of a national survey of aviation students found a significant difference between novices (particularly novice women) who were just starting their university experience and those who were farther along in their training (Turney et al, 2002). These differences are summarized below.

1. Some notable differences were identified between male and female students in pilot training.
2. Differences were noted between novice women pilots (freshmen/sophomores) and more experienced women pilots (juniors/seniors).
3. Novice women had greater desire for role models.
4. Novice women were less confident than either men or experienced women pilots.
5. Novice women preferred to work in teams.
6. Novice women were concerned about working in a male dominated career.
7. Generally men had fewer family concerns than did women.
8. Women who remained in pilot training responded more like men after their second year, suggesting that they may have adopted to the male-oriented learning environment.

Research Recommendations

As outcomes of the data analysis and findings, the following recommendations were developed to integrate into the final model:

1. Identify and communicate a variety of issues that may concern a diverse group of students, particularly to faculty and flight instructors.
2. Advise entry-level students that learning differences exist.
3. Intervene with specific, tailored actions to address differences while students adapt to the aviation culture.

Interventions

The interventions derived were data-driven by expressed student concerns during the retention research. The interventions (Figure 18.2) were divided into those focused on the faculty and flight instructors, and those directed toward the peer group (Karp et al, 2002b).

Faculty and Program Commitment

1. Gain understanding of how, what and when students need to adopt and adjust to the aviation learning environment.
2. Indicate strong support for individual student goals and needs.
3. Facilitate classroom discussion.
4. Maintain the same standards for all students.
5. Provide hands-on learning, in addition to visual and auditory learning environments.
6. Include 'observational learning' classroom opportunities.
7. Insure that classroom instructional pace does not exceed students' learning pace.
8. Do not talk down to students or use gender, racial, or culturally insensitive language.
9. Offer faculty workshops to underscore why we need diversity in aviation and to detail the model components.
10. Facilitate faculty recognition and support of areas that affect learning and retention which are different among various culturally diverse groups.
11. Insure the program supports a change in marketing, recruiting, and retention effort, to include all groups of people in aviation.

Data-driven interventions

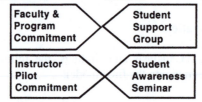

Figure 18.2 Data-driven interventions

Instructor Pilot Commitment

1. Gain understanding of how, what and when a variety of students may adopt and adjust to the aviation learning environment.
2. Indicate strong support for student's goals and needs.
3. Be receptive to all students' questions to assure that they understand subject before performing a maneuver.
4. Insure that flight instructional pace does not exceed a student's learning pace.
5. Consciously maintain the same standards for everyone.
6. Do not talk down to students or use offensive language.

7.   Discuss flight objectives in detail on the ground, but use a big-picture approach and demonstrations in the air.

Student Support Group

1.   Establish entry-level support group for new students.
2.   Recruit mentors from aviation industry to support student needs.
3.   Recognize that individuals may progress differently. This can lead to misunderstanding and different prioritizations.
4.   Recognize the existence of issues regarding children and family values.
5.   Understand that for most women, people and relationships are frequently more important than the job, while the opposite is true for most men.
6.   Provide adequate scholarships for flight training for everyone because many may be less financially risk-tolerant.

Student Awareness Seminar

1.   Explain adaptation and adjustment process that generally takes place after the initial training stages.
2.   Explain need for a highly structured academic and flight program.
3.   Identify issues of self-confidence in a competitive environment.
4.   Communicate the need for clear, concise speech.
5.   Discuss discomfort that may be associated with a predominately white male environment.
6.   Identify strategies for coping with attention (negative and positive) from classmates.
7.   Recognize the benefits of mentors to support goals and needs.
8.   Recognize that gender sensitivity may cause discomfort among males in the faculty.
9.   Understand that one individual does not have to prove himself or herself more than another.
10.   Discuss methods of developing confidence.

Model Development

The results of the review of the literature were placed as an overlay on the data-driven interventions to develop the Diverse Workforce Model (Figure 18.3). This model can be customized for each aviation training provider, but the individual components should always be integrated together to keep the focus on retaining diversity awareness in aviation programs.

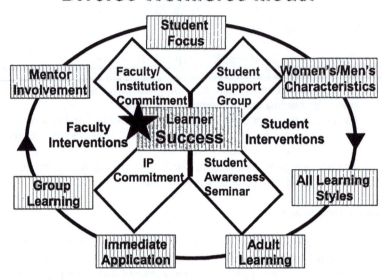

Figure 18.3 Diverse Workforce Model

Summary

The retention of diversity in aviation programs is a particularly important factor to consider in meeting the future needs of the aviation industry. Multi-cultural and multi-national populations comprise a large resource pool from which the commercial aviation industry can draw. In order to retain the best talent in aviation programs, aviation academic providers should design their academic curriculum and delivery vehicles to meet their students' specific learning needs, whomever they are. The investment in time for curriculum development to include the elements of the Diverse Workforce Model should pay high dividends in expanding the aviation learners' knowledge base and enhancing their flexibility to address new situations, while increasing the retention of talent in aviation.

References

Cross, K. (1979). 'Adult Learners: Characteristics, Needs, and Interests', in R. Peterson and associates (eds), *Life learning in America*, San Francisco: Jossey-Bass.
Emanuel, R. and Potter, W. (1992). 'Do Students' Style Preferences Differ by Grade Level, Orientation toward College, and Academic Major', *Research in Higher Education, 33*, 395-414.

Filipczak, B. (1995, March). 'Different Strokes: Learning in the Classroom', *Training, 32*, 43-48.

Karp, M.R., Turney, M.A., Green, M. Sitler, R., Bishop, J. and Niemczyk, M (2002a). 'Retaining Women in Collegiate Aviation Programs: Implementing Learning Style Considerations', *International Journal of Applied Aviation Studies*, 2 (2), 117-133.

Karp, M., Turney, M., Green, M., Sitler, R., Bishop, J. and Niemczyk, M. (2002b). 'Retaining Women in Collegiate Aviation: a Data-Driven Model', *Proceedings of Aviation Communication Conference, March 3-5,* Mesa, AZ.

Knowles, M. (1980). *The Modern Practice of Adult Education: From Pedagogy to Andragogy* (2nd Ed), New York: Cambridge Books.

Kozma, R. and Johnston, J. (1991, January). 'The Technological Revolution Comes to the Classroom', *Change*, 16-18.

Machado, R. (1994, January). 'A Happy Cockpit: Reducing Cockpit Stress between the Sexes', *Flight Training, 5,* 50-52.

Seymour, E. and Hewitt, N. (1997). *Talking about Leaving,* Boulder, CO: Westview Press.

Stuart, R. (1999). Gender Differences in the Cockpit. New Zealand Wings.

Tannen, D. (1990*). You Just Don't Understand: Women and Men in Conversation,* New York: Ballentine Books.

Turney, M. (1995). 'Women's Learning and Leadership Styles: Impact on CRM', *Proceedings of the 21st Conference of the European Association for Aviation Psychology, Volume 1, Applications of Psychology to the Aviation System*. Aldershot, UK: Ashgate.

Turney, M., Bishop, J., Karp, M., Niemczyk, M., Sitler, R., and Green, M. (2002). 'National Survey Results: Retention of Women in Collegiate Aviation', *Journal of Air Transportation, 7 (1)*.

Turney, M., Karp, M., Green, M. and Sitler, R. (1999). *Report: Maximizing Retention of Women Students Enrolled in Collegiate Aviation Programs*. New York: Alfred P. Sloan Foundation.

Weiss, M.J. (1993, Fall). 'Integrating Communication and Gender in the Medical Setting', *Proteus, A Journal of Ideas, 10,* 55-59.

Zemke, R. and Zemke, S. (1995, June). 'Adult Learning, What Do We Know for Sure'? *Training, 32,* 31-40.

Index

acculturation, 23
air traffic control
    communication. *See*
      communication:radio
AIRSPEAK, 143, 144, 147, 149
Avianca accident, 100
Avianca Flight 052, 100

Charkhi Dadri, India accident, 100
communication
    eye contact, 155
    gender differences. *See* gender
      differences
    information transfer, 210
    motor skill, 138
    nonverbal, 139. *See* nonverbal
      communication
    physical space, 154
    protocol, 162, 166
    protocols, 161
    radio, 35, 143
    reflexive, 105, 114
    status, 23, 161, 165, 167, 175
    subcultures, 208, 214, 218
communication and culture, 22, 106,
    110, 116, 166, 207
communication and safety, 21, 29
communication problems, 29
communication style, 112
communication styles, 64
Computer-Based Instruction, 54,
    188, 189, 224
CRM and communication, 162
CRM and culture, 18, 66, 106, 111,
    112, 180
CRM and learning, 190
cultural differences, 14, 30, 110,
    156, 174, 174, 175, 177, 183
cultural diversity

communication, 155
crews, 110, 111
management, 3, 4, 5, 19
cultural groups, 15
cultural meta-message, 109
cultural misunderstanding, 23
cultural orientation, 11
cultural problems, 36
culturally diversity
    communication, 116
culture
    defined, 107
    organizational, 3, 5, 9, 11, 12, 15,
      18, 23, 24, 31-39, 61, 65, 71,
      80, 105-110, 119, 120, 126,
      147, 161, 166, 167, 173, 177,
      178-181, 190, 207-209, 216
    subculture bias, 214
culture and assertiveness, 14, 164
culture and harmony, 16
culture and humor, 120
culture and job satisfaction, 108
culture and learning, 37
culture and maintenance technicians,
    208
culture and safety, 173, 182
culture and time, 15
curriculum
    cultural learning module, 193
    diverse workforce model, 228
    integrated aviation learning, 53

demographic trends, 6
demographics, 10
diverse culture, 18
diverse students, 185
diverse talent, 9
diversity, 3
    cultural, 3

diversity and crew communication, 105

English competency, 38
ergonomics and diversity, 197
eye contact, 156

flight deck design, 198
  anthropomorphics, 199
flight instructor stress, 32
flight instructor training, 26
flight training
  aircraft design, 198, 200
  instructor, 25, 28, 39, 72

gender
  job satisfaction, 65
gender and humor, 120
gender and learning, 186, 222
gender and speech, 141, 147
gender differences, 65, 69, 70, 77, 82, 157
  achievement, 78
  cognitive, 79
  humor, 123
  military and civilian pilots, 68
gender role, 81
globalization, 3, 101

Hofstede, 12, 13, 15, 21, 22, 23, 24, 29, 30, 35, 36, 37, 39, 40, 43, 107, 185
humor and cultural context, 119
humor and gender, 123
humor and leadership, 125
humor and power, 122
humor and social Norms, 124

ICAO, 4, 38, 91, 92, 93, 94, 95, 96, 97, 98, 99, 104, 177, 181
ICAO language requirements, 144
ICAO language requirements, 93
illocution, 146

individualism, 13

Kolb, 48

language, 139
  assertiveness. *See* culture and assertiveness
  commissive speech, 166
  confidence, 4
  convergence, 165
  intonal contour, 133
  intonation, 132, 136, 141, 146
  paralinguistic cues, 135
  performative speech acts, 167
  pitch, 132, 135, 146
  prosody, 129, 131
  standard English, 101
language and culture, 5, 6, 12, 17, 94, 95, 96, 111, 129, 131, 143, 148, 165
language and gender, 81
language and power, 157
language barriers, 4, 24, 26, 31, 34, 40, 176
language choice and status, 165
language fluency. *See* non-native English
language skill, 102, 180
learning
  competition and performance, 187
  cooperative, 54
  group, 224
  inclusive strategies, 189
  preferences, 72
  student-centered, 188
learning and instruction, 23
learning model, 52
learning styles, 27, 46, 47, 49, 50, 51, 54, 55, 63, 66, 67, 70, 186, 187, 188, 220, 223
  adult, 220, 221
learning theory, 54

maintenance and communication.
See communinication: subcultures
masculinity, 13
memory
   short term, 137
mental blocks, 12
miscommunications, 25

non-native English, 21, 22, 23, 24,
   25, 26, 27, 28, 29, 30, 31, 32, 34,
   35, 36, 37, 38, 39, 40, 41, 96, 98,
   102, 145, 175, 180
non-standard phraseology, 28
nonverbal behavior, 17, 156

politics
   flight deck, 182
power distance, 13
prosody in aviation communications.
   See language
psychosocial sex Differences, 80

reflexive communication
   components, 114
runway incursion, 161

silence, 11
silent messages, 158
standard aviation English, 41, 101,
   103

standard operating procedures, 178
status and power, 31

talent pool, 8
Tenerife, 22, 100
training
   cultural, 4
training aircraft design, 199

uncertainty avoidance, 13

values
   differences, 11, 16, 108, 206

women
   flight training, 77, 83, 86, 199
   leadership, 63, 64
   learning, 49, 51, 61, 62, 66, 83,
      85, 185, 187, 192, 222
   speech, 168
women instructors, 31
women pilots
   aggression, 84
   safety, 85
workforce
   diverse, 5, 6, 7, 8, 9, 10, 45, 61,
      125, 185, 190, 197, 199, 205,
      220